PRAISE FOR *EFFECTIVE DATA G*

"Many data governance efforts fail from over complication with too many 'shoulds' and 'musts'. Nicola Askham addresses this issue head-on in a succinct and clearly presented fashion. Her six principles need to be pasted in your cubicle."
John Ladley, author of *Data Governance*

"Nicola Askham has managed to write the definitive text on data governance. It covers every established element of the discipline in a highly practical way and introduces new ideas which other writers will want to quote and build upon for years to come. This book carries the personality of the author in a way which is very engaging, with her honesty about mistakes that she learned from and her clarity on what works and what doesn't, giving the book real gravitas."
Robert Hawker, Data and Analytics Consultant, Meloro Limited and author of *Practical Data Quality*

"Nicola Askham is an expert in her field and has helped many companies set up their data governance functions from the ground. All her knowledge is now found within *Effective Data Governance*. This book is a must-read for anyone new to data governance or wanting to enhance their data governance function."
Shaymoly Mukherjee, Data Leader, Guardian News and Media

"I love how Nicola Askham has broken *Effective Data Governance* down into three distinctive parts, which makes the whole process easy to follow. Her vast knowledge and experience shines through in her explanation of data governance and its relationship to other areas of data. I love her practical approach, tools and real-world examples, to make data governance easy to implement in your own organization. I am also happy to see data quality discussed; while it's not the same as governance, the two work hand in hand, and this book will be a great resource to help keep your data dirt-free."
Susan Walsh, Founder and MD, The Classification Guru

"Nicola Askham is one of the most prominent and brightest voices in the data governance space – a true pioneer who has shaped how we think about governing data in the modern world. When she says she wished she had this book when she started in data governance, I couldn't agree more. I wish I had it too! This is the one-stop shop for everyone who wants to get started or improve their data governance in today's fast-paced, data-driven landscape. Whether you're a seasoned data professional or just beginning your journey, Askham breaks down complex governance concepts into practical, actionable insights that you can apply immediately. This isn't just another theoretical framework—it's a real-world guide from someone who's been in the trenches and knows what actually works. Truly a must-read for everyone who works in data."
Tiankai Feng, author of *Humanizing Data Strategy*

"You need a coach, whether you are new to the data game or a seasoned pro and Nicola Askham is the one you want! Now, given the intense focus on Artificial Intelligence, there has never been a more critical time to read *Effective Data Governance*."
Scott Taylor, The Data Whisperer

"Nicola Askham's *Effective Data Governance* is a triumph; an indispensable guide that transforms a complex discipline into a clear, actionable journey. Askham takes the reader through every aspect of building a data governance program that will actually work. Her writing is crisp, her insight hard-won and her commitment to clarity shines through in every chapter. From the brilliant chapter summaries to the real-world examples, she delivers on every promise. Askham's six principles (opportunities, capability, custom-build, simplicity, launch and evolve) are both memorable and transformative. *Effective Data Governance* is a masterclass from the queen of data governance herself, earning five stars from me, without hesitation."
Joe Perez, data analytics expert, bestselling author and international keynote speaker

Effective Data Governance

*Design a framework that works
for your organization*

Nicola Askham

KoganPage

First published in Great Britain and the United States in 2026

Kogan Page

Kogan Page Ltd, 2nd Floor, 45 Gee Street, London EC1V 3RS, United Kingdom
Kogan Page Inc, 8 W 38th Street, Suite 902, New York, NY 10018, USA
www.koganpage.com

EU Representative (GPSR)

eucomply OÜ, Pärnu mnt 139b -14 11317, Tallinn, Estonia
www.eucompliancepartner.com

Kogan Page books are printed on paper from sustainable forests.

ISBNs

Hardback	978 1 3986 2419 1
Paperback	978 1 3986 2417 7
Ebook	978 1 3986 2418 4

British Library Cataloguing-in-Publication Data
A CIP record for this book is available from the British Library.

Library of Congress Cataloging in Publication Data
A CIP record for this book is available from the Library of Congress.

Typeset by Integra Software Services, Pondicherry
Print production managed by Jellyfish
Printed and bound by CPI Group (UK) Ltd, Croydon CR0 4YY

CONTENTS

PART TWO
Design

ABOUT THE AUTHOR

Nicola Askham is known as The Data Governance Coach and has spent over two decades helping organizations transform their relationship with data. She specializes in helping companies reduce costs and inefficiencies by turning their data from a liability into a strategic asset. Her practical, results-driven approach has helped clients across diverse sectors establish robust data governance frameworks that actually work in the real world.

Nicola's data governance journey began at a leading UK bank, where she gained deep insights into the challenges of managing data at scale. In 2009, she transitioned to consultancy, allowing her to apply her expertise across a broader range of industries and data challenges. This experience has given her unique insights into what works (and what doesn't) when implementing data governance across different organizational cultures and contexts.

Beyond her consulting work, Nicola is passionate about education and skill development. She runs training courses designed to equip professionals with the practical skills needed to use data effectively for problem-solving and decision-making. Her teaching philosophy centres on making complex concepts accessible and actionable.

As a respected thought leader in the field, Nicola served as a Committee Member of DAMA UK for 13 years, contributing to the advancement of data management practices across the UK. She regularly shares her expertise through writing, speaking engagements, videos, blogs and her popular podcast on data governance best practice: The Data Governance Podcast.

PREFACE

I wish I'd had this book 24 years ago.

Back then, I was grappling with data governance challenges at a major UK bank, trying various approaches and making plenty of mistakes along the way. There was very little available to read about the topic and I found myself struggling with the practical reality: how do you actually implement data governance in a way that works for your specific organization?

That struggle shaped everything that followed. When I moved into consultancy in 2009, I was exposed to organizations across different sectors, each with their unique cultures, challenges and constraints. Through this journey, I began to understand what works across different contexts and, perhaps more importantly, what doesn't. Every failed attempt, every successful implementation and every lesson learned the hard way has contributed to the approach you'll find in this book.

The turning point in my career came when I realized that I didn't want to simply do data governance for my clients. I wanted to give them the capability to do it for themselves. This shift towards training and coaching rather than traditional consulting has become central to my work. It's also why writing this book felt like a natural evolution of what I do.

Data governance is hard to implement in practice because it has to be different for each and every organization. There's no one-size-fits all solution, no standard framework that you can simply adopt wholesale. This reality is both the challenge and the opportunity. When John Ladley's seminal work on data governance was published in 2012, it brilliantly covered the theory and has been on my bookshelf ever since. However, I wanted to create something more practical: a guide that helps you work out how to design and implement a data governance framework that is pragmatic and actually works in your organization.

This book is built on the lessons I've learned through experience, both my own mistakes and the insights gained from working with countless organizations over the years. My goal is simple: to save you from making the same mistakes I did in the early years and to help you create what I call 'effective data governance': an approach that delivers real results rather than just good intentions.

Whether you're just starting your data governance journey or looking to improve what you already have, this book is designed to be your practical companion. It won't give you all the answers, because your answers will be unique to your situation, but it will give you the tools, frameworks and confidence to find those answers for yourself.

That's what effective data governance is all about.

ACKNOWLEDGEMENTS

Writing this book has been a journey that I could not have completed alone and I am grateful to the many people who have supported me along the way.

First and foremost, I want to thank the team at Kogan Page, especially my editors Charlie Lynn and Ellen Capon. Their support, guidance and expertise have been instrumental in making this book a reality. From the initial concept through to the final manuscript, they have helped shape my ideas into something that I hope will genuinely help others navigate the world of data governance.

I also owe a huge debt of gratitude to the team at Bright Lights Business Services Ltd, who have been invaluable in bringing this book to life. Not only did they help with the admin and diagram creation for the book, but more importantly, they took on many of the day-to-day tasks of running my business, freeing up the time I needed to focus on writing. Without their support, this book simply wouldn't exist.

I am deeply grateful to the countless colleagues, data friends and clients who have shared their experiences, challenges and insights with me over the years. While there are too many to mention individually, each conversation, initiative and collaboration has contributed to my understanding of what works in data governance and, perhaps more importantly, what doesn't. Many of the lessons and real-world examples in this book exist because of their willingness to share their experiences and allow me to learn alongside them.

To my fellow data professionals who have helped me develop and refine my thinking on data governance: your questions, feedback and perspectives have been invaluable. You've challenged me to find clearer ways to explain complex concepts and pushed me to focus on what truly matters when implementing data governance in practice.

On a personal note, I owe enormous thanks to my husband and sister for their unwavering support and belief that I could write this book, especially during the moments when I wasn't so sure myself. Their encouragement kept me going through the challenging parts of this journey.

I'm also grateful to my 'non-data' friends who, despite not working in this field, have cheered me on throughout the writing process. Their enthusiasm and interest in what I was doing meant more than they probably realize.

Thank you all for being part of this journey. Your contributions have made this book richer, more practical and hopefully more useful for everyone who reads it.

PART ONE

Prepare

01

What is data governance?

Introduction

Data is everywhere. It should be considered the lifeblood of our organizations; however, for many organizations, data remains poorly understood and inadequately managed. In an era of artificial intelligence (AI), digital transformation and increasing regulatory scrutiny, the need for effective data governance has never been more crucial.

But what is data governance? Why do so many organizations struggle to get it right? And how can we implement it in a way that delivers real business value rather than just creating bureaucracy?

This chapter will provide clarity on what it is (and isn't), why it matters and how it relates to other aspects of data management. Whether you're just starting your data governance journey or looking to enhance your existing framework, we'll explore the essential concepts, benefits and challenges you need to understand. From defining data governance in practical terms to examining its relationship with data quality and other disciplines, this chapter lays the foundation for everything that follows.

By the end of this chapter you'll have a clear understanding of:

- what data governance really means in practice
- why organizations need it now more than ever
- the key benefits it can deliver
- common challenges you might face
- how it relates to other data management disciplines

Most importantly, you'll learn why explaining the 'why' of data governance is more important than the 'what' – and how this understanding can help you build support for your data governance initiative.

A reasonable data governance definition

Data governance is a term that is rapidly growing in popularity, but there is much confusion about what the term means. When I was first working in data governance there was very little on the topic on the internet to help me. Now a quick search will unveil a whole host of definitions and explanations that range from really useful, through confusing, to the downright wrong. And I'll be honest a lot of them are… well… a little bit boring! If you are new to the topic, how are you supposed to know which are useful and which are not?

That is why the best way to start off this book is with an explanation of what data governance is.

I am a great fan of the Data Management Association (DAMA),[1] having been a director and board member of the UK Chapter for 13 years. It is a great organization providing support for data management professionals and if you are not already a member of your local chapter, I recommend that you consider joining.

DAMA offers lots of useful resources, including the Data Management Body of Knowledge (DAMA–DMBOK).[2] The DAMA–DMBOK has a section dedicated to data governance and defines it as being:

> The exercise of authority and control (planning, monitoring and enforcement) over the management of data assets.

While this is a good starting point for a definition, it feels a bit vague and does not give enough detail about what you will actually be doing. When I have to write a formal description of what data governance is, I describe it as:

> A collection of processes, roles, standards and metrics that ensure the effective and efficient use of data within an organization.

Data governance is all about establishing the necessary processes and responsibilities to ensure that we understand what data we have across our organization and whether it is good enough for us to use.

Having a definition is important. We need to be able to describe what we are doing, after all. But having just given you a definition, my next action is to tell you not to use it! It's not a bad definition, it just won't work for the business users you need to influence. Think about it from their viewpoint – does it sound like something that is going to help them do their job better; or does it sound like more rules and regulations that hinder them from doing their job? My experience is that if you use a definition similar to these when first introducing the topic to them you are likely to get the latter reaction.

Experience has taught me that you need to explain why your organization is (or should be) doing data governance first. The 'what data governance is' can come afterwards once your audience has agreed that they want it. I learnt in the early years of doing data governance that stakeholders are more interested in outcomes. Senior stakeholders care about delivering your organization's strategy, so I use the following definition when I first start having conversations about data governance:

> Data governance is all about proactively managing your data to support your organization to achieve its strategy and vision.

How many senior stakeholders wouldn't want to know more about something which is going to help their organization achieve its strategic objectives? Of course, after sharing such a definition, you need to be able to explain it in more detail if asked. So make sure you have done your preparation and know what benefits your organization could achieve if they implement data governance. More on that later in the chapter...

Are there better names to call it?

Before we go any further, I want to address the issue of the name.

A question I get asked frequently is: does it have to be called data governance? The answer is a bit more intricate than a simple yes or no.

Data governance as a term often carries a weight of misunderstanding. It's not the snazziest of terms and some consider it downright boring. So, calling it a different name could make adoption easier. If 'data governance' doesn't resonate with your team, consider a name that speaks to them. For instance, if your focus is on enhancing data quality, why not name your initiative the 'data quality initiative'? (We will look at the relationship between data governance and data quality at the end of this chapter.) This approach draws attention to tangible outcomes and makes it easier for business stakeholders to understand what you are trying to achieve.

A number of my clients have successfully renamed data governance as 'data enablement'. However, I have heard that 'data excellence' has been less well received, the title giving the impression that all data must be perfect and stakeholders being unwilling to embrace the amount of effort required to make it so.

My personal view is that as long as the scope and purpose of your data governance initiative has been made clear from the outset, a name change can be helpful in some cases.

Why are there so many definitions?

I mentioned right at the start of this chapter that there are numerous definitions of what data governance is. Don't you think it's strange that a data management discipline that, amongst other activities, actively promotes defining data has so many definitions of what the discipline itself is? It's bewildering and, to be honest, very frustrating. It is vital that we all mean the same thing when we are talking about data governance. Sadly, this is not yet the case. This means that whenever I am presenting or running a course on data governance, I start each and every one with a section on what data governance is.

So why are there so many different data governance definitions? Pick up a data governance book (this one included!) and very early on you will get a definition of data governance or an explanation of the concepts behind it. But if you pick up a data quality book they don't define data quality, they dive into what causes poor data quality and why we may want to improve it. They don't need to define it as we all understand and agree what the term means. So why as a data management profession have we not yet agreed and universally understood what data governance is?

I don't know the definitive answer, but I believe that it could be down to the following factors.

Name

It could be due to the choice of name of the discipline. After all, the definition of 'governance' is fairly vague. The Cambridge Dictionary defines it as:

> the way that organizations or countries are managed at the highest level and the systems for doing this

So from that rather woolly definition we can infer that 'data governance' is the action of governing data, but that can mean any number of things. I believe this is a reason why many take it to mean governing access to data and hence the common misunderstanding that it is another term for data security. Others take it to mean governing how long we hold data and confuse it with data retention.

I think (or hope) that the term is used to mean the correct thing the majority of the time. Its inclusion in such things as the DAMA–DMBOK and various regulations has got to be helpful. However, while a number of data security and data protection software vendors persist in labelling their products 'data governance' confusion will persist.

Framework or foundation

Data governance is a framework or foundation which underpins or supports the other data management disciplines (indeed it features at the centre of the DAMA–DMBOK wheel which I discuss later in this chapter).[3] Although there are activities and processes to follow, data governance is all about putting in place a framework for who does what to manage data. Other disciplines are much more about a specific set of activities, e.g. data modelling or data security, and can be considered in isolation. We do not do data governance in isolation just for the sake of 'doing data governance', it is always in connection with at least one other data management discipline.

Relationship with other disciplines

I mentioned previously that many data management activities can be viewed on a standalone basis, but data governance is rarely undertaken for its own sake. It has a close relationship with some other data management disciplines and provides a foundation for all other data management disciplines. We will look at these relationships in more detail later in this chapter, but I believe this interrelatedness is the cause of some of the confusion.

I don't think this issue is going to disappear overnight, after all even data management professionals can't agree on the definition. Over the years I have had a number of discussions with a well-respected data management author who, despite my best endeavours, still firmly believes that data governance is a term interchangeable with data management. We must however all strive for consistency in the use of the term and its meaning. That will make life easier for all of us. There will be one less hurdle in selling and implementing the concept if there is a common understanding of what it is in the first place.

The importance of explaining why you need data governance

If you plan to implement data governance in your organization, it is crucial to understand why you are doing it. It can be a long and thankless process and some might argue it's not for the faint-hearted, so understanding 'why' is vital in order to get the most out of your data governance journey.

Everyone needs to ask (and answer) why their organization needs data governance very early on in their initiative. If you don't know 'why', it can be easy to get side-tracked and distracted. The 'why' is what will guide you in your journey and ensure your organization is getting what it needs from your data governance initiative. I've seen people make the mistake of spouting things like, 'We're doing it because it's best practice' or 'We work in a regulated industry and it is required.' If you commence data governance because it's best practice, you are doomed to failure. I can tell you from my experience that the vast majority of your organization will not want to do data governance because it's 'best practice'. In order to persuade them to support your initiative you need to be able to explain what is in it for them, their team and the organization.

You might be thinking that it will be easier to do if there is a regulatory requirement for data governance. However, having spent many years helping companies implement it to comply with regulation, I've found that many organizations are only interested doing the minimum to meet their regulatory requirements. I was lucky to only work with companies that saw the bigger picture, but if you take the bare minimum approach, you are going to miss out on most of the benefits that are to be had from implementing data governance.

People often spout generic benefits like 'There will be efficiencies' or 'There will be better opportunities if we do data governance', but they can't explain the what and why when challenged. When you meet your senior stakeholders at the start of a data governance initiative, they will want to be able to know 'What's in it for me?' and if you can't answer that, they're just not going to engage and support the initiative. Ultimately that means that you will not get the support or funding you need and everything you've done to date is wasted effort.

So, what do you do? This is slightly more complex because the answer will depend on your organization's specific circumstances. Each and every organization is different and why your company is doing data governance will be different from another and probably even different from your closest competitors. This means there is not one standard approach. I cannot give you a detailed approach that will work for everybody.

What I can do is tell you how to work it out for yourself.

Figuring out why your organization needs data governance

There are three things you need to do to figure out your 'why'. The first is to look at your corporate strategy. Look at the objectives listed and work out if your data is currently well understood and good enough quality to help deliver those objectives. If the answer is no, then you have a great way of explaining why data governance is needed to help you achieve your corporate strategy.

The second thing I would do is look at your data strategy (if you have one). In order for a data strategy to be successfully implemented it needs to include a section on data governance, since this is what will provide the framework for managing and using data effectively. If your organization's data strategy does not mention data governance, you need to work with the person responsible for the data strategy to get them to understand this and to work with you.

Finally, go and search for your data quality horror stories. I use this term to refer to real-life scenarios where poor data management or quality issues have led to disastrous outcomes for organizations. For example, a company celebrates a successful new system implementation only to realize much too late that the data migrated into it was riddled with inaccuracies, or a disastrous decision was made on the basis of a report that is later found to contain incorrect data. Sound familiar?

If you gather and analyse all this information, you will be able to identify the drivers for data governance in your organization. With that information in hand, you'll be able to talk to anybody, whether they are senior stakeholders or the business users down at the coal face. You will be able to articulate what the benefits of data governance are going to be for them and why their part of the organization needs it. Being able to explain why your organization needs to do data governance is going to enable you to engage your stakeholders and ultimately design the right framework.

What data governance is not

Now that we have explored what data governance is, we need to spend some time looking at what it is not. That might seem a strange way of looking at things, but, given the number of misunderstandings around the topic, it's worth clarifying a few things.

Data protection

Though undeniably linked to your data governance framework, data protection (also known as data privacy) is often confused with data governance. It specifically revolves around the protection of personal information and although data protection regulations like the General Data Protection Regulation (GDPR) do have requirements that are more easily met if you have a data governance framework in place, data governance is a separate discipline supported by a different expert team in your organization.

Data retention

Likewise, data retention, which focuses on how long you should hold onto data before deleting it, is something which your data owners should be consulted on but is a fundamentally different discipline. Data owners are senior stakeholders accountable for one or more dataset. We will explore the role in detail in Chapter 6.

Data security

As already mentioned earlier, the term 'governance' implies control and oversight, which can lead many to equate data governance directly with the safeguarding of data access and security. I was very worried early in my career as an independent data governance consultant when a new client cheerfully announced that their data security manager was looking forward to working with me. In classic imposter mode, I assumed that the client had mistakenly hired me to help with something I had no experience with! It turned out that their data security manager was struggling to get anyone at the company to make decisions about encryption levels and access management. He had recently joined from another organization which already had data governance and knew how much easier his job was when there was a clear framework of data roles and responsibilities in place (something which data governance gives you).

Records management and information management

Records management or information management (two names used to mean the same thing) do bear some similarities to data governance, as their principles are aligned. Records and information are collections or compilations of related data. For example, a date field is just a random date without context, but in a customer details record you realize that it is a date of birth. This discipline focuses on the handling of complete records (whether they are analogue or digital) rather than electronic data which are the building blocks of records/information. To be successful at information management, you need to manage the underlying data as well.

While these separate disciplines all carry value in their own right and can (and should) be aligned with your data governance framework, they are ultimately separate practices usually undertaken by different specialist teams.

Unfortunately, the confusion surrounding the links between these different areas can feed into the misconception of data governance as a Big Brother-esque surveillance programme designed to watch business users' every move with their data.

This isn't the case at all! Data governance is actually more about getting your business users to care about their data and its quality. When any monitoring is undertaken, it will be because our business stakeholders have asked us to.

Benefits of data governance

Increasing numbers of organizations are striving to become data driven and digital transformation is high on the agenda for many. Not to mention that nearly every organization I speak to wants to implement some form of generative AI, if they haven't already. These really are exciting times from a data point of view. The landscape in which we work is changing rapidly, with generative AI increasingly influencing our daily lives. Hopefully, I do not need to convince you of the importance of data governance to support digital transformation and AI. Right now is not only a good time but a necessary time to embrace data governance. Any attempt to implement generative AI or digitalization is sure to fail if we use the wrong data, or if it is not good enough quality to be used for that purpose. However, supporting and enabling such initiatives to be successful are not the only benefits to be had from embracing data governance.

You need to be confident that you know the benefits that data governance will deliver for your organization. You need to be able to articulate them to whoever you talk to, explaining what's in it for them. I have already mentioned that you need to work out the specific reasons that your organization should be doing data governance and not just use generic benefits, but I do understand that if you have never done data governance before that it can be helpful to understand the types of benefit you can expect to achieve.

Efficiencies

Probably the biggest benefit that most organizations can achieve from implementing data governance is improved efficiency. When you start looking at the processes and activities ongoing in your organization, it can be quite amazing how much time is wasted on manual workarounds and fixing poor-quality data. If these activities are reduced or even eradicated, you immediately save huge amounts of time, enabling your business users to spend more time using their skills to add value to your organization. For example, I've had numerous analytics teams tell me that at least 50 per cent of their time is spent finding and correcting data before they can even start to analyse it and produce reports. At one client, I was told by someone that they spent two weeks every quarter cleansing and fixing the data in a spreadsheet they received from another department before they were able to use it in an important process. Think about how much money that company was paying for someone to spend two weeks, every quarter, just to correct that spreadsheet. That was just one of numerous manual workarounds we found and corrected at that company.

Better decisions

The quality of reporting and therefore the decisions made on the back of them will be improved. Every company should want this.

Executives and senior managers in your organization are making decisions based on reports every day. I like to think that most people do not deliberately make the wrong decisions. However, in my experience, poor decisions are frequently made because they are based on wrong or poor-quality data in reports. Some are easily spotted and rectified, many result in poor customer service and I am aware of quite a few which have had a major impact financially on the organizations concerned.

If you make sure your data is understood and of good enough quality, you get great reporting that senior stakeholders can use to make the right decisions for your organization.

Regulatory requirements

It seems that more and more regulators are asking that companies in their sector ensure that data is of good enough quality for them to be able to monitor compliance against certain standards. As mentioned earlier, I recommend putting in place a solid data governance framework to deliver wider business benefits and not just the minimum to meet the regulatory requirements.

Protecting reputation

We have already established that poor data can lead us to make poor decisions. Many of those decisions can lead to bad customer service and frustrating relationships with suppliers. Your organization needs to maintain good relations with both customers and suppliers. However, I have come across countless examples of reputations damaged as a result of poor-quality data or even the wrong data being used. This includes one major supplier who gave my client six months to improve their data or they were going to stop supplying them (an ultimatum that prompted them to commence implementing data governance!).

Supports strategy

I mentioned earlier that you should look at your corporate strategy to understand where your data is not currently good enough for the strategic objectives to be achieved. It follows that identifying these areas and working to improve that data will facilitate achievement of your organization's strategy and objectives.

Single version of the truth

Finally, a lot of organizations wish to create a single version of the truth, a single customer view or perhaps a master list of product data. A *single version of the truth* refers to a principle where everyone in an organization operates using the same, consistent dataset. It implies that all data and information across various departments align, creating a unified understanding of facts and figures.

If that is important to your organization, you are going to need to have a good understanding of your data. This is crucial to be able to select and merge the right data fields. It is also vital that the data you are trying to merge is of good quality. I am sure by now you will not be surprised to learn that data governance helps you achieve that.

Challenges of doing data governance

By now, you understand what data governance is, and hopefully I have convinced you that there are numerous benefits to be achieved from implementing it. If everybody understood this, surely it would be easy to put data governance in place? Well, sadly, that is rarely the case. This is because there are a number of challenges which we face when implementing data governance.

Culture change

The first and biggest challenge that you will face is that of achieving the cultural change needed.

The trouble with data governance is that people expect that it is a project, a one-off initiative. You will fix everything, then data governance will be completed and done. Unfortunately, that is not the case.

Data governance is an ongoing process which needs to be embedded in everything your organization does. We need to achieve an underlying change in the behaviours of our business users. We need them to start thinking and caring about the quality of their data. To do that takes a considerable amount of time and effort. It is definitely not a one-off project. Your business users need to understand that this is an ongoing change in the way they think and behave around their data. It is something that they have to adopt going forward.

Boredom

The second challenge that I frequently encounter is that data is just not viewed as something that is exciting to be working on. People are often not thrilled to find out that they have been assigned to work on a data governance initiative. Now, I don't understand this and I hope that you don't either, because data is the lifeblood of all organizations. As we have already seen, improving how we manage our data brings with it huge benefits. Despite that, sadly data governance does have a reputation for being a dull topic.

I liken it to foundations. When amazing architectural buildings are constructed it takes many months of building strong foundations below ground level, before a beautiful building emerges. We may admire the architecture, but we do not think about the foundations. We do not appreciate everything they are doing to support the building. Data governance is a lot like that. It provides a strong foundation for everything else we want to do with data. However, most people get excited about the amazing insights and generative AI that we have enabled and not the data governance framework that we put in place. I don't think this is something we are going to change easily. We just have to be aware that this is the case and make sure that we tackle this with lots of good-quality communications and training.

Prioritization

I believe that data underpins everything we do in our organizations, but, despite that, it is rarely the top priority of the business users you will be talking to. On a more positive note, things have definitely improved in recent years. Not too long ago data was rarely even on the agenda!

So how do we overcome the fact that our stakeholders have got other things which they are more concerned about? Personally, I believe that we have to accept that data governance will never be the top priority for the vast majority of people. The only way to get it on their agenda is to link data governance inextricably to the things which the organization is prioritizing. And do not think that if you work in a sector that has regulatory requirements for data governance that it will be any easier.

Over the past decade or so, a lot of regulation in Europe has put data firmly on the agenda of financial services institutions, but even that has not made doing data governance as easy as you might hope. In my career, I have helped numerous organizations in the financial services sector. It remains difficult to get their stakeholders to consider the data governance element of the regulation. That's because the requirement for data governance is not the primary thing that the regulation is asking for.

For example, Solvency II is a regulatory framework for insurance companies operating in the European Union. Its objective is to ensure that insurers have enough financial resources (solvency) to meet their obligations to policyholders. Some of its requirements ask for data governance to be in place over the data that is used to calculate the solvency of a firm. This sounds like good news to those of us advocating for the benefits of data governance, but of course the majority of the regulation is about how solvency is calculated, rather than the data used in the calculations. This meant that when I naively first spoke to senior stakeholders in the industry about doing data governance activities, I expected them to want to work with me. After all, I was going to help them meet a critical regulatory requirement. I was shocked to discover that selling the idea of data governance was no easier than before. I had failed to consider that the stakeholders had been tasked with meeting all of the Solvency II requirements and to them the data part was less important. This was a valuable learning experience for me, as I had thought that the regulatory requirement would make everyone want to work with me. What I discovered was that, whatever the situation, you will struggle to convince stakeholders to prioritize data governance unless you can explain how it is going to help them deliver what they consider to be their highest priorities.

Defining scope

Another challenge is that at the start of a data governance initiative, it is really difficult to define the scope of what you want to achieve. When I started doing data governance I felt that all data should be perfect and that we needed to tackle it all straight away! Of course, with the benefit of hindsight, I realize that I was naive in telling senior stakeholders that. I was presenting them with something that was really big, complicated and required a lot of effort. While I was getting carried away with the enthusiasm of what I wanted to do, I did not realize that what I was describing was scary and costly! No wonder they said no.

You must identify a manageable scope and roadmap, but this in itself is a challenge. All organizations these days have huge volumes of data, how are you going to identify and agree on what to focus on first?

Legacy systems

The final challenge I see frequently is that of legacy systems. Regardless of size or sector, nearly every organization has challenges dealing with legacy systems. This is because companies tend to focus on running their business, be that making things or selling things or services, but not on the systems that support them. Changing old systems that are part of a complex architecture of other systems becomes a costly and complicated process. It is an activity that is often deferred until there is no option but to upgrade or replace a failing system.

This means that you can start a data governance initiative with the best of intentions. You can identify some simple fixes to systems which would improve the quality of your data. However, these are not always implementable because of the constraints of legacy systems and often a lack of knowledge of where the data goes downstream of that system.

Data governance vs data management

I mentioned earlier some of the other data management disciplines which data governance is frequently confused with. However, there is a bigger misunderstanding that it is important to clarify.

It is a very common misconception that the terms data management and data governance mean the same thing and are interchangeable.

This is not the case.

Data management refers to the management of the full data lifecycle needs of an organization. Data governance is the core component of data management, tying together the other disciplines, such as data quality, master data management and data security. Data governance stands prominently at the centre of the DAMA–DMBOK wheel, as you can see in Figure 1.1.

FIGURE 1.1 DAMA–DMBOK wheel

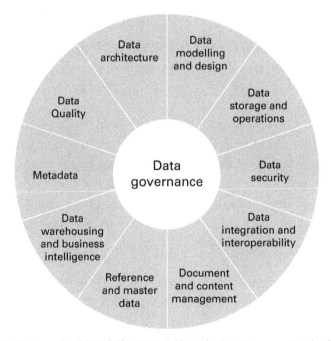

SOURCE DAMA International (2024) *The DAMA Guide to the Data Management Body of Knowledge (DAMA-DMBOK2R)*, 2nd edn, Technics Publications, LLC, Sedona, AZ

This placement causes confusion regarding its role and relationships with other data management disciplines. The central positioning is very intentional; it highlights that data governance is not just another discipline within data management, but rather a foundational framework that underpins and supports all other data management disciplines. However, many people come across this image and don't understand the context. They see the words in the middle of the diagram and assume, incorrectly, that everything on the wheel is data governance. At its core, data governance comprises a variety of processes, roles and standards that ensure effective and efficient use of data across an organization. It is about defining who can take what action upon data and in what context. This clarity is essential for managing data effectively and aligns closely with various other disciplines, creating a well-established ecosystem within data management.

Interconnections with other data management disciplines

Data governance fosters collaboration across various data management practices, so let's look at each of these in turn.

DATA ARCHITECTURE

Data architecture is a vital framework that outlines how data is collected, stored, organized and integrated within an organization. It is similar to the blueprint for a building, ensuring that every piece is in its right place to support the functionality of the entire structure. Just as a well-designed building accommodates the needs of its occupants, a robust data architecture caters to the data needs of an organization.

I have often introduced myself to the data architecture team as their new best friend! It's a great icebreaker, but I mean it. In my experience, if the data governance and data architecture teams work together they can achieve so much more than working in isolation. While they want to create an overall structure of data that meets your business needs, we ensure that that data is understood and of good enough quality to meet those same needs. Working together we supercharge our ability to help our organizations deliver value and better outcomes by being able to use the right data, of the right quality, at the right time.

If your organization has a data architecture team (sadly many do not), it is likely that they will run a design authority. This is a regular meeting where new projects have to present their proposed approach and the design authority reviews to ensure that new initiatives are aligned with the target architecture which has been designed to facilitate the organization's business goals. As a data governance manager sitting on such a forum, you get early access to the projects which will be making changes to data. This will give you the opportunity to influence them before decisions regarding the data have been made. This is a good escalation point to raise systemic issues with systems which you become aware of in your role. A design authority often has the opportunity to influence projects that may be able to apply simple fixes for you as part of their initiative.

DATA MODELLING AND DESIGN

Data modelling is the process of discovering, analysing and scoping data requirements, then representing and communicating these data requirements in a data model. Sadly, although many consider data modelling an essential data management discipline, I have worked with numerous organizations who do not have a single data modeller, let alone a team. This is a pity as it helps improve data understanding. Data models provide clear, structured representations of data. They make it easier for business users to understand how data is, or should be, organized and related.

My data modelling skills are basic, but I like to create conceptual data models for every business department in an organization early in a data governance initiative. It helps stakeholders engage, it helps them articulate their data challenges and start thinking about which data they might want to own. If your organization has any data modellers, they will have been capturing data definitions and attempting to standardize naming conventions and data formats long before anyone thought to introduce data governance! So you can see why they are good allies and often are happy to share resources and experiences.

DATA STORAGE AND OPERATIONS

This is about the design, implementation and support of stored data to maximize its value. Data engineers often support these activities.

Data governance defines standards and guidelines for how data should be stored and managed. It is the data engineers who implement these policies by configuring storage systems and operational processes to align with the standards and guidelines.

The two must work in harmony to ensure that data is well managed.

DATA SECURITY

Data security is one of the most mature data management disciplines and one of which we are all aware. Absolutely every organization has a data, information or cyber security team in their information technology (IT) department that is tasked with preventing the unauthorized access, use, modification and destruction of data. No small task in these days of increasing cyber attacks!

As mentioned earlier in this chapter, having data governance in place makes it easier for your data security team to quickly identify the correct stakeholders to contact regarding sensitivity classifications and access requests. Data governance also provides the mechanism to document what we know about our data. We will cover the data glossary in detail in Chapter 8, but from a data governance point of view one of its main purposes is to document what data terms mean and who is responsible for that data. However, I would not expect my data security team to refer to the data glossary just to identify who to speak to about the data. I want the data glossary to be the single source of everything we know about our data (think how much easier it is for our users if everything is in one place) so why not also include those sensitivity classifications in the data glossary?

DATA INTEGRATION AND INTEROPERABILITY

These activities are also usually undertaken by data engineers. This time they are concerned with managing the movement and consolidation of data within and between applications. Having read the chapter to this point, I'm sure you will not be surprised when I tell you that data governance supports these activities by creating and enforcing standards for data formats, structures and definitions. This ensures consistency and compatibility across systems, making it easier to integrate and share data.

DOCUMENTS AND CONTENT MANAGEMENT

This discipline encompasses all the activities required for the lifecycle management of information (sometimes called information management or records management). The team responsible for these actions is primarily responsible for documents, emails, images and other unstructured content often called *information* or *records*. These records consist of a collection of related data, so it follows that managing records and the data that they contain, requires similar principles. A data governance team needs to work closely with the team responsible for document and content management to ensure that there is no overlap or ambiguity between their approaches.

In one role early on in my career, I discovered what happens if they do not work together. I had been making good progress in implementing data governance and my data owners were engaged and supportive. Then one day one of the data owners became very cross and frustrated. I was summoned to meet him to explain why I had sent someone to speak to him, who had told him he was not a data owner, he was an information owner! I had no idea what he was speaking about, but a little investigation revealed that the organization had recently hired an information manager who was implementing a records management policy. This caused much confusion and consternation amongst my data owners. By speaking to and building a good relationship with the information manager, I was able to resolve the issue, making sure our approaches were aligned. As mentioned previously, information management needs data governance to be successful and it is likely that the same person would cover the role of both data and information owner for related data/information. In this instance, we agreed to both use the role title of 'data owner' to cover the respective responsibilities, to avoid confusion.

REFERENCE AND MASTER DATA

Master data management (MDM) focuses on identifying an organization's key data and then improving the quality of this data to enable consistent use across systems. Master data is an essential concept in the realm of data management that provides the foundational reference points for business operations. The term is described by the *DAMA Dictionary of Data Management* as:

> The data that provides the context for business activity data in the form of common and abstract concepts that relate to the activity. It includes the details (definitions and identifiers) of internal and external objects involved in business transactions.[4]

At its core, master data encompasses the critical information entities that businesses rely on, such as:

- customer data: identifiable details about customers necessary for understanding engagement and transactions
- product data: information about products offered by the business, enabling consistency across multiple channels
- employee data: key personnel information, vital for human resource management
- supplier data: details about suppliers and partners critical for supply chain management

Reference data is an important subset of master data. It is the data used to categorize or define other data. It often consists of standardized lists or codes and their corresponding definitions, such as ISO country codes or product categories.

Of course, I am biased, but MDM is rarely successful without proper data governance. Data governance defines the master data models (the definitions of a customer, a product, etc.), provides definitions of individual attributes being mastered and the standards of quality that the data needs to meet, as well as defining roles and responsibilities for data authoring, data curation and deletion.

Put simply, MDM initiatives require a strong data governance framework to succeed and I have often seen MDM tasks undertaken by the data governance team.

DATA WAREHOUSING AND BUSINESS INTELLIGENCE

Every organization wants to make decisions based on the correct data and have at their disposal a team of people able to provide valuable insights into their data. This is where data warehousing and business intelligence teams have a part to play: processing and storing data for analysis and performing that reporting and analysis.

However, if there is no data governance in place, such teams waste considerable time and effort trying to locate the data required to produce a report or perform analysis. When they finally get the data they often find it is poor quality and some data cleansing is needed before it can be used. Early on in this chapter I mentioned that such teams often waste at least 50 per cent of their time in these 'data wrangling' type activities, instead of using their skills to deliver useful reports and insights. One lead data scientist told me recently that his team spent approximately 90 per cent of their time trying to source and fix data!

Data governance helps improve this situation with the creation of a data glossary, which documents what data the organization has and where it is held, as well as helping understand and improve the quality of the data.

METADATA

Metadata management is an interesting discipline that has no clear single owner. It is the capture, documentation and management of data about the data our organization holds. It is rare to come across a metadata management team. These activities tend to be split across the data architecture, data modelling and data governance teams. The first two teams focus on capturing the more technical characteristics about the data. This technical metadata is primarily used by IT teams, database administrators and developers. From a data governance perspective, we are more interested in capturing the context, meaning and usage of data from a business perspective.

There is the potential for more insight and value to be gained if we are able to store all metadata in a single place. However, unless your organization has a specialist tool to support this, it is not possible to easily integrate and interrogate multiple spreadsheets, which is how organizations tend to document metadata in the absence of a specialist tool.

DATA QUALITY

Data quality management is about ensuring that data meets quality standards and remains at those levels. Data governance supports this by putting in place the roles and processes necessary for monitoring and improving data quality. The relationship between data governance and data quality is so important that I cover it in more detail below.

BETTER TOGETHER

Data governance stands as a crucial bridge between the various data management disciplines. Many data management activities can and do operate independently, but they are far more effective when aligned under a robust data governance framework, which clarifies roles and establishes consistent practices across the board.

REAL-WORLD EXAMPLE
An overwhelmed client

The confusion between data management and data governance is unfortunately fairly common, and I have started work with many new clients over the years who are extremely relieved when I explain that these are not interchangeable terms.

At one such client, the head of an existing team was told she had also been given responsibility for data governance. While she was recruiting a data governance manager, she did some research and was horrified at what looked to be the extent of this new responsibility. She decided to hire a contractor to help get started on the enormous task during the lengthy recruitment process for the permanent role. Unfortunately, the contractor was also under the same misapprehension and spent most of their engagement researching and writing papers on the huge variety of activities to be done. Finally, feeling extremely stressed and overwhelmed by the enormity of the task, she contacted me. I was quickly able to reassure her and advise her of the true extent of her responsibilities.

Of course, given the supporting role that data governance has for the other data management disciplines, it is not always easy to work out which team should be responsible for which activities. I recommend that you take time to speak to everyone undertaking any of the data management disciplines outlined here and agree on who is responsible for which activities. This is a vital step to ensure that there is no misalignment, duplication or gaps. It also gives you the opportunity to build good relationships with the other data teams, who will be your allies in designing and implementing a data governance framework.

The relationship between data governance and data quality

When we talk about data governance, we often end up talking about data quality at the same time. We use both terms in the same conversation. This causes a lot of confusion about whether they are the same thing or not. As we already covered, they are not considered to be the same data management discipline, but in my experience they are best done by the same team.

Most organizations have been doing data quality management activities long before they even consider implementing data governance. Some will have a data quality team, and even if they do not there will be manual cleansing and fixing of data before reports are produced or processes followed. There may even be some regular reports that are produced by the business intelligence or analytics team to highlight when certain exceptions happen.

However, if you do data quality without data governance in place, your data quality efforts are reactive and tactical at best. If you do not identify and fix the underlying cause of the poor-quality data, next month your report or data will be wrong once more and need fixing again. There may be regular reports of things that need to be fixed, but again they are fixed each time the report is run and nothing is done to stop the issue from recurring. Or, even worse, the person who requested that the reports be set up is no longer in that role and the reports are produced but ignored.

Having data governance in place solves this problem. It establishes the roles, responsibilities and processes to ensure that the root causes of issues are identified and resolved. It is about being proactive and strategic in how we look after our data.

Data governance enjoys a symbiotic relationship with data quality. While data governance supports all of the data management disciplines, the primary reason it is implemented is to understand and manage data quality. You would not want to do one without the other. No one implements data governance just for the fun of it, and I hope I have convinced you that doing data quality without data governance is just a huge amount of effort for limited value.

HOW DO A DATA QUALITY AND DATA GOVERNANCE FRAMEWORK RELATE TO EACH OTHER?

Having established that they are two separate disciplines, it seems logical to many people that you need a different framework for each set of activities. But think about it, data quality is the degree to which data is accurate, complete, timely and consistent with your business's requirements. Data governance provides a framework to help you proactively manage your data to help your organization achieve its goals and business objectives by improving the quality of your data.

So, why would you want two frameworks relating to data quality? The simple answer is you would not. You do not need to think about aligning two frameworks. You should only have one framework covering both data quality and data governance. Remember, their relationship is based on mutual interdependence. It does not matter whether you call it data quality or data governance as long as it gets your business users engaged and understanding what the framework is about.

I am going to say this a lot in this book, but to deliver effective data governance that delivers value to your organization we need to make things simple, so definitely fewer frameworks to confuse our business stakeholders is a good thing!

Conclusion

As we have explored throughout this chapter, data governance is far more than just another corporate initiative or compliance requirement. It is a fundamental framework that enables organizations to understand, trust and effectively use their data. While often misunderstood as simply being about control or restrictions, effective data governance is actually about enabling and empowering organizations to derive maximum value from their data.

We've seen that data governance:

- is distinct from but supportive of other data management disciplines
- provides the foundation for successful data quality initiatives
- delivers tangible benefits, from improved efficiency to better decision-making
- requires cultural change and sustained commitment rather than just technical solutions

The challenges of implementing data governance are real, from achieving cultural change to competing priorities and legacy system constraints. However, these challenges are far outweighed by the risks of not governing data effectively, especially in an era where artificial intelligence and digital transformation are reshaping how organizations operate.

Most importantly, we've learned that successful data governance is not about starting with complex frameworks or technical solutions. It starts with understanding and clearly articulating why your organization needs data governance and how it will support your business objectives. This understanding provides the foundation for everything that follows.

As we move forward in this book, we will build on these foundational concepts to explore the practical aspects of designing and implementing a data governance framework. We will examine how to establish the right roles and responsibilities, develop effective processes and create a simple sustainable data governance framework that delivers real value to your organization.

Data governance is a journey rather than a destination. While the path is often challenging, the rewards of getting it right, from improved efficiency and better decision-making to enhanced regulatory compliance and risk management, make it a journey well worth taking.

Notes

1   DAMA International. dama.org (archived at https://perma.cc/ZGT6-2594)

2   DAMA (2017) *DAMA–DMBOK Data Management Body of Knowledge*, 2nd edn, Technics Publications, Sedona AZ

3   DAMA INTERNATIONAL (2024), DAMA-DMBOK 2R Wheel Images. dama. org/dmbok2r-infographics (archived at https://perma.cc/N9NT-8WD2)

4   DAMA (2011) *DAMA Dictionary of Data Management*, 2nd edn, Technics Publications, New Jersey

02

Planning your data governance approach

Introduction

In this chapter we explore the critical relationship between your organization's corporate strategy and your data governance initiatives. Many data governance efforts fail not because of technical shortcomings, but because they lack strategic alignment with what truly matters to the business. We will examine why understanding your organization's strategic objectives is the foundation for successful data governance and how this alignment enables you to secure and maintain the executive support essential for long-term success.

You'll learn how to build a compelling business case that speaks directly to stakeholders' priorities, whether that's improving operational efficiency, enhancing decision-making, ensuring regulatory compliance or driving digital transformation. We'll also discuss the rise of formal data strategies, their relationship to data governance, and practical approaches to measuring and advancing your organization's data governance maturity.

You will come to understand that data governance is not just about maintaining clean data; it is about enabling your organization to achieve its strategic goals through better data. You will gain practical advice to create a roadmap that aligns your data governance efforts with organizational priorities, ensuring that your initiative delivers tangible value from the start and continues to evolve alongside your organization's needs.

After reading this chapter, you will have a clear understanding of:

- why aligning data governance with corporate strategy is essential for gaining and maintaining senior stakeholder support
- how to identify and articulate the business value of data governance specific to your organization's objectives
- the distinction between a data strategy and a data governance approach and when each is appropriate
- how to build a compelling business case using data quality 'horror stories' from your organization
- the purpose and value of data governance maturity assessments
- how to create an effective data governance roadmap that allows for flexibility and iteration
- practical approaches to secure resources and drive cultural change around data management

Your corporate strategy is key

Aligning your data governance approach with your organization's corporate strategy is essential if you want to succeed. You may have read the last sentence and wondered if you really need to worry about your corporate strategy if you're focusing on data governance. This is a fair question and I'll be honest, the first few years that I was doing data governance, I didn't think that the corporate strategy of the organization was relevant to me as a data governance manager. However, in my first few attempts at data governance, I learnt the hard way that the key to the success of your data governance initiative is to engage your senior stakeholders and gain their support.

The only way you are going to get and keep senior stakeholders engaged is to focus on the things they are interested in. They are unlikely to be interested in sorting out small data niggles that impact only a small part of the organization. They are interested in delivering the corporate strategy and, specifically, the objectives for which they are personally responsible. If you can talk to them about how you are going to help them with this, then I promise you they will want to hear what you have to say and how they can support you.

Too many people start data governance talking about best practices, the presentation from the conference they recently attended or an article they have read. Doing this will not engage your senior stakeholders. You must talk about how doing data governance will help your organization achieve its corporate strategy. In other words, talk about data governance in the language of the business.

A vital piece of work you should be doing very early on in your data governance journey is to spend some time looking at your organization's corporate strategy and objectives. Find out whether your data is currently good enough to help meet those objectives. A classic example of how data governance helps meet strategic objectives is the often-present objective to *reduce costs by x per cent* over the next few years. If your data isn't good enough and a lot of costs are incurred through manual data workarounds or rework, then it is clear where you need to focus your initial data governance efforts. More importantly, undertaking this analysis enables you to explain the benefits of data governance in ways which will make your stakeholders want to work with you.

As you start implementing data governance in your organization, you will soon realize that a significant amount of time, effort and money is wasted because data has not been considered and managed as an asset. Because of this, we have the cost of mistakes, rework and dealing with customer complaints. There will also often be a considerable amount of time spent doing what I call 'data wrangling'. I use this term to cover all the time spent finding and fixing data, manually transferring data between systems or even maintaining extra spreadsheets because the system does not hold all the data needed.

As you implement data governance, you will be able to identify and resolve such issues and reduce the amount of time wasted on data wrangling activities. By doing that you will reduce costs and improve efficiency. When talking to your finance director or any other senior stakeholder responsible for cost reduction, you can highlight some of these issues and explain how data governance will help solve them and reduce costs. Presented with that information, most people are happy to support the person who offers to solve the issues and help them deliver their objectives.

Taking the time to review the corporate strategy and identify how data governance supports it is vital. Doing this ensures that you focus on the specific data which is of strategic importance to your organization. It also means you will be in a much stronger position to get senior stakeholder buy-in and sustained engagement.

Maintaining alignment with your corporate strategy to ensure that you continue to focus on the right things is also vital. Corporate strategies change and you need to make sure that your approach evolves to continue to support the needs of your organization. With technologies rapidly changing, many organizations are reviewing and updating their strategy more frequently, reducing the update period from five years to three or even less. So, be aware of the update cycle of your corporate strategy and make sure that your data governance approach evolves and continues to support it.

My personal experience

When I first started doing data governance I did not give corporate strategy much thought, and at that time no one was talking about the need for a data strategy (they are a more recent development which we will cover shortly.) If I thought about it at all, I felt that the corporate strategy was just not relevant to me as a data governance manager. I was just one person in a very large organization. I felt that the corporate strategy was not my concern because my primary focus was on establishing a better way of managing our data. I believed that the high-level business direction covered in the corporate strategy belonged to the executive leadership's domain, not mine. I felt that I needed to be designing the data governance framework and starting to implement it. I was impatient to make things happen and start delivering better data!

With the benefit of hindsight, I realized that I had missed the point. I needed to align all of my activities with the corporate strategy. Not aligning with the corporate strategy led to limited and unsustainable successes. I started fixing issues which had caused me pain when I had been a user of the data. However, senior stakeholders were not interested in the issues I decided to fix, so they did not engage with or support my efforts. Without their backing, I struggled to move my initiative forward. I discovered the hard way that the key to the success of a data governance initiative is bringing along senior stakeholders and keeping them engaged. As already mentioned, the only way to do this is to focus on the things that interest them. That means solving data issues which will, in turn, help achieve the strategic objectives for which they are responsible. Explaining how data governance can help achieve these objectives changes the narrative. It changes the conversation from best practice to enabling organizational objectives.

Do you need a data strategy and a data governance strategy?

There is growing recognition across most industries that data is an asset. I would go as far as saying that there has been a remarkable evolution in how companies view data over the past 20 years. When I was first starting my data governance career, most organizations viewed data merely as an operational by-product. If they thought about data at all, it was as something that was needed for compliance or reporting purposes. In the first 10 to 15 years of my data governance career it was very rare to work with a company that wanted to manage their data better for strategic reasons. The vast majority of data governance initiatives were focused on regulatory compliance.

Thankfully, that is changing and companies are realizing that having the right data of the right quality is integral to making good decisions and building good customer relationships, and is essential for digital transformation and the successful adoption of AI.

Operational efficiencies, improved risk management and revenue generation are all enabled once we start managing data as an asset. As a result, there is an increasing trend of companies developing data strategies.

This, in turn, has led to a considerable number of people asking me if they need both a data strategy and a data governance strategy. Before addressing that, it is important to get the basics straight.

What is a data strategy?

A data strategy is like a game plan for how a company uses its data to reach its business goals. Think of it like a recipe book – it lays out exactly what data is needed, how it needs to be prepared (collected) and the processes followed to make sure you have the right results, i.e. good-quality data that can be used across your organization.

A good data strategy will typically include:

- vision and objectives: the big picture of how the company wants to use data to support its goals
- data governance framework: the rules, roles and processes to keep data understood and organized
- data quality management: what is needed to make sure the data is of good enough quality to deliver the vision and objectives
- technology and tools: the systems and software that help collect, store and analyse data

A data strategy is important because it acts like a map in a world overflowing with data. Without it, organizations can easily lose direction. With a clear strategy, businesses can make smarter, faster decisions because they are working with accurate and reliable data. A solid data strategy turns scattered data into meaningful insights that drive success.

Where does a data governance strategy come in?

As the focus on data has increased, there has been a shift from individual data management disciplines to the broader, more joined-up approach of a data strategy. Data governance should be a key part of the data strategy. Sadly, this is not always understood and you may have to work with the owner of your data strategy to ensure that it is. There are a number of reasons why organizations neglect to include data governance in their data strategy. These range from a lack of understanding that it enables everything else data-related to a misconception that it slows innovation, as well as a tendency to focus on short-term gains. It is likely that you will have to overcome such

hurdles to ensure that data governance is recognized as the fundamental foundation for all other data activities and given the
appropriate focus in the data strategy.

Even before data strategies became a thing, I was never a fan of
having a document called a data governance strategy. Of course, I've
always documented the approach I'm planning, but I discovered that
keeping this light touch and high level is more useful. Calling it a
'data governance approach' means that I can quickly pull together
the document and use it to engage with stakeholders, amending it
quickly based on their feedback. If it is called a data governance
strategy, I find that questions are asked about who owns it. In addition, a number of people will want to review and approve it before I
can start doing anything. You need an iterative approach to implement data governance successfully. Think about it. You do not want
to waste hours seeking approval for small amendments to a strategy.
You want to spend as much of your time as possible on the activities
which add value to the organization.

As a data governance lead, your job is to make sure your governance practices fit within the broader data strategy and align with
your organization's corporate strategy and goals. I do not think you
need a separate data governance strategy.

I am not prescriptive above this, though. You can call your plan or
approach a data governance strategy if you want to, and in some
cultures or organizations doing so may mean that it is taken more
seriously. Personally, I rarely do as I prefer to keep things simple and
focus as much effort as possible on solving data problems and delivering business value.

Building the business case for data governance

While ensuring your efforts are aligned with corporate strategy is
critical, it is only part of the story. Building a compelling case for data
governance is essential. It is a bit like constructing a strong building;
without a solid foundation, everything is at risk of collapsing.
Aligning with corporate strategy is not enough, you need to be able

to explain to stakeholders at all levels what is in it for them and why it is important.

Making the case for data governance is not easy. In addition to strategic requirements, we have to demonstrate an immediate need for it. Explaining that you will find and fix problems and save money sounds good. However, when you clarify that you will not know which problems and how much you will save until you get going, you are unlikely to gain many supporters. Believe me, I have tried that! Instead, we have to take a more objective approach and plan how we will answer the inevitable questions about return on investment.

As mentioned in Chapter 1, while we need to understand what data governance is, it is more important that we can explain the value it will deliver. Therefore, our business case should not contain lengthy sections on roles, processes and standards. Of course, you should mention that it will enable you to turn unmanaged data into an asset, but this must be explained in terms of what it means to your organization.

Let's look at the key elements to consider when making this case.

Compliance and risk management

If regulatory requirements mandate data governance within your organization, this obligation must be clearly communicated.

There is a growing list of regulations that require data governance in place over at least some of an organization's data (usually the data used in reports to the respective regulators). These include BCBS 239 and Solvency II for the financial services and insurance sectors, along with a whole raft of regulations requiring it in the healthcare, pharmaceutical, telecoms and energy sectors. The public sector is not immune either, with both the UK and US governments requiring government departments and agencies to have data governance in place. Not forgetting that, as covered in Chapter 1, GDPR requires all organizations holding data on European citizens to have some data governance fundamentals in place.

Of course, data governance supports risk management beyond regulatory compliance. The framework you will put in place will strengthen the identification and mitigation of data related risks. It does this by:

- Identifying clear accountability for data. With data owners in place, risks are properly managed rather than falling through gaps.
- Providing a clear understanding of data. The documentation and availability of definitions considerably reduce the risk of the wrong data being used, which is a common cause of data quality issues.
- Documenting the flow of key data. Data lineage, which is covered in Chapter 7, provides a clear record of how data moves through your organization. This is a valuable tool in identify when data is most at risk and when mitigating controls need to be introduced.

That said, remember the example in Chapter 1 and be sure to explain that a solid data governance foundation will not only enable regulatory compliance and improved risk management, but also deliver business value.

Improved data quality

Of course, you will deliver improved data quality, but in a business case you cannot be generic. Remember, the senior stakeholders who must approve the business case require specific, substantiated claims rather than generic statements. They will need specific examples. This, in itself, creates a challenge. Without approval to start doing data governance, you are not in a position to start a massive discovery exercise that will uncover all the ways data is being used poorly. When making the case, we will not have a complete list of data quality issues, but we do need enough organization-specific examples to convince stakeholders that there are enough problems to warrant this initiative. We need to identify some data pain points, or, as I like to call them, data quality horror stories.

Over the years, I have heard many data quality horror stories. Some are humorous upon re-telling but all have been painful for those involved to resolve. Most have resulted in unexpected costs or losses. One of my favourites is an organization that wrongly matched and combined the customer records for 800 separate customers into one customer, because a call centre agent had entered their own mobile number for each customer rather than ask each customer for their mobile number! Or, there was the company who discovered that around a quarter of their customers had the same date of birth. When investigating this, a business analyst who had been with the company years remembered that a default value had been added for all records with a missing date of birth when customer records had been migrated to a new system in the past.

If you are at the stage of creating a data governance business case, you should undertake some stakeholder engagement at every level of the organization and encourage them to share their data quality horror stories.

If you are able to, this is a good time to create the conceptual data models mentioned in Chapter 1. I doubt you will be able to do them for every business department at this stage. However, if you can do them for two or three key functions, you will easily collect enough horror stories for your business case. In a 90-minute workshop with a handful of data subject matter experts from one business function, you will be able to create a valuable conceptual data model. During the workshop, attendees will often tell you about the challenges they currently have or have previously faced with the data they are telling you about. If they don't, without prompting, I always ask! Attendees are always keen to vent their frustrations with the data they deal with. I often liken it to a data therapy session. For 90 minutes of your time, you will gain the examples you need for your business case, plus a conceptual data model which will be used as you progress your data governance initiative. Throughout the remaining chapters of this book, I will explain how you will use it more.

Operational efficiency

Senior stakeholders care about efficiency and wasted time! Some of the horror stories you collect will demonstrate how much time is wasted data wrangling. Use these in a separate section of your business case to highlight some of the operational inefficiencies arising from poor data. Some organizations I've worked with have used these to estimate the amount of time being wasted by one team and then, assuming that every area of the organization wastes a similar amount of time data wrangling, they extrapolate to show the potential amount of time being wasted across the organization. The numbers can quickly become scary and are extremely helpful in getting business case approval!

Building trust and accountability

One of the many benefits of data governance is that when roles and responsibilities are defined, it fosters a culture of accountability. Employees are more likely to value data when they understand its importance and their role in maintaining it. Most people want the issues they face with data resolved, but without clear responsibilities no one is clear who can make decisions about that data. So, no one makes the decision and the data wrangling continues. It is really useful if one or more of your horror stories illustrates this point.

Better decision-making

Senior stakeholders are not stupid people, but sometimes poor decisions are made because they believe that the data in a report given to them is correct. With a robust governance framework, leaders can make informed decisions backed by reliable data. Trust in data equates to trust in decisions, which in turn drives organizational success.

Can you find and share examples of poor decision-making because of poor data? Perhaps there are multiple reports which all show, for example, a different number of customers? In my experience, a significant amount of time is wasted in endless debates about why 'my number is right and yours is wrong'. It is extremely useful to find and expose a few of these in your business case.

Pilot proposal

By covering these points, you should be able to build a compelling business case, but it often goes wrong when we ask for too much!

Every successful data governance initiative begins with small, tangible steps. Although you might envision a grand, all-encompassing framework, initiating a small pilot project can yield quick wins. For example, select one critical data domain, establish clear definitions and ownership and demonstrate measurable improvements in data quality. This can create momentum and enthusiasm for broader implementations.

Building a compelling case for data governance calls for clear communication, stakeholder engagement and a strategic approach. By illustrating the benefits and starting small, you are more likely to get approval. And when your pilot is successful, you will gain invaluable momentum to expand your data governance initiative.

Data governance maturity assessments

At an early stage of your data governance journey (either as part of building the business case or soon after), it can be extremely useful to undertake a maturity assessment. A data governance maturity assessment is a structured evaluation designed to gauge an organization's current level of data governance capabilities. Much like assessing your garden's health after a long winter, this assessment helps you understand what is thriving, which areas are struggling and which need more attention.

The primary aims of a maturity assessment are as follows:

- Identify strengths: Highlight the areas where the organization excels in managing its data.
- Spot gaps: Pinpoint weaknesses and areas that require improvement.
- Establish a roadmap: Create a clear path for improving the organization's data governance practices.

There are several different data governance maturity assessments available that you can find online, some of which are reasonably straightforward and others which are more complex and onerous to complete. They all use a structured approach and a defined set of criteria to assess maturity levels. Which you select, or whether you design your own, will come down to which best meets the needs of your organization. However, do keep in mind that there is great value in repeating these assessments at regular intervals and more value will be gained from repeated assessments against the same criteria. Therefore, choose an assessment which you will be happy to repeat. For example, will you get approval or buy-in to repeat a complex, time-consuming process at regular intervals?

One thing they all have in common is that the main objective is to generate actionable insights. Undertaking such an assessment should lead to practical recommendations on how to improve data governance practices.

Why you should conduct a data governance maturity assessment

From the description above, you would be forgiven for thinking that the main reason to undertake a data governance maturity assessment is to identify strengths and weaknesses. Of course, this is an important part of why we do them, but they deliver much more than that. They are valuable tools in helping progress your data governance initiative.

I have found that they can be extremely helpful in facilitating cultural change. Other more mature disciplines, for example data security, have used maturity assessments for many years. Many business users may be used to regular data security maturity assessments and understand that they are undertaken because data security is important. Using the same approach when it comes to data governance sends a very clear message that it is not just the security of our data that is important.

On numerous occasions, I have found they can also be useful in obtaining resources to support your initiative. One client presenting on data governance to their executive committee was asked what 'their number' was. The data governance manager had to ask for clarification of what was meant. It was explained that at the previous meeting, the data security team had presented the results of their latest maturity assessment, along with recommendations of what was needed to enable the organization to meet the desired level of maturity. The data governance manager explained that he did not have enough budget to undertake such an assessment. The committee instructed him to determine the implementation cost. This was later approved and the assessment undertaken. A few months later, the data governance manager presented the results and the target level of maturity. He was asked to come back with plans and costs to achieve that, which were subsequently approved.

Assessments are valuable in monitoring and improving communication. The first time I ever created a simple maturity assessment, I was frustrated by some results. Two of the business areas assessed had selected the criteria to say there were no data owners in place. I felt offended and defensive. I had put considerable effort into identifying and engaging the data owners in both areas. Initially, I blamed the stakeholders in those areas for completing the assessment questionnaires incorrectly! Then, I realized that the results had highlighted something important. While the data owners and I knew that they had accepted the role, we had not communicated the fact very well. Since then, I am much more open-minded when reviewing the results; they are an excellent way to gauge how effective your communications are, or even whether you have been doing enough of them.

Frequency of assessments

Conducting a maturity assessment should ideally occur once a year. This frequency allows enough time for meaningful changes to be implemented and ensures that stakeholders are not overwhelmed with too frequent evaluations. Many people seriously underestimate the speed at which they will be able to implement data governance. As such, repeating a data governance maturity assessment can help identify progress made, as well as areas to focus on in the next phases of the initiative.

Doing an assessment more frequently than annually is not recommended. It is unlikely you will have made enough progress to justify it. You do not want your stakeholders to use too much of the time they have for data governance activities completing questionnaires instead. As already stated, they provide valuable insights, but running them too frequently can cause disengagement in key stakeholders. This is something which we need to avoid at all costs.

Data governance maturity assessments can be very powerful tools when used correctly; just do not do them too frequently.

Creating a data governance roadmap

A roadmap was mentioned earlier and you may be wondering what it is, and, with everything else you need to do, whether you really need one. Many people take this to mean a project plan. To be clear, when I use the term 'roadmap' I do not mean a project plan. There are two reasons for this.

Firstly, it is not and should not be a project plan because data governance is not a project. It is not a once-and-done activity. Your organization is always going to need data governance to ensure that its data continues to be managed as an asset. The data governance manager role is not a temporary one. They are responsible for supporting data governance and ensuring that the approach evolves so that data continues to meet the changing needs of the business.

For example, a few years ago, no data governance managers would have been wondering how to fit AI governance into their data governance framework, but today they all are (or should be). Since data governance is not a project, we do not want to have a project plan. We do not want to do anything that gives the impression to the rest of the organization that once the 'plan' is completed, we can stop doing data governance.

The second reason we do not want a project plan is that they are very detailed. A project plan will have activities broken down into detailed tasks, specific dates, dependencies, resource allocations and critical paths. As a former project manager, I like a good project plan, but they are not useful when it comes to implementing data governance. To succeed with data governance, we need to be flexible and iterative, amending our approach as we discover what is working and what is not. Additionally, a project team usually undertakes most of the work in a project, with some consultation with business stakeholders. In contrast, in a data governance initiative, we guide and support the business users while they do most of the work. We do not have the authority to tell them when tasks must be completed. We need to convince them to work with us. Presenting them with a detailed plan containing arbitrary timescales will have the opposite effect.

This does not mean that I recommend that you do not have any documented plans. If you do not, it is unlikely that anything will progress. If we say we will identity data owners or agree some data definitions 'sometime', it will never happen. This is where the road-map comes in.

A roadmap is a very high-level plan. It's an idea of the direction of travel, the order in which we are going to do things, and includes some target dates to be agreed with our stakeholders. A roadmap will not have numerous detailed tasks. The level of activity that I include would be for example to: complete data discovery and create concep-tual data models for five key business functions by the end of June. The next activity would be to: identify and train data owners by the end of September. We do not want a great deal of detail, we just want to provide an overview of what we will be doing, the order and approximate timelines. A roadmap gives us something to help explain what we are doing. It gives us a structure to discuss with stakehold-ers. It helps ensure that our plans are aligned with their own plans and expectations.

A data governance roadmap is a valuable tool; it documents the actions we want to take and is useful for structured discussions with stakeholders.

Conclusion

Strategy is the cornerstone of successful data governance. Throughout this chapter, we have seen that aligning your data governance initia-tive with your organization's corporate strategy is not just beneficial; it is essential. By focusing on the strategic objectives that matter to your senior stakeholders, you transform data governance from being seen (incorrectly) as a technical initiative into a business enabler that commands attention and support.

Remember that the most successful data governance programmes start small, demonstrate value quickly and grow incrementally. Your business case should highlight specific pain points that resonate with decision-makers, while your maturity assessments provide both a baseline and a roadmap for improvement. Whether your organization has a formal data strategy or a more simple data governance approach, make sure that it supports your organization's goals. The key is to remain flexible, responsive and focused on delivering tangible business value.

As you move forward, keep your roadmap high-level and adaptable, remember that data governance is not a project with an end date but an ongoing capability which will evolve with your organization. By maintaining this strategic focus, you will ensure that your data governance initiative not only starts strongly but continues to deliver value long into the future.

PART TWO

Design

03

What is a data governance framework?

Introduction

A data governance framework provides the essential structure that enables organizations to understand and manage their data effectively. Much like the framework of a house that prevents collapse, a well-designed data governance framework ensures your data management approach delivers real business value without unnecessary complexity. This chapter explores what constitutes an effective framework and why simplicity is crucial for successful implementation.

In this chapter, you will learn:

- why a structured approach to data governance is necessary
- the importance of documenting your framework
- how simplicity drives stakeholder adoption and success
- why custom-building a framework for your organization is essential
- lessons from real-world implementation successes and failures

Creating a framework that works for your organization requires balancing comprehensiveness with accessibility. Through real-world examples and practical guidance, this chapter will show you how to avoid common pitfalls and develop a framework that drives adoption rather than resistance.

A structure that describes what we are implementing

If you are responsible for implementing data governance at your organization, there is a high chance that you have googled the term 'data governance framework'. If you have, you probably received a whole myriad of answers back. You may also have seen many diagrams, some of which were very complex and, let's be honest, a bit scary! If you look up the term 'framework' you will find a range of definitions, but most sources agree that it is a basic structure underlying a concept or system. Data governance is definitely a concept and, more importantly, it is a system. It is a way of managing and looking after data that we want people to adopt at our organization.

However, a data governance framework should not be scary, complex or confusing! A data governance framework simply provides a structured approach that enables organizations to understand and manage their data effectively. As I mentioned, it resembles the framework of a house; without it, the building can collapse or may not serve its purpose. I like to think of a data governance framework as a way to describe our approach to data governance. Done well, it provides a helpful illustration of what we are doing.

So, what does a data governance framework consist of? I think it should consist of just three components: a data governance policy, processes, and roles and responsibilities. I like to think of each as follows:

- data governance policy: what we will be doing
- processes: how we will be doing it
- roles and responsibilities: who will be doing what

We will be covering each of these in depth in later chapters, but for now I want to focus on the framework itself.

One of my biggest frustrations is that when we work in data governance, we spend a lot of effort getting business stakeholders to document and agree on data definitions (which we will cover in Chapter 7). However, data governance practitioners rarely explain what they mean by the various terms used. As a result, they are often used to mean different things. This only adds to the confusion of those new to a data governance role, as well as the business stakeholders trying to understand what is being implemented.

I use 'data governance framework' as the overarching term which describes what we are implementing. I have worked with many organizations that like to call the entire documentation of their data governance approach their data governance framework. If that works for your organization and its culture, go for it. I frequently use the term as a label for the diagram which illustrates the structure we are putting in place. Alongside the diagram, I have several documents that describe in detail the components of the framework. The diagram can be something like Figure 3.1 in its simplest form, or a more complex one along the lines of Figure 3.2.

I use the simple version primarily when teaching training courses, but it can be useful in organizations when a previous overly complex approach to data governance has failed. Alex Leigh (a data governance and data strategy consultant I have worked with on numerous occasions) and I created the first version of Figure 3.2 when we worked together several years ago, and I have used versions based on this many times since.

FIGURE 3.1 Simple data governance framework diagram

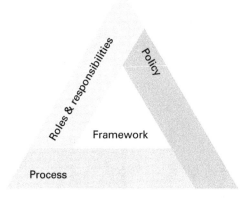

Why we need a structure

Having a structured approach enables us to articulate our initiative clearly and to educate our business stakeholders on their role.

FIGURE 3.2 Detailed data governance framework diagram

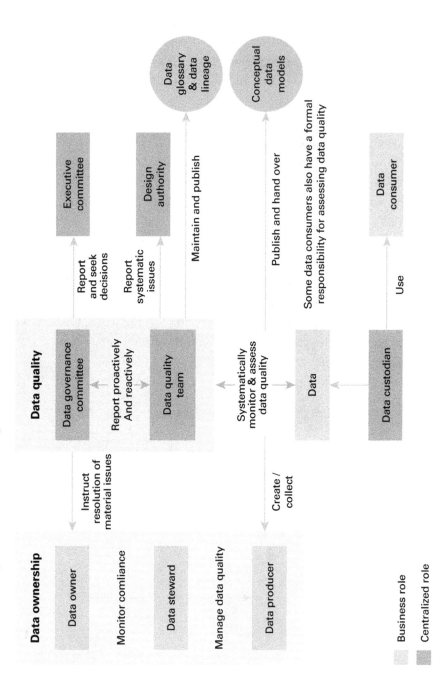

If you follow the advice in Chapter 2 you will be able to engage stakeholders and inspire them to want to do data governance. If we can articulate the benefits it will bring, it is a relatively straightforward (although please note I do not say easy!) task to gain support. However, it is impossible to get everyone to do things consistently if you do not give them a structure, i.e. the data governance framework, to follow. We need a policy which explains what we are doing, we need instructions (processes) to describe how to do it and we need to make it very clear who will be following these processes.

Early in my career, I discovered what happens when we do not have that structure. I convinced some people to support me and agree to be data owners. I impressed upon them the importance of identifying and fixing data quality issues. However, I did not give them a documented process to follow which would ensure that all impacted stakeholders were identified and consulted. I was thrilled to discover that some data owners were being proactive and solving data quality issues. But then came a problem. One team fixed a data quality issue but unwittingly caused an issue for another team that used the same data. I learnt that if we do not have a clearly documented process for dealing with data quality issues, they can be fixed in a way which may cause a problem for other users of that data. Having a structure is vital when it comes to successful data governance. It makes it much easier for everyone to both understand and do the right things when it comes to data.

Why it is important to document the framework

Documenting your framework should not be considered something optional. I've found that a documented data governance framework serves as the backbone of successful initiatives. A documented framework helps us with the following:

- Strategic alignment: Diagrams help us to explain abstract data concepts in terms of business value by explicitly connecting data governance activities to business context. Without this link, data governance becomes a technical exercise disconnected from business outcomes, which will result in a failed implementation.

- Operational clarity: A documented framework helps establish clear accountability, defining who makes decisions about what data and under which circumstances. A role description in isolation is not enough. A diagram that shows roles in action helps our stakeholders to understand what is required of them. It also helps them comprehend how their role fits into the bigger picture.

- Consistent implementation: I have learnt that good diagrams and communication materials go a long way to ensuring that data governance is applied uniformly across departments. This prevents the fragmented approaches that often emerge when you rely solely on verbal explanations or lengthy formal documents.

- Cultural transformation: In Chapter 1, we discussed how culture change is the biggest challenge you face when implementing data governance. A documented framework signals a commitment from senior stakeholders that data is considered a strategic asset. This will help shift mindsets from viewing data as a by-product to recognizing it as a valuable resource requiring intentional management.

- Support education and communication: When you start implementing a data governance framework for the first time, you might be implementing lots of new ideas and concepts that have not existed in your company before. When we meet new stakeholders, it is not helpful to talk randomly about processes, roles and responsibilities. This is new territory for them and we are covering concepts they have never heard before. However, a diagram showing the things you are implementing and how they relate to each other can be a game changer. You have a diagram to talk through logically and it gives the person you are speaking to some structure. This makes it easier for them to follow along and gain an understanding of what you are talking about. Many stakeholders over the years have said that they find such a diagram useful, not just in that initial meeting but also as something which they can refer to afterwards.

Why simplicity is key

A framework is something you can make as complicated as you want to. I have seen many very complex examples over the years. In my experience, your framework needs to be as simple as possible to be successful. I recommend simplicity when doing data governance above all else. Sometimes, circumstances necessitate a more involved framework, but start with a simple approach and build in additional details as and when needed. Simplicity is one of the key principles for successful data governance, which we will cover in more detail in Chapter 11.

It is important to recognize that we are trying to enable our business stakeholders to use their data better. We want them to understand what data they have and whether it is good enough quality to use. We need them to know what to do if data quality issues are found. If we create a convoluted framework, will anybody want to follow it? We must remember that we are doing this to deliver real business value. A complex approach will be perceived as an obstacle stopping people from getting on with their day jobs. Even if you are telling them that this is going to make their job easier in the future, why would they believe you if the framework looks very complicated?

My mantra is to make a data governance framework as simple as possible. That does not mean that you cannot add more details or alternatives approaches to cover particular circumstances as you go along, but always start with something simple that your business users can get their heads around. That way, they are more inclined to adopt it and work with you.

REAL-WORLD EXAMPLE
A prospective client with an overly complex approach

I have seen many overly elaborate frameworks over the years, but I will always remember a video call I had with one particular prospective client. The person I met was the newly appointed data governance manager at a medium-sized financial services company in Portugal. My initial impression was positive; he was incredibly enthusiastic and knew he could make a difference. He was new to both the company and to data governance. He spent three months speaking at length to every business function about the various data challenges they were experiencing. He then sat at his desk for another three months, researching online and designing the perfect data governance framework for his company. You could not fault his research skills and attention to detail. He finally shared the framework with his stakeholders and was crestfallen at their reaction to it. The feedback was almost instantaneous and mainly consisted of 'no'. I was intrigued and asked if he minded sharing the diagram with me before we continued our discussion. He happily agreed; he was very proud of it and wanted to share it with someone who would appreciate it.

The diagram was incredibly detailed and intricate. It mentioned numerous roles, committees and processes. There were various different icons to represent the assorted data governance deliverables which will be covered in Chapter 7. It tried to cover every possible eventuality with data in that company. Even if it had been printed on A3 paper, it would have been hard to read. Honestly, I felt overwhelmed and confused! If I found it off-putting, it is no surprise that his stakeholders reacted negatively. The sad reality was that this person had been in the role for over 6 months and had not managed to progress his data governance initiative at all. Instead, all he had achieved was to alienate his stakeholders.

I advised him that the complex diagram was scary and had probably made his stakeholders feel stupid. Over the years, I've observed a psychological barrier that undermines even technically sound frameworks. I realized that people exhibit resistance when something makes them feel intellectually diminished. We need to make data governance feel simple, eminently doable and connected to business value. You will not be surprised to learn that I recommended that he create a significantly simplified version of his diagram, focusing only on the basics, before attempting to engage with his senior stakeholders again.

Understanding the resistance

Early in my data governance career, when I wondered why my stakeholders were not responding as expected, I decided to put myself in their shoes and consider it from their perspective. Had I instantly grasped the principles of data governance when I was first working in it? The answer to that question was a resounding no. I would even go as far as saying that for quite a while, I felt overwhelmed with what

I trying to do and struggled to explain it in a way that got other people to support me. So, if I had not instantly understood the concept and value, why was I expecting my stakeholders to do so?

While researching what I could do to overcome this obstacle, I came across the idea of the competence threat response. Psychologists explain that when professionals encounter situations which challenge their existing expertise, they see this as a 'competence threat', i.e. a perceived attack on their professional identity and capability. I was unwittingly triggering this response in my senior stakeholders and I've seen many others (not just in the data governance space) doing the same. The lesson to be learned is that we must not make our stakeholders feel stupid and overly complex diagrams and frameworks are a sure way to do this!

Why you must custom-build for your organization

At a basic level, humans seem wired to seek efficiency. I am sure that initially it was about survival. Using less energy to get food, avoid danger or solve problems meant a better chance of thriving. But now, in modern life, that same instinct shows up in our constant search for shortcuts, tools, automations… anything to save time and effort. So, of course, in an attempt to speed up data governance implementation, a number of different standard data governance frameworks have been created.

Increasingly, I am being asked by clients to help them implement a standard data governance framework, but I'll be honest: I am not a great fan of them. Over the years, I've made that view clear in my social media posts, but still a question I get asked regularly is: 'Do I really need to design my own data governance framework?'

My answer is always a resounding yes. The best way that I can think of to explain this is to use an analogy. We are all individuals and each have unique challenges when it comes to exercise. If we follow a generic exercise routine not designed for us personally, it may not help us and may even harm us. This was the case recently for my husband. After slowly recovering from shoulder replacement surgery, he wanted to get fitter and, for various reasons, decided not to work with his old personal trainer but to join a group programme instead. He thought the camaraderie of others might help motivate him as he got back to exercising. Unfortunately, although the group leader asked at the start if anyone had any injuries, no allowances or alterations were made for those who did declare injuries. He found that he was either not able to physically do many of the exercises or they were movements which he had been told to avoid. Consequently, he had to sit out a number of the exercises and his fitness levels did not improve much. This was a standard programme that was inflexible and made no allowance for the constraints of the individuals undertaking the programme. I suspect my husband was probably not the only person in the group not to achieve the hoped for benefits.

This perfectly illustrates what can happen if you try to adopt a standard framework. Standard frameworks are just like that standard exercise programme – not designed for the specific organization. They are a theoretical idea of what should be done but make no allowance for the specific needs or constraints of an organization. They can and should give us inspiration for what we could be doing, but if we try to follow them rigidly they do not deliver the expected benefits.

I understand that when you are just starting your data governance journey, copying an existing framework may seem like an easy and sensible option, but please bear in mind that standard frameworks have several constraints:

- Reality gap: Just like the standard exercise programme, a standard framework is unlikely to align with your organizational structure, culture and challenges.

- Resourcing: Because they are theoretical, no consideration is given to the resources required to implement them. As a result, they often require considerably more resources than many organizations ever have available to implement data governance.

- Culture change: As already mentioned, this is the biggest challenge when implementing data governance, yet standard frameworks focus primarily on what will be done and not on the culture change required for it to happen.

- Maturity misalignment: A standard framework has to be designed to cover everything you may wish to do, but only an organization which is very mature in its data governance practices would be able to implement some of the practices mentioned in the standard frameworks available online.

Data governance success does not come from having a perfect initial design. It comes instead from starting with something simple which has been designed to meet the needs of your organization. It can and should evolve over time as your organization itself evolves and achieves a more mature approach to data governance. A data governance framework is not a static thing, it should continue to change and grow.

Designing your own data governance framework is not as hard as it may initially seem, and over the remaining chapters we will cover all the things you need to consider. By all means take inspiration from standard data governance frameworks, but please do not rigidly adopt them. Use them to help you tailor something that is right for your organization at this moment in time, as well as provide some ideas of what to aspire to in the future.

REAL-WORLD EXAMPLE

A client who implemented a standard framework

I have helped many clients over the years whose first attempts to implement data governance had used a standard framework and failed, but one in particular stands out. The company, a large financial services company based in London and providing services globally, was taking the topic very seriously. They had executive sponsorship, dedicated resources and had spent a significant amount of effort to do data governance correctly. Unlike many others, they had not chosen to implement a standard data governance framework as a quick fix. They believed that following a standard framework would be the best practice and ensure that they did it correctly.

I first met them when two members of the data and analytics team and the executive sponsor of the data governance initiative attended a public training course I delivered. I noticed immediately that the questions they asked were not the typical questions that those new to data governance typically ask. Their questions were diving into the thinking and reasoning behind the concepts. I also found it odd that, although obviously very engaged, at some points during the course they just sat nodding their heads while at other times they were frantically taking notes.

At the end of the day, one of the three (whom I subsequently discovered to be the executive sponsor of the initiative) asked if I could spare a few minutes to speak to her. She explained that the course had been very illuminating for them. The company had been trying to implement data governance for 18 months but had struggled to make progress. They decided that attending the course might help them identify what they were doing wrong. Some of what I taught made perfect sense and they were already doing these things. However, other things were new to them, or I recommended implementing in a different order than they had tried (explaining why sometimes they took lots of notes and at other times none). We agreed to speak the following week for them to share some details of their approach.

On that call, they explained that they were implementing a standard data governance framework, one they had chosen carefully after conducting extensive research of the options available. It was a framework of which I was aware but did not have detailed knowledge about. I was asked if I would work with them to help them identify what was going wrong and why. I agreed; I love working out how to make data governance successful in different circumstances, and my first step was to purchase the framework they were implementing.

My initial thoughts were that it was not an intrinsically bad framework, but there was one glaring omission. It went to great lengths to explain what you need to have in place, but it did not provide any guidance on who should be doing any of the activities it described. The success of a data governance initiative hangs on the roles and responsibilities. If no one is responsible for undertaking the tasks, is it likely that they will happen? We will look at roles and responsibilities in Chapter 6.

Having familiarized myself with the standard framework, I spent a few days with the client. I interviewed key stakeholders on the team implementing data governance and senior stakeholders from across the company. I was keen to understand the company and the data challenges that each department faced. Armed with pages of notes, I sat down to analyse the situation. I determined that not only were there no data governance roles and responsibilities in place, but that some sections of the framework were too mature for the company to achieve at that point. My main conclusions were:

- The only people undertaking data governance activities were the data and analytics team.
- Most business areas were unaware of the initiative.
- Some parts of the framework were unachievable without some basics in place first.
- Some parts of the framework would only be appropriate for an organization much more mature in its existing data governance practices.

Having spent significant effort on the initiative by that stage, it would not have been well received if a U-turn was announced and the standard framework abandoned. However, with some guidance, the team created a modified version of the framework. They focused their efforts on getting the roles and responsibilities agreed upon and stakeholders engaged with the initiative. They postponed implementing those parts of the framework that were just too mature for them at that time, including the section on measuring process improvements arising from better-quality data. The framework also included a section on 'data-related support' which covered data architecture management, data transfer management, data operations management and data security management. As covered in Chapter 1, these are not data governance activities and added to the confusion over the scope of the initiative. Removing them provided clarity for both the team and their stakeholders on what the data governance initiative covered.

After a rocky start, this company went on to have a very successful data governance initiative, growing the team and the scope of their activities over the years as demand for their services and support grew. Unfortunately, that is not always the case, and many initiatives are cancelled because they are not working and it is sometimes years before another attempt is made. And, of course, subsequent attempts to implement data governance are even harder if a previous attempt has failed.

Trying to implement a standard framework rigidly is the reason that many data governance initiatives fail, so please design your own framework based on your organization and its needs. Failing that, adapt and tailor a standard framework to make it appropriate for you. Above all, please keep it simple!

Conclusion

Creating an effective data governance framework is about balance – providing enough structure to guide your organization while keeping it simple enough to encourage adoption. Your framework should evolve as your organization matures in its data practices.

Remember these key principles:

- Start with simplicity – complexity leads to resistance.
- Custom-build for your organization's unique needs.
- Document your framework to ensure consistent implementation.
- Focus on culture change as much as technical implementation.
- Prioritize stakeholder understanding over theoretical completeness.

A well-designed framework empowers your organization to treat data as the valuable asset it is. By providing clear guidance on what to do, how to do it and who is responsible, you create the foundation for lasting data governance success that delivers real business value.

The real-world examples in this chapter demonstrate the pitfalls of overcomplicated frameworks and rigid adherence to standard models. When stakeholders feel overwhelmed or incompetent, they resist change. Conversely, when they understand the framework and see how it addresses their specific challenges, they become advocates for your data governance initiative.

As you move forward in designing your own framework, remember that perfection is not the goal – progress is. Begin with addressing your organization's most pressing data challenges, document your approach clearly and build from there. Allow your framework to mature alongside your organization's data capabilities and culture.

With this solid foundation in place, you will be ready to explore the specific components of your framework in greater detail in the chapters ahead.

04

Writing your data governance policy

Introduction

Developing a data governance policy is a crucial step in your data governance journey. This foundational document sets the stage for how your organization will manage its data as a valuable asset. While it may be tempting to skip this step when faced with the multitude of tasks in implementing data governance, a well-crafted policy provides the mandate and direction needed for success.

In this chapter, we'll explore:

- what a data governance policy is and why it's distinct from standards
- why creating a custom policy is essential rather than copying from others
- the critical importance of having a policy to drive adoption
- the real consequences of attempting data governance without a policy
- key components to include in your policy document
- the difference between a policy and an operating model
- how to engage stakeholders in the policy creation process

Through my years of experience implementing data governance in various organizations, I've learnt that a concise, clear policy developed with stakeholder input becomes the foundation for sustainable data governance. This chapter will guide you through creating a policy that works for your unique organizational context rather than overwhelming your stakeholders with unnecessary complexity.

What is meant by a data governance policy?

Organizations typically have several types of policies that guide their operations, governance and employee conduct. You will be familiar with several of them; they cover areas such as human resources (HR), recruitment and IT usage. If we want our organization to start managing its data as an asset, we should have a policy that covers how we do that.

A data governance policy is a formal document that outlines an organization's approach to managing data, ensuring that data is understood, of good quality and usable. Think of it as the roadmap guiding how an organization interacts with its data, ensuring that every team member knows their roles and responsibilities when it comes to handling data.

When I use the term 'data governance policy', I mean a high-level document which mandates that your organization embraces data governance. I've seen many examples where someone has spent a lot of time and effort researching data governance and what they think they ought to have in their framework. They then dump everything they find into their data governance policy. The result is a lengthy document – some I've seen are like small novels! Honestly, I wrote some that length early in my data governance journey but soon learnt that long-winded documents can be more of a hindrance than a help to your efforts. When you come to share it with stakeholders, they will be put off by the sheer level of detail. You are likely to fall at the first hurdle and not persuade senior stakeholders to approve the policy in the first place.

Another thing I frequently see is people thinking that they can fast-track this part of a data governance initiative by copying an existing policy, either looking on the internet or asking a contact doing a similar job at another organization if they can have a copy of theirs. Please do not do this. A policy should be written to reflect how *your* organization wants to do data governance. If you take another company's policy, it is extremely unlikely to be useful or even relevant for your organization. As with all things data governance, there is no such a thing as a successful standard approach. There certainly is not one for a data governance policy. Think about it this way: if a standard data governance framework is not going to facilitate success, why would you think that a policy written for another organization would work for you?

I am often asked if I will share a template of a data governance policy. I have never created or used one as I believe that for a policy to be useful (i.e. help you implement data governance successfully), it needs to be written with your organization in mind. You should consider the following:

- What is the scope of your data governance programme?
- What is it that your organization is going to do to manage its data better?
- What roles and responsibilities do you need to manage your data better?
- What kind of processes are you going to implement as a result of having data governance?

The answers to these questions will not be the same for all companies. Every organization I have ever worked with has been unique in its approach to data governance. I admit that sometimes the differences are subtle, but for a policy to be valuable, these subtleties must be addressed. These slight differences can be different role titles or the inclusion of a less common process, but they can make all the difference in whether the policy is accepted and approved.

The difference between policies and standards

I have been asked what the difference is between data policies and data standards numerous times over the years and had some interesting discussions on the topic! But before I dive into my thoughts on the matter, there is another question which needs to be asked (and answered) first: why do these two terms cause so much confusion?

After all, they are commonly used business terms. It is not as though they are specialist data management terms. The Cambridge Dictionary defines these two terms as follows:

> Policy: A set of ideas or a plan of what to do in particular situations that has been agreed to officially by a group of people, a business organization, a government or a political party.

> Standard: A level of quality.

The way I use these terms in the context of data governance follows the above definitions. Nevertheless, confusion arises as many people use the term 'policies' when I use 'standards'. I would say that an organization will have one data governance policy and many data quality standards. However, I am aware that a lot of practitioners say that an organization will have many data quality policies. So, to clarify, the definitions I use and apply throughout this book are:

> Data governance policy: A formal document which describes an organization's approach to managing data quality, i.e. what will be done.

> Data quality standard: The standard that a certain field or dataset needs to achieve, e.g. that a field must always be completed or the value sits within a defined range.

So which definitions should you use? I believe that it is fine to use them however you wish (and whichever fits best with your organization's culture). The important thing is to define what you mean and communicate those definitions with your audience. As with most things, confusion only arises when no explanation of what we mean is provided and those on the receiving end of your messages are left to make their own varied interpretations. Not defining terms is a common mistake or omission that many people make when starting in data governance.

Why you really need a policy

There is so much to do when you first start a data governance initiative that it is tempting to look for things that are not needed or can be postponed. As a result, I am frequently asked whether a data governance policy is really needed.

I am rarely able to give a definite answer to a data governance question. Usually, my answer is 'It depends' because so many aspects of data governance are nuanced and depend very much on the organization. In this case, however, the answer is yes. You do need a data governance policy if you want to effectively implement data governance in your organization.

Corporate policies of any type are approved by senior stakeholders in your organization to mandate certain types of activity and behaviour. It is vital that we also have one of these for data governance. If we don't, we are trying to implement data governance on a best-efforts basis. You might be thinking that this is a bit odd, given that, so far in this book, I have been telling you that you should emphasize the benefits and sell the value of doing data governance. Now I am telling you that you need a formal document, which is akin to a big stick, to make people do data governance!

Let's be clear: I want you to spend the vast majority of your time focusing on and selling the benefits of data governance. However, if we don't have a data governance policy, no one 'has' to do it. We must create a data governance policy which sets out the scope of what data is going to be and what activities we will be doing. The policy will make it very clear what it is that you are requiring people to do in your organization to manage their data better.

Having a data governance policy in place also sends a clear message that senior stakeholders understand that data is an asset and have provided guidance on how it needs to be managed.

REAL-WORLD EXAMPLE

The consequences of not having a data governance policy

For the first three or four data governance initiatives I worked on, I didn't have a data governance policy in place, or not until it was too late. I had worked out that I had to sell the benefits or value of doing it and I focused all my efforts on meeting people and enthusing them to support my initiative. As anyone who has met me will confirm, I am passionate about the topic and my enthusiasm often gets people to agree to what I am asking. Things went well in the early stages of these engagements. I mistakenly thought that my enthusiasm, along with some influencing skills, were all I needed to progress things. Often, I met with stakeholders who confirmed that they were still supportive of the idea but were very busy with other priorities. After another enthusiastic discussion with me, they agreed to try to find the time in the coming weeks. I noticed that the pattern kept occurring and that sooner or later somebody would ask, 'Do I really have to do this?'

The people I was speaking to were not being deliberately obstructive. They were asking because, like most of us, they had too much on their to-do list and did not have time to do everything. They reasoned that if they would not get into trouble for not doing data governance, then it was an easy activity to drop off the bottom of their to-do list. Passion and enthusiasm cannot help you overcome such logic. If, however, you have a data governance policy in place, it sends out a clear message that senior stakeholders have committed to it. More importantly, once you have a formal policy in place, your audit function will include it in their regular reviews and no one wants a bad report from an audit because they are not complying with company policy.

Data governance can deliver amazing benefits to your organization. You do not want your initiative delayed or even stopped because you did not take the time to get a data governance policy in place.

What to include in your policy

When drafting a data governance policy for clients, the policy needs to look and feel familiar. This helps make the stakeholders reviewing it feel more comfortable and, therefore, more likely to approve it. To make it look familiar, you need to match the format and house style used in other policies in your organization. If you have a risk team, they can usually provide a template, but if not, just find an existing policy to copy the format and generic headings from. It is also a good idea to review a few of your existing policies to get an idea of the style, level of detail and general length of the policies. Generally, as stated previously, shorter and more succinct policies are better.

However, on more than one occasion, I have been told that a short policy would not be taken seriously at that company and I have had to add more detail to the policy to get it approved.

Implementing a comprehensive data governance policy is imperative for the reasons previously articulated. However, navigating the approval process demands strategic planning, as policy adoption typically involves multiple stakeholders and approval checkpoints. Therefore, making the data governance policy look and feel as much like the existing policies with which your senior stakeholders are familiar is key to making the process as smooth as possible.

Once you know your format and style, you need to add the components specific to data governance to your policy. My preference is to start the policy writing with a meeting of senior stakeholders to brainstorm and agree on the principles by which they wish data to be managed. This is an easy way to get them engaged early in the process. Senior stakeholders are much happier to approve a policy if they feel they provided input. A frequent misstep in data governance implementation, one I initially made myself, involves presenting a fully drafted policy to stakeholders who have had no prior engagement in its development. No wonder they ask endless questions and request multiple rewrites and changes, making the sign-off process lengthy and painful for all concerned!

Running a short workshop to gather some data principles is an excellent way to get your stakeholders engaged in the policy and you will find it so much easier to get the resulting policy approved. Of course, if your organization has never had data principles before, they may not know what they would like them to be, so you need to be ready to ask questions to help them come up with some useful principles. Such questions could include:

- If data disappeared overnight, what would be the immediate impact on our operations and decision-making?
- When you think about our most valuable business assets, where does data fit in?
- Who should have the final say when different departments disagree about data?

- When data quality issues arise, who currently takes responsibility for resolving them?
- What level of confidence do you have in the data that informs your strategic decisions?

It will not surprise you to learn that I like to keep things simple and only have a short list of principles. These can include such things as:

- Data is an asset.
- Data is managed.
- All data has an owner.
- Data is fit for purpose.
- Data issues are fixed at the source.

Naturally, you will need a sentence or two to explain the rationale behind each, but I have found that succinct principles work better. I include the agreed principles at the start of the policy (after the introduction/purpose section) and then the rest of the policy document describes what your organization must do to comply with those principles.

What you will include in the rest of your policy will depend on why you are doing data governance and what you want to achieve, but I usually include something on each of the following.

Scope

I mentioned in Chapter 2 that, to be successful, you must iteratively implement data governance. Therefore, you need a section in your policy describing the data which is currently in the scope of your initiative, i.e. what data you must have data governance over. Naturally, this will expand over time and this section should be updated to reflect the latest scope during each review cycle of your policy (for most organizations, corporate policies get reviewed and updated annually).

The scope can be described in different ways, including by data domain, business function or systems in which the data resides. Select the method best aligned with how you are implementing data governance.

Roles and responsibilities

In keeping with my desire to keep the policy as short as possible, I do not recommend including full role descriptions in your policy. However, the roles must be mentioned, as it is the policy which mandates that they exist. I recommend listing the new roles with a short description of each and an idea of who the role holder will be. We will cover the roles in detail in Chapter 6, but this is an example of how a data owner could be described in the policy:

Data owners are senior stakeholders accountable for:

- the quality of the data they own and approving any changes to that data
- taking appropriate action to resolve any data issues with the data they own
- ensuring sufficient resources are available to support data governance activities

It is important to include enough detail to make it clear what each role is responsible for, but not to cause alarm about workloads. Some of the stakeholders who will be signing off on the policy may become data owners. It is unlikely that they will approve something that gives them an onerous additional workload!

In this section, you should also mention any data governance committee, working groups or forums you are setting up to support these roles. I recommend including a simple diagram to show how the groups relate to each other and other existing committees, as well as which roles attend each (see Figure 4.1). More details on these forums can also be found in Chapter 6.

Criticality

Early on my data governance journey, I worked out that not all data is equally important and that we need to focus our data governance efforts on the most important data. Not all your data needs to be as

FIGURE 4.1 Example committee structure diagram

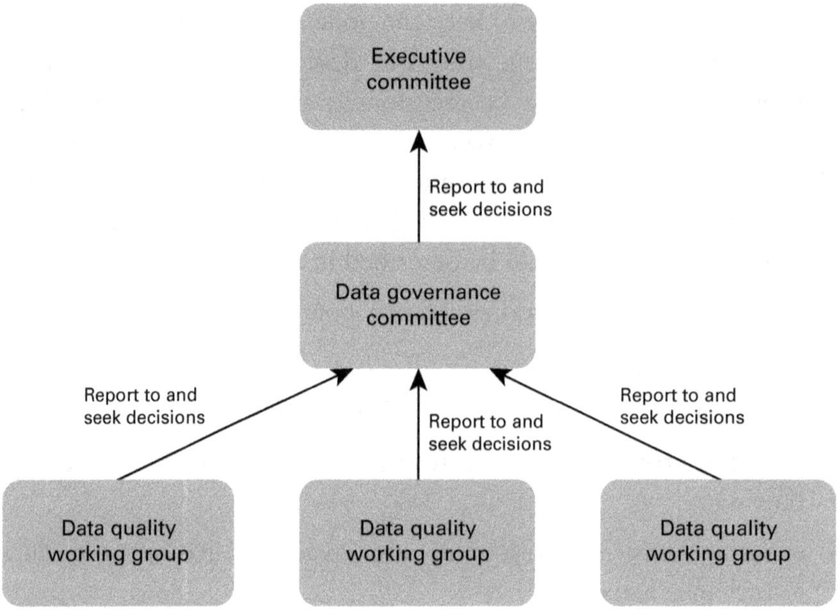

proactively managed, monitored and controlled. To do so would make data governance a burden or an obstacle to people carrying out their day-to-day activities. This is never the point of data governance. I believe that the point of data governance is to identify the most important data and manage that data proportionately to the value it has to your organization.

REAL-WORLD EXAMPLE
How regulation taught me to prioritize data governance efforts

Between 2011 and 2017, I worked primarily with insurance companies. One of the insurance sector regulations is Solvency II. It primarily deals with the capital adequacy of insurance firms but also requires that data governance is put in place over all data used in capital calculations. The regulator realized that in those complex calculations, some data is extremely important, while other data is included just for context. If context data is wrong or missing, it has a negligible impact on the final calculation. With this in mind, the regulator said they did not expect you to have the same level of data governance over the data used mainly for context. They wanted insurance firms to ensure that they were proactively governing the data, which is critical to the calculations and which, if wrong, would result in the wrong numbers being calculated.

This made perfect sense to me. Focusing your efforts on the most important data was the right thing to do, and since that time I have encouraged every client, regardless of which sector they operate in, to adopt this approach.

Solvency II gave a name for this approach: materiality, i.e. it is about identifying your most material data and managing that appropriately. However, calling it 'material data' may not work for your organization. I was told in no uncertain terms by a German manufacturing client that the term materiality most definitely does not work if your company uses materials to make something. In that context, 'material data' means something else entirely. That client, and most others since, have chosen to call it critical data.

I recommend that the approach you take to identify and manage your critical data is detailed in your policy. This should include an overview of the different levels of critical data. I recommend using something along the lines of:

- high criticality: the data that is the most valuable to your business, supports critical business processes and would have a considerable impact if it were of poor quality

- medium criticality: data which is important but would not have such a significant impact if it were of poor quality

- non-critical: data that is useful but would not cause great problems if it were not of the best quality

Including this section in your policy is key to enabling you and your organization to prioritize effort on the most valuable data.

Data definitions

Understanding what data you have and what it means is crucial for any organization that wishes to manage and leverage its data effectively. Data definitions play a key role in this as they provide clarity of what specific terms mean within your organization, which in turn leads to better decision-making and communications. However, it is likely that your organization has thousands of data fields across multiple systems. You will not gain supporters by declaring that every data field needs to have a definition drafted! Instead, you should use this section to describe which data must have definitions. This could be all high-criticality data and/or data used in new systems. Whatever you decide, make sure that it supports your iterative implementation of data governance.

One important final note on data definitions is that the actual definitions should not be documented within your policy. This section of your policy should only explain which data must have definitions in place. The definitions themselves will be held in your data glossary, which will be covered in Chapter 8.

Data quality dimensions and standards

As one of the primary purposes of implementing data governance is to understand and, if needed, improve the quality of our data, it makes sense that we should cover how we will measure data quality in our policy.

DATA QUALITY DIMENSIONS

There are many ways to measure the quality of data, which are called data quality dimensions. While I was serving on the DAMA UK board, I chaired a working group which sought to make sense of the confusing myriad of different dimensions being quoted online and in various books. Over 18 months, the working group distilled everything we could find on the topic and recommended six basic dimensions: accuracy, completeness, uniqueness, consistency, timeliness and validity. These dimensions are described in detail in the whitepaper published by the working group and were subsequently incorporated into the data quality chapter in version 2.2 of the DAMA–DMBOK.[1] The UK government used these DAMA UK recommended data quality dimensions as part of their Government Data Quality Hub.[2]

If your organization does not operate in a regulated sector, consider keeping your policy simple by omitting data quality dimensions. However, if you do work in a sector subject to regulation, I recommend including the data quality dimensions which your organization uses, along with a description of what your organization means by each dimension. When you are audited (by your audit team or the regulator), your data governance policy, as an approved formal document, is considered strong evidence that you are doing the right things and complying with regulatory requirements.

STANDARDS

As mentioned earlier in this chapter, a data quality standard is the specification that a certain field or dataset needs to achieve, e.g. that a field must always be completed or the value sits within a defined range. Data quality standards define what constitutes good data and generally use a data quality dimension to describe the level that needs to be attained, e.g. a date of birth field that must always be completed would have a standard of 100 per cent completeness, but perhaps the field is only used for trend analysis and we do not care so much about the accuracy of the data so another standard for the same data could be that it is 80 per cent accurate.

You should use your policy to identify the data which must have data quality standards in place. Again, I usually explain this in terms of how critical the data is. As with the data definitions, the actual data quality standards will be documented elsewhere, usually in your data glossary.

Processes

Finally, you should include a section in your policy to describe the processes you will have in place. We will cover these in more detail in Chapter 5, but one that I recommend everyone has early in their data governance implementation is a data quality issue resolution process. It is a simple process that helps you identify and solve data quality issues.

I do not propose that you include a detailed description of the processes, but it is extremely useful to have a high-level description of each process you are implementing and why it is needed. Once approved, all processes mentioned in the policy are mandatory, which can make it easier to get some stakeholders to adopt them.

A high-level description of a data quality issue resolution process would be:

- The data governance team logs data quality issues and will work with the data consumers and data owner(s) to investigate and take appropriate action to rectify the issue.
- The data governance team monitors and reports on progress to the data governance committee.
- The detailed process for data quality issue resolution can be found in data governance operating model.

Many of the terms in the above description may be new to you, but don't worry, they will be covered in the following chapters.

Policy vs operating model

You will have noticed that, in describing what to include in your policy above, I have used the words 'overview' and 'high-level' several times. You may be wondering where the detailed criticality approach, process documents and role descriptions will be documented. This is where an operating model comes into play.

As mentioned earlier, if we put everything in our data governance policy then it becomes too big. With so much detail you will find it hard, if not impossible, to get it approved. So for many years now I have made sure I only put in the policy a high-level description of what we must do to govern our data. I detail how we will achieve that elsewhere in a document, or a collection of documents, which I call a data governance operating model.

Your data governance policy is an overview of what we want people to do and the data governance operating model provides detail on how to do it.

Many organizations have the concept of an operating model and you may have several different operating models covering disparate activities at your organization. If you do, it will make sense to also have a data governance operating model, as it will be a concept that is familiar to your stakeholders.

However, I've worked with some organizations that do not like the concept of operating models, and having a data governance operating model in such cultures would cause confusion or result in increased resistance. Sometimes I find that renaming your single document to a data governance framework can be a viable alternative, but please remember, as I described in the previous chapter, this is not how I usually use the data governance framework term.

If having all this information in one document does not work for an organization, another approach is to create a collection of shorter documents each covering different aspects, for example processes or detailed role descriptions.

If calling either a single or a collection of documents an operating model is going to make your organization resistant to it, then don't do it. We have to make this as easy as possible for our stakeholders to accept.

Another reason for not putting everything in your policy is that, once approved, you are going to have to go through the same hoops and over all the hurdles every time you need to get your policy changed. Most organizations have an annual review of existing policies and it is simpler if you do not need to get a policy updated outside of that review cycle. If we keep the policy at a high level, it is less likely to change as quickly as the details on how we do data governance.

The details do not need such strenuous oversight and approval. I recommend that changes to your data governance operating model are reviewed and agreed by the committee that is primarily made up of your data owners (we will discuss this committee in Chapter 6). That will make it much easier for you to evolve and iterate your data governance framework.

Who to involve in writing it

I encourage you to get your data governance policy drafted fairly early in your initiative, as it sets the stage for success. However, you should not be writing the policy in isolation – this is a great opportunity to get your senior stakeholders involved and engaged with your initiative. This is not just a nice-to-do activity; it is essential. Over the years, I've seen numerous instances where a data governance manager has drafted the policy alone before sharing it with senior stakeholders. Invariably, the policy is not well received and significant effort and rewrites are needed to achieve approval. This is a frustrating experience for everyone involved, and the senior stakeholders are then prone to view data governance as something challenging. This sets the stage unfavourably for everything that then follows.

I discovered through trial and error that when individuals actively participate in determining changes they develop psychological ownership that transforms them from passive recipients into invested stakeholders. This principle is particularly critical in data governance initiatives, where success depends on behavioural change. I worked this out by making mistakes and learning from them. It would have been helpful if I had been aware of organizational psychology before I started working in data governance!

Kurt Lewin, the German-American psychologist, is considered the 'father' of participative management. Lewin's pioneering work in the 1940s first established the empirical basis for participatory change approaches. His landmark studies demonstrated that groups who participated in decision-making implemented changes more effectively and with less resistance than those simply instructed to change.

Of course, this is a long-winded way of explaining that if you get your senior stakeholders involved in drafting your data governance policy, they are significantly more likely to be engaged in the data governance initiative as a whole and also to approve the policy which they helped draft.

Invariably, if you are the data governance manager or lead for your organization, a lot of the drafting of the policy will be done by you, but you need the input of your senior stakeholders. I do not recommend that you send an email to the people who are your prospective data owners and ask for their input. You are unlikely to get a good response to such an approach, and your email will probably be ignored. It is rare that they will have experience of writing (or even reading) a data governance policy before. Gathering your senior stakeholders in a small workshop and asking questions to brainstorm some data principles (as mentioned earlier in this chapter) is a far more effective way of getting them engaged and feeling that they have input to the policy development.

As mentioned above, it is useful to start the whole policy drafting process off by running a workshop with your key stakeholders. At this point you may not even know who your data owners will be. Identify the senior stakeholders who, if engaged, would be able to help you further your data governance initiative. I like to bring the group together and get them to brainstorm the principles by which they would like data in your organization to be managed, i.e. the principles already discussed earlier in this chapter.

This initial workshop makes a huge difference to engagement and support levels, and most senior stakeholders do not wish to be further involved until it comes to reviewing the first draft of the policy, but some do want to be more involved, so always ask. The more involved they are, the easier it will be to get your policy approved.

Conclusion

A data governance policy is a critical foundation for successful data governance implementation. Creating a well-crafted policy early in your journey provides the mandate needed to drive adoption while clearly communicating your organization's approach to managing data as an asset. Remember that your policy should be concise and tailored to your organization's unique needs.

Key takeaways from this chapter include:

- A data governance policy mandates data governance activities and provides legitimacy to your initiative.

- Keep your policy concise and in a familiar format to increase chances of approval.
- Customize your policy for your organization rather than copying or using templates.
- Engage senior stakeholders in creating the policy to build psychological ownership.
- Differentiate between your policy (what to do) and your operating model (how to do it).
- Focus on critical data by establishing a criticality framework in your policy.
- Review and update your policy regularly as your data governance initiative matures.

By investing time in developing a thoughtful data governance policy and involving key stakeholders in the process, you'll set a strong foundation for your data governance journey. This investment pays dividends when you need stakeholder support for implementing processes and assigning responsibilities in the later stages of your initiative.

Notes

1 DAMA (2024) *DAMA–DMBOK Data Management Body of Knowledge*, 2nd edn, Technics Publications, Sedona AZ
2 Government Data Quality Hub. Meet the data quality dimensions, Gov.uk, 2021. www.gov.uk/government/news/meet-the-data-quality-dimensions (archived at https://perma.cc/RC7V-GD6R)

05

Identifying the right processes

Introduction

Effective data governance requires more than just roles and responsibilities – it demands well-designed processes that provide clear guidance to stakeholders throughout your organization. This chapter explores why documented processes are essential for successful data governance implementation and how to develop the right processes for your organization's specific needs.

Processes serve as the operational backbone that transforms abstract data governance concepts into practical, day-to-day activities. Without clear processes, even the most enthusiastic stakeholders will struggle to translate good intentions into consistent actions.

Key aspects we will explore in this chapter include:

- why processes matter: understanding the critical role of documented processes in ensuring consistent data governance practices
- essential starting processes: identifying the core processes needed in the early stages of your data governance initiative
- data quality issue resolution: developing a structured approach to identify, document and systematically resolve data issues
- process documentation best practices: creating accessible, user-friendly process documentation that drives adoption
- moving from reactive to proactive: shifting your organization toward preventing data issues rather than repeatedly fixing them

The right processes, implemented at the right time, create the foundation for sustainable data governance that delivers tangible business value. In this chapter, we'll explore how to build that foundation in a way that engages your stakeholders and addresses your organization's most pressing data challenges.

Why we need data governance processes

Data governance practitioners and consultants spend considerable time debating role definitions and responsibilities, yet give surprisingly little attention to the operational processes that turn those roles into effective data governance. Indeed, I have often been asked if we really need data governance processes. Roles and responsibilities are vital to the success of your data governance initiative and we will explore these in the next chapter, but clearly documented processes are also essential.

This is because data governance requires active implementation, not just role assignment. Until people begin following established processes and making decisions about their data, data governance remains theoretical.

The reason for this is that, until your initiative begins, people in your organization have not been practising data governance. It is essential that we provide them with clear, practical guidance. If we ask stakeholders to write definitions or resolve data quality issues without proper guidance, they are unlikely to know where to begin. Even if they are willing to take on the task, without clearly defined and agreed-upon processes, we risk inconsistency and things are unlikely to progress as intended. The hoped-for benefits are much less likely to be delivered, and in the absence of any value delivered you risk your stakeholders becoming disengaged and no longer supporting your initiative.

Writing this chapter has made me recall an instance fairly early on in my career when I was working at an insurance company. By sheer enthusiasm, I persuaded a data owner that they needed to fix their data quality issues. They had a seemingly endless list including

misspelled company names, outdated contact information, conflicting classifications and data entry errors that were causing their
monthly reports to be questioned by the finance department. At that
stage, though, I had not designed and shared the data quality issue
resolution process. This particular data owner was inspired to take
action by themselves. They dived in and fixed some issues. In particular, they agreed with their team a new format to capture some key
information that was often captured incorrectly. This sounds like
good news, right? Unfortunately, because they had had no guidance,
they did not do this in a holistic manner. They did not identify all of
the consumers of the data. They spoke only to the stakeholders who
initially raised concerns about the data. A resolution was identified
and implemented. The person who had flagged the issue was happy.
However, in changing the format of the data to solve an issue for one
team, an issue was caused for other users of the data. In fact, the
unexpected change in format caused a system to crash! This was not
something that the data owner expected. Fixing a data issue in isolation from other users of the same data had unintended consequences.
It was a lesson that we need clear and simple processes so that our
stakeholders understand what they need to do and, more importantly,
how to do it.

The processes you might need

In the previous chapter I mentioned that, when answering questions
about data governance, I often begin with the words 'It depends', and
this is one of those occasions.

Data governance can encompass a range of different activities. It is
unlikely that you will need to do them all at any one time. Instead,
you'll need to focus on what your organization needs right now. You
can work out which processes you need by understanding why your
organization is doing data governance and what problems you are
trying to solve. Hopefully, you found answers to these questions
while you were reading Chapters 1 and 2. Once you are clear on the
problems you are trying to address, you can identify the activities

needed. You are then in a position to agree and document the processes required to support those activities.

While there are many processes you might eventually need in a mature data governance programme – such as data definition approval, data catalogue maintenance and changes to data – at the start of a data governance initiative I recommend focusing on just two key processes:

- data quality issue resolution
- data quality reporting

The reason for this focused approach is that stakeholders can only cope with so much change at any one time. Introducing too many new processes simultaneously can overwhelm our stakeholders and lead to poor adoption or outright resistance. By starting with these two fundamental processes, you build confidence and establish good habits before expanding your data governance framework. At the end of this chapter I'll cover other processes to consider as your initiative matures.

I recommend these two in particular because business users are already acutely aware of data quality problems and are likely to have experienced frustration trying to get these issues resolved through informal channels before data governance was in place. They probably found it hard to get data quality issues addressed before the data governance initiative started. There will be other activities that we need to move forward with, but business stakeholders care more about the quality of the data than documenting definitions for it. In the early stages it is crucial to engage stakeholders and maintain their interest by making progress on the issues they care about while simultaneously laying strong data governance foundations like clear data definitions.

A key process: Data quality issue resolution

Why this process is critical

The first process you should implement in your data governance initiative is a data quality issue resolution process. This is not a nice-to-have element, it is foundational to achieving tangible improvements in your data quality. Organizations require a structured, repeatable approach to identify, document and systematically resolve data issues that arise throughout the business. Without this process, data quality efforts become fragmented, inconsistent and ultimately ineffective.

A data quality issue resolution process serves multiple purposes:

- It creates accountability by clearly defining who is responsible for what.
- It ensures consistent handling of issues across departments.
- It provides visibility into recurring problems that may indicate systemic issues.
- It facilitates prioritization of issues based on business impact.
- It creates an audit trail of issues and their resolutions.
- It builds organizational confidence in the data governance initiative by demonstrating actionable results.

I am sure you will agree that this all sounds good, but why do I recommend that it is the first process to be implemented? The reason is that every other process and document that you will deliver as part of implementing a data governance framework will take a considerable amount of time and effort before they start to deliver business value and benefits. If you are not solving any problems during this time, your stakeholders are likely to become disillusioned and disengaged. That is where this process comes into play. We can use it from very early on in our data governance initiative to identify and fix business issues. It is a part of a data governance framework that every organization should have. It is the first thing that delivers true business value and solves real business problems.

The role of the data governance team

A common and potentially damaging misconception is that the data governance team will solve data quality issues. I have encountered many situations where newly formed teams struggle with this expectation. While the data governance team do play a crucial coordination role, they are not responsible for determining remedial actions or performing manual data cleansing. These activities are undertaken by data owners, data stewards and data producers (which are all covered in the next chapter). Of course, in the early days of your data governance initiative you may want to provide more hands-on support, but it is useful to understand what your team will ultimately be responsible for in this process.

The data governance team's responsibilities in the issue resolution process include:

- identifying data owners: determining which data owner is responsible for the affected data elements, if this has not already been identified and documented

- maintaining the data quality issue log: creating and managing a centralized repository for all data quality issues, ensuring nothing falls through the cracks

- monitoring and reporting on open issues: tracking progress against agreed timelines and providing regular updates to stakeholders

- facilitating discussions between stakeholders: acting as mediators when needed to drive consensus on impact assessment and remediation approaches

- supporting the impact assessment process: helping business users and data owners quantify the business impact of identified issues

- assisting with root cause analysis: working with IT teams, data owners and other business stakeholders to determine why issues are occurring

- ensuring communication flow: making sure all stakeholders remain informed about issue status and resolution progress

Over time, you and your team will develop extensive knowledge and expertise about the data which your organization creates and uses. This expertise will enable them to provide valuable guidance and support throughout the issue resolution process, even though they do not directly implement fixes.

As a word of warning, once your team has developed this knowledge, do not let your key stakeholders assume that means you will do their role for them! I have seen this happen on numerous occasions. Ultimately, it can result in your business stakeholders disengaging from the roles (which we will cover in the next chapter), believing they do not have to do anything as the data governance team will handle everything. Data governance is only successful when business stakeholders understand and commit to their role in it. This is a scenario to be aware of and avoid at all costs.

A simple four-step process for data quality issue resolution

At this stage in the book, you will not be surprised to learn that I recommend using a simple approach for your data quality issue resolution process, as Figure 5.1 illustrates.

FIGURE 5.1 Simple data quality issue resolution process

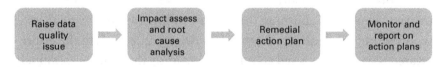

Let's have a look at each of the four stages.

1. RAISE DATA QUALITY ISSUE

The identification and formal documentation of data quality issues establishes clear accountability and ensures proper oversight. Business users typically initiate this process when encountering data that fails to meet their operational needs. They serve as the frontline detectors of data quality issues. Once notified of an issue, the data governance team documents it in a centralized data quality log, capturing details from the individual who reported the issue.

The data governance team then identifies the appropriate data owner(s) for the affected data and formally notifies them of the issue. This may include gaining agreement to ownership if that has not already been agreed upon. The process culminates with reporting to the data governance committee, providing visibility into all open critical issues and maintaining appropriate governance oversight.

2. IMPACT ASSESSMENT AND ROOT CAUSE ANALYSIS

The resolution of identified data quality issues follows a structured, methodical approach that ensures accountability while driving toward effective remediation. The data owner and their team assume primary responsibility for investigating the issue's root cause, collaborating closely with relevant stakeholders to develop a comprehensive understanding of underlying factors. Once causes are identified, the data owner is responsible for considering options for remediation. This stage concludes with formal documentation of progress in the data quality issue log.

3. REMEDIAL ACTION PLAN

This stage focuses on planning and preparing for the implementation of the resolution and begins with data owner(s) proposing an approach that not only resolves the immediate issue but also implements preventive measures to address root causes rather than merely treating symptoms. Business validation follows as the original issue reporter and other affected data users review and confirm the appropriateness of the proposed action plan, ensuring the solution genuinely addresses actual business needs.

If there are differences in opinion on the most appropriate remediation, the data governance team mediates discussions between different business teams to reach an agreement on the approach. Throughout this process, the data quality issue log is updated by the data governance team with agreed actions, responsible parties and target completion dates.

A risk assessment evaluates potential implementation impacts, considering downstream systems vulnerabilities and business process disruptions. Finally, the remediation plan is approved, with significant changes requiring formal approval from change management boards or other governance bodies, as well as data owner sign-off.

4. MONITOR AND REPORT ON ACTION PLANS

The final stage ensures that planned actions are executed properly and yield the desired results, recognizing that remediation complexity varies significantly, from straightforward interventions like training a new team member to complex system modifications requiring substantial resources and coordination. Implementation execution begins with data owners and their teams undertaking the agreed remedial actions. This sometimes requires specialized IT support for system changes or data corrections. Progress tracking maintains accountability as the data governance team monitors against target dates and key milestones. They also provide regular stakeholder updates to both affected business users and the data governance committee. The data governance committee oversight provides strategic direction as they review progress regularly and intervene on prioritization or resource allocation for critical issues when necessary.

Lessons learnt during the process are documented to inform future improvements to data quality practices. The process culminates with issue closure in the data quality issue log.

The data quality issue log

The log is central to managing the process effectively. It is not merely an administrative tool. It is a critical operational asset. A well-designed log serves as the single source of truth for data quality issues as well as a tracking mechanism for resolution progress. It is an analytical tool for identifying patterns and trends and finally, it is a key reporting source for governance committees.

I recommend including the following fields in your data quality issue log:

- ID: I use sequential numbers (001, 002, 003) as identifiers. This approach has the dual benefit of simplicity and provides an immediate count of identified issues since the process was implemented. This is a metric senior stakeholders will inevitably request.

- Date raised: Critical for tracking issue age and analysing average resolution times.

- Raised by [name and department]: Records who identified the issue, which serves multiple purposes:

  ○ It helps identify key data consumers for specific datasets.

○ Provides contact information for further clarification if needed.

○ Facilitates communication about resolution progress.

- Short name of issue: A concise issue name significantly enhances communication efficiency. When presenting updates to governance committees or discussing issues with stakeholders, a descriptive label like 'Duplicate customer issue' is much more effective than 'Issue #067' or lengthy descriptions.

- Detailed description: A comprehensive description of the issue as provided by the person who identified it. This should include:

○ the specific data elements affected

○ how the issue manifests in business processes or reports

○ when it was first noticed

○ any patterns or conditions that trigger the issue

○ examples or evidence demonstrating the problem

- Criticality: As mentioned earlier in this section, this classification drives prioritization decisions.

- Data owner: Identifying who is responsible for investigating and fixing each issue is essential for accountability.

- Status: Use status tracking to facilitate monitoring and reporting. Beyond basic 'open' and 'closed' designations, consider these additional statuses:

○ new: recently logged, not yet assigned or assessed

○ in analysis: under investigation to determine root cause

○ action planned: solution identified but not yet implemented

○ in progress: solution being implemented

○ verification: solution implemented, awaiting confirmation of effectiveness

○ accepted: issues that cannot be fixed due to technical limitations or cost constraints

○ closed: successfully resolved

The 'accepted' status is particularly important for issues that cannot be reasonably fixed. Rather than leaving these as permanently open (which distorts your metrics) or closing them (which loses visibility), this status acknowledges the issue while indicating a business decision to accept the risk or limitation.

- Update: A chronological record of progress, including:
  - notes on investigation findings
  - decisions made about remediation approaches
  - actions completed toward resolution
  - obstacles encountered
  - next steps and responsible parties

This field becomes an invaluable historical record of the issue resolution journey.

- Target resolution date: Records when the issue is expected to be resolved.

Communication is key

As with all aspects of data governance, effective communication determines the success or failure of your data quality issue resolution process. To maximize the adoption and effectiveness of your process, the following actions as part of implementing the process are important:

- Create a simple high-level diagram of your process that clearly illustrates the flow and key responsibilities.
- Develop role-specific guidance that helps stakeholders understand their specific responsibilities.
- Regularly share success stories where issue resolution delivered tangible business benefits.
- Make the process and supporting documentation simple and easily accessible to all stakeholders.

- Conduct brief training sessions for business units about the new process and how to effectively report issues.
- Establish regular reporting cadences to governance committees and affected stakeholders.
- Regularly report and communicate on your successes.

Remember, simplicity is essential – overly complex processes will be ignored or circumvented. Your goal should be a process that stakeholders can easily understand, remember and follow. By implementing a data quality issue resolution process, you create a powerful mechanism for systematically improving data quality while building confidence in your overall data governance initiative.

Data quality reporting

Data quality reporting is a critical aspect of any data governance framework, because it provides the visibility needed to maintain trustworthy and useful business data. Without regular reporting, poor data quality can silently undermine decision-making. Imagine discovering that your customer retention analysis was based on duplicate records, or that budget forecasts were wrong because of inconsistent data entry across departments. Data quality reporting acts as an early warning system, highlighting issues before they impact critical business processes. However, it does take considerable time and effort to get a reasonable number of data quality reports in place. To produce these reports, the following activities need to take place:

- Identify critical data: In the previous chapter, we determined that not all data within an organization is equally important. It is not useful to put data quality reporting in place over all data, so before we do anything we need to identify which data is considered critical to the business and therefore needs its quality monitored.
- Confirm data owners: It is the data owner who will approve the data quality rules, so it is vital that they have been identified and are engaged.

- Agree on data definitions: Before we can agree on what makes the data good enough to use, we need to agree on what it is. Different stakeholders often interpret terms differently. For instance, what one department considers 'customer data' might differ from another's perspective. Many organizations waste considerable effort developing data quality rules, which are later deemed incorrect because there had been a misunderstanding over what the data actually represents. For example, assuming that 'customer' means active customers only, when the database actually includes prospects and inactive accounts as well.

- Agree on data quality rules: Before we dive into creating data quality rules, it's crucial to understand a fundamental principle: your data doesn't need to be perfect, it needs to be 'good enough' for its intended use. This concept, often called 'fit for purpose', can save your organization from endless perfectionism and help focus your data quality efforts where they truly matter.

  Think of data quality like a tool: a hammer doesn't need to be precision engineered to drive a nail, but a surgical instrument requires extraordinary accuracy. Similarly, your data quality requirements should match your business needs. Customer addresses for marketing campaigns need to be accurate enough to ensure delivery, but minor formatting inconsistencies won't derail your strategy. Financial data for regulatory reporting demands near-perfect accuracy, while rough estimates might suffice for initial budget planning. Historical sales data for trend analysis can tolerate some gaps, but missing recent data could invalidate your conclusions.

  With this 'fit for purpose' principle in mind, we need to agree on what constitutes 'good enough' data for each specific use case. Stakeholders who use a critical dataset need to explain what makes that data fit for purpose. These business requirements must be approved by the data owner before they can be converted into data quality rules using the data quality dimensions mentioned in Chapter 4. For example, a rule for customer data might state that the date of birth must be completed and in a valid date format. Similarly, product data rules might specify that product codes must follow a standardized format, product descriptions cannot be blank and prices must be greater than zero.

Understanding this approach will help you create data quality rules that actually serve your business rather than creating impossible standards that frustrate everyone involved.

• Create data quality reports: Once the data quality rules are agreed upon, reports can be created to assess how well the data meets these standards. These reports should be distributed regularly to the data owner as well as all stakeholders who use that data.

Data quality reports typically present information in a clear, actionable format that business users can understand. a well-designed report might include:

  ○ summary dashboard: shows overall data quality scores as percentages or traffic light indicators (red, amber, green) for each dataset

  ○ rule-by-rule breakdown: details how the data performs against each specific quality rule, such as 'customer date of birth completeness: 92 per cent' or 'product code format compliance: 87 per cent'

  ○ trend analysis: shows whether data quality is improving, declining or remaining stable over time

  ○ exception details: lists specific records that fail quality checks, making it easier for data stewards to investigate and fix issues

  ○ business impact assessment: explains what the quality scores mean in practical terms, such as 'poor address quality affects 15 per cent of marketing campaigns'

Meeting your data quality standards doesn't necessarily mean achieving 100 per cent perfection. Remember the 'fit for purpose' principle – success looks different depending on your business context. For instance:

  ○ A customer database with 95 per cent complete email addresses might exceed standards for general marketing but fall short for automated email campaigns.

- ○ Product data with 98 per cent accurate pricing meets standards for catalogue displays but needs improvement for financial reporting.
- ○ Historical sales data with some gaps from five years ago might still meet standards for trend analysis.

The key is defining acceptable thresholds for each rule based on business requirements. Your reports should clearly indicate whether each dataset meets, exceeds or falls below these agreed-upon thresholds, giving stakeholders confidence in the data they're using and highlighting areas that need attention.

- Test and iterate: It is rare that stakeholders with no prior experience in defining data quality requirements get the rules right on their first attempt. There is usually a phase of testing and adapting the rules to get them right. This is done by running exception reports against the rules. These reports are shared with the business stakeholders to review. Commonly, they see items on the reports that they would not consider to be poor quality and the rules need to be amended so that these are excluded next time the report is run.

- Monitor and take action: It is not sufficient to simply produce reports; actions must be taken based on findings. Data owners and their data stewards (we will cover both roles in Chapter 6) must regularly review reports and initiate remediation activities for any identified exceptions to the required standards.

Seeing the steps laid out like that, I am sure that you will understand that it takes many months to develop data quality reports. In the meantime, there is a considerable danger that our stakeholders will get bored with the other data governance activities and become impatient for some value to be delivered or problems to be solved. This is where the other process I prioritize comes into effect.

We need to start demonstrating value to our stakeholders as quickly as possible. A key way we can do this is to solve some data quality issues that are causing an impact on the business. Once we start saving time and money, our stakeholders will start to understand the bigger benefits to come as we move forward with our data governance initiative. This is the main reason why I recommend implementing a data quality issue resolution process very early in your initiative.

Why a proactive approach to data quality is vital

Maintaining high-quality data is becoming more important for all organizations. However, many organizations find themselves stuck in a cycle of reactive data quality measures, which often lead to short-term fixes rather than long-term solutions. This reactive approach creates several serious problems: it prevents organizations from building trust in their data because stakeholders never know when the next quality issue will surface; it wastes significant time and resources as teams repeatedly firefight the same types of problems; it damages credibility when reports or decisions based on poor data have to be corrected or retracted; and it creates a culture where data quality is seen as someone else's problem rather than everyone's responsibility.

A particularly wasteful aspect of reactive data quality management is that the same data often gets cleansed or fixed multiple times. Once when it's used for a report, again when it's loaded into a data warehouse, and yet again when it's needed for another analysis. And, of course, as the source of the issue has not been fixed these cleansing activities have to be repeated on a weekly, monthly or quarterly basis. This repetitive fixing wastes enormous amounts of time and effort because the root cause is never addressed. In contrast, proactive data quality issue resolution identifies the source of the problem and fixes it once at the point of origin, preventing the issue from propagating or having to be repeatedly resolved.

Perhaps most critically, reactive approaches prevent organizations from leveraging their data as a strategic asset because leadership loses confidence in data-driven insights when they've been burned by quality issues in the past.

The data quality issue resolution process detailed earlier in this chapter is a key step in achieving the shift from reactive to proactive data quality management using a data governance framework. By implementing systematic processes that identify and address data quality issues before they impact business operations, organizations can break free from the costly cycle of crisis management and start building the reliable data foundation that modern organizations need. Additionally, regular data quality reports enable users to check that the data is good enough for their specific purpose before they use it, preventing quality issues from affecting critical business decisions and analyses.

Shifting from reactive to proactive data quality

While most organizations now understand that data quality matters, many still struggle with how to manage it effectively. They are likely to have data cleansing routines as data is loaded into data warehouses, data lakes or data platforms. However, these efforts are typically tactical fixes addressing issues only when they are detected. For example, missing fields might be defaulted to a placeholder value, which may be better than an empty field, but does not ensure that the data is actually correct.

Proactive data quality involves preventing data issues from occurring in the first place. This shift requires more than just addressing problems as they arise. It means having a strong approach to managing data quality, which can be achieved through data governance. Implementing a data governance framework is crucial for proactive data quality. Data governance establishes the roles, responsibilities and processes needed to manage data quality consistently across the organization. It ensures that data quality is maintained at the source, reducing the need for repeated data cleansing and enabling more reliable data usage.

Advice on documenting your processes

Different organizations, and different people within them, tend to document processes in different ways. Some of these are better at creating support and engagement than others when it comes to data governance.

When I first got involved in data governance, I worked for a bank that was pretty good at documenting processes. They used an internationally recognized standard approach called the Business Process Model and Notation (BPMN) specification, which provides a graphical notation for specifying business processes in a business process diagram.[1] These are more commonly known as swimlane diagrams. I like them. They have nice, logical rows with roles listed in each swimlane, and you can see who does what, when and how the process gets passed on to the next stage. As a data governance geek, I find them logical and easy to read.

I worked with some colleagues at the first consultancy I joined who were experts in BPMN, and they taught me how to do it properly. That just deepened my love for it. I think swimlane diagrams are a fabulous way of documenting your processes.

However, not all organizations embrace that format. And, even if yours does, there is something important to be aware of: the way you formally document your processes is not always what business users like to see. Maybe I was an unusual business user liking swimlane diagrams. I discovered that they are a bit of a 'marmite' thing – you either love them or you hate them.

So it is important to understand that your business users may not respond well to them. They may look at them and think, 'What *is* this?' That is why we need to find a way to make processes accessible. If your organization does not use swimlane diagrams then I would recommend documenting your data governance processes in the same format your organization uses for documenting all other processes. Remember what I said in Chapter 4: where possible, we want our formal data governance documents to look like existing formats in use in your organization. We do not want to rock the boat or do something completely different. It is important to make sure that we do not make our stakeholders feel uncomfortable. The key thing is to make sure that they will want to engage with us and follow the process we have worked hard to document.

I have a further piece of advice when it comes to documenting data governance processes: whether you are using swimlane diagrams or a different format, keep that as your formal way of documenting processes. Do not use it as your primary communication tool with business users. Instead, take the information you have documented and create simple diagrams. Something that fits on a single PowerPoint slide (without needing a magnifying glass to read!). You need something simple, high-level and accessible, so that your stakeholders can readily understand it.

Time and time again, I have found that business users respond well to simple, pictorial diagrams. I encourage you to make your formally documented processes more accessible when you are communicating them to others, by creating simple diagrams.

In Figures 5.2 and 5.3, you can see the difference between a swimlane diagram and a pictorial diagram for the same data quality issue resolution process. I hope you agree that Figure 5.3 is more visually appealing and more likely to be engaging for stakeholders.

Usually, I create a swimlane first and, once the new process is approved, I create the diagram version for communications about the process. When sharing that diagram, I also mention that a swimlane version is available if desired. They are usually in the minority, but there are business users who like them and would like to see them.

Processes to consider in the future

When I am talking about or presenting data governance processes, a lot of people ask why I am not recommending a process for the maintenance of a data catalogue (the inventory of data definitions, which will be covered in more detail in Chapter 8) as the first one you need. Let's be clear, this is a process you will need, but you will not need it in the early phases of your data governance initiative because you have not captured any data definitions yet.

I have never found it useful to create a process for documenting and approving data definitions until your stakeholders have been doing it for a while. I want them to be happy to work with me.

FIGURE 5.2 Swimlane diagram for a data quality issue resolution process

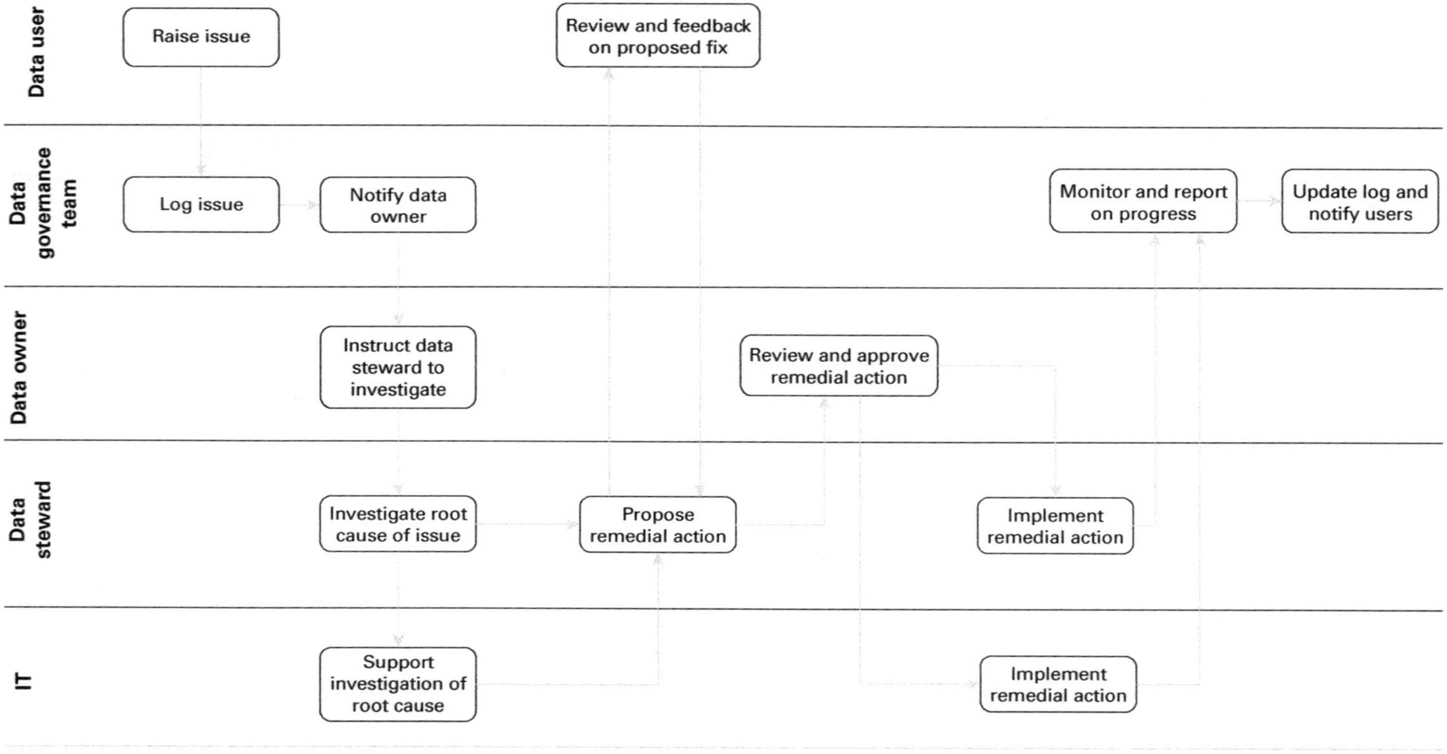

FIGURE 5.3 Simple pictorial diagram for a data quality issue resolution process

Data quality issue resolution process

Process

1. Raise data quality issue

2. Impact assess and root cause analysis

3. Remedial action plan

4. Monitor and report on action plans

People involved

Data governance manager

Data consumer

Data governance manager

Data producers

Data stewards

Data governance manager

Data owner

Data stewards

Data governance manager

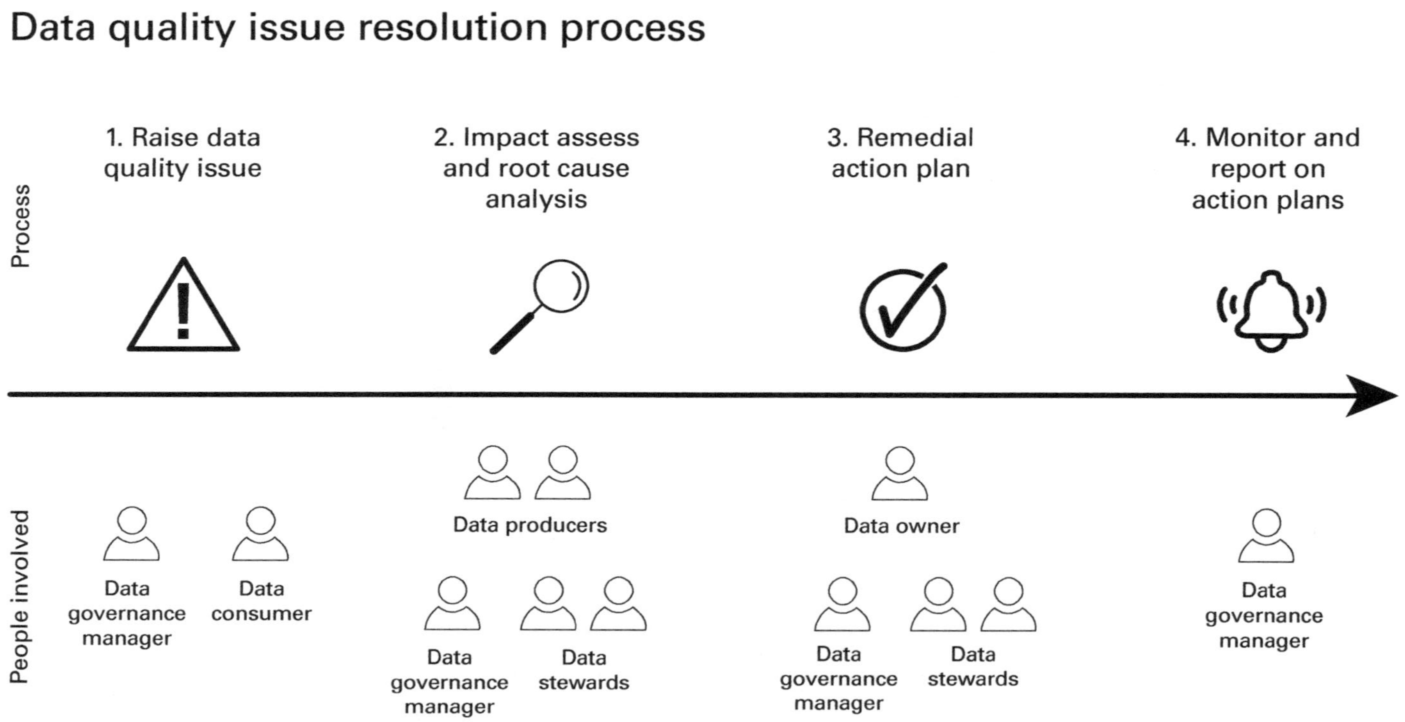

Giving them a complex formal process is likely to scare them off in the early days. I am happy to just start getting them to document some definitions and once I have their feedback about what works and, most importantly, what does not, I can get them to agree on a formal process.

As for a process to make changes to existing definitions, you will want one in the future. As mentioned, in the early days of your data governance initiative, you need to focus on getting the initial batches of definitions documented. Once you have got a reasonable number documented, then I would recommend that you introduce a maintenance of definitions process. This is often split into two separate processes. One would be a regular review of existing definitions. For example, on an annual basis, you ask the data owners to confirm that the definitions for their data are still correct or whether they require updating. The second process is for when a business user wants to amend an existing definition. Perhaps a business process has changed, or the company has started selling a new product. Many things can cause the need for data definitions to be amended and you will need to have a process for sharing the proposed changes with data owners to review and agree (or possibly reject).

Focus on building momentum in the early stages of your initiative, rather than creating processes that will not be needed immediately. As your data governance initiative matures, you will have a clearer understanding of which additional processes will deliver the most value and you will be able to design them based on real-world experience rather than theoretical assumptions.

Conclusion

Establishing the right processes for data governance represents a critical success factor in transforming how your organization manages its data assets. As we have explored throughout this chapter, documented processes provide the operational clarity and consistency needed to translate governance principles into practical actions.

The journey from initial process design to mature data governance involves balancing immediate value delivery with long-term strategic development. By starting with essential processes focused on data quality issue resolution, you create a foundation that demonstrates tangible benefits while laying groundwork for more sophisticated governance activities.

Key takeaways from this chapter include:

- Process prioritization matters: Focus initially on processes that solve immediate business pain points, particularly data quality issue resolution.

- Simplicity drives adoption: Design straightforward, accessible processes that stakeholders can easily understand and incorporate into their daily work.

- Communication is essential: Supplement formal process documentation with simplified visualizations that engage business users effectively.

- Clarify team responsibilities: Establish clear boundaries around the data governance team's coordinating role versus ownership responsibilities.

- Build for sustainability: Develop processes that foster progressive movement from reactive data fixes toward proactive quality management.

- Plan for evolution: Recognize that process requirements will mature alongside your governance initiative, requiring periodic reassessment.

Remember that the ultimate goal is not perfect process documentation, but practical application that delivers measurable improvements in data quality and decision-making capabilities. When implemented pragmatically, data governance processes become powerful enablers that transform organizational data culture while systematically enhancing data quality and value.

Note

1 Object Management Group Standards Development Organization. www.omg.org/bpmn (archived at https://perma.cc/7X9Z-G63V)

06

Roles and responsibilities

Introduction

One of the most fundamental challenges in implementing data governance is determining who should be responsible for what. Without clear roles and accountability, even the best data governance framework will struggle to deliver meaningful results. This chapter provides a practical approach for identifying, engaging and structuring the human elements that make data governance work.

Success depends less on perfect role definitions and more on finding the right people who understand both the importance of data quality and their specific responsibilities within the data governance framework. The key is matching organizational culture with role design while maintaining clear lines of accountability.

In this chapter, you'll discover how to establish six critical role categories that form the foundation of successful data governance:

- executive leadership: securing senior-level sponsorship and strategic direction for your data governance initiative
- data ownership: establishing clear accountability for business decisions about data domains and quality standards
- data stewardship: implementing day-to-day governance activities and managing data quality processes
- data producers: engaging those who create and capture data at its source to prevent quality issues
- data consumption: involving stakeholders who use data for decision-making and analysis in defining requirements

- data governance coordination: providing dedicated resources to design, implement and facilitate the governance framework
- data governance forums: bring stakeholders together to share ideas, solve problems and agree on actionable strategies

Each role serves a distinct purpose in creating a comprehensive data governance ecosystem. The challenge lies not in the theoretical design of these roles but in the practical work of identifying the right individuals, gaining their commitment and helping them understand how their contributions drive success.

Getting started with data governance roles and responsibilities

If you're just starting out on your data governance journey, you may very well feel like you are playing the classic 1980s board game 'Guess Who?' when it comes to sorting out who should be doing what.

There are a number of different roles and responsibilities needed when you are designing and implementing a data governance framework and it is easy to get confused over which roles you really need and what you should be calling them.

When implementing data governance, there will be many challenges and one of these will be the naming of the different roles. What if someone tells you that the term 'data owner' won't work at your organization? Well, you certainly don't need to panic if this does happen. In this chapter, I'm going to share what I consider a starting point, but you do not need to stick to the names of the different roles rigidly. The role titles I use in this chapter are what I have in mind when I start designing a data governance framework, but you do not have to use them. Go with what will work for the organization you work for.

It is much better to use terms that suit the culture of your organization rather than fighting to use role titles that you have read in this book or found with the help of an internet search. It is what the roles do that is the important part. In the early part of my data governance career, I wasted countless hours trying to persuade senior stakeholders to be data owners. Eventually I realized that many of the people I was speaking to were telling me what to do if I only took the time to listen to and understand what they were saying. It was not the responsibilities that they were objecting to, it was the role title. That objection is easily overcome by selecting an alternative title.

Executive support

Many people assume that the chief data officer (CDO) role is a data governance role. Instead, the CDO should be considered more of a strategic partner to the data governance initiative. The CDO position typically focuses on strategic data utilization, analytics innovation and data monetization rather than the operational discipline of data governance.

However, you'll still need executive sponsorship for your data governance initiative. It is the only way to make the initiative truly effective. You need someone senior on your side advocating for resources, removing organizational barriers and demonstrating leadership commitment. A CDO champions data as a strategic asset at the executive level, securing investment for data initiatives. If your organization has a CDO, they are well placed to be the executive sponsor for your data governance initiative.

If your organization does not have a CDO, do not panic. Many organizations implement data governance frameworks successfully without a CDO by identifying an appropriate executive sponsor from their existing leadership. What matters most is not having this specific role, but rather ensuring that rather that someone at the executive level supports your data governance initiative. This executive doesn't need to have a background in data, what's essential is that they understand the importance of data to your organization and are willing to support you and champion data governance. I have helped more organizations successfully implement data governance that do not have CDOs than those that do! What is important is that your data governance initiative does have an executive sponsor.

Data owners

Data owners play such a critical role in any data governance framework that their role is given a larger proportion of this chapter than the rest of the supporting roles. These senior stakeholders are accountable for the quality of one or more datasets within the organization. Their position carries significant weight because they ultimately make critical decisions about how data is managed and used.

Key responsibilities of data owners

Data owners bear ultimate accountability for their assigned data domains. Their primary responsibilities include ensuring data quality and discoverability while maintaining compliance with relevant regulations and organizational policies.

Specifically, data owners must ensure appropriate definitions exist for their data, oversee the resolution of data quality issues, allocate resources for data improvement initiatives and provide strategic guidance on data usage. They serve as the final authority on decisions regarding their data domains and represent their data at data governance committee meetings (which are covered later in this chapter).

The data owner role extends beyond tactical data activities to encompass strategic considerations regarding how data supports business objectives. They must balance immediate operational needs against long-term data quality goals, often making difficult prioritization decisions with limited resources.

Identifying effective data owners

One of the most common challenges when working with organizations on their data governance journey is the question: 'How do we work out who should be data owners?' It's a deceptively simple question that often leaves teams pointing fingers at other stakeholders, or worse, assuming that IT owns all data since they support the systems on which a lot of data resides. Adding to the confusion, many people expect data owners to come from the data team or have 'data' in their job title, when in reality, data owners are typically business leaders who understand how the data is used to drive business outcomes.

To be effective, data owners must possess sufficient seniority within the organization. They need the authority to make changes to business processes and systems and they must have access to budget and resources for implementing those changes. Without these capabilities, they will struggle to fulfil their responsibilities.

Agreeing on the right data owners requires careful consideration of organizational structure, business processes and political dynamics. Ideally, ownership aligns with operational responsibility and authority. Those who direct the business processes that create or heavily consume the data are often the most appropriate owners, but there are some occasions when a team which is not a direct user or producer of the data is the best data owner. One example of when this can occur is when a head of compliance agrees that they are the most appropriate owner of data which is collected for regulatory reporting processes. Even though they are not involved in the collection of the data or production of the reports, the head of compliance is the person who best understands the data and what it is used for. Furthermore, they do not want any other teams making decisions about that data.

A common challenge when identifying appropriate data owners is when multiple departments use the same data. Initially, I used the following approach for identifying the right data owners:

1 Identify which business area feels the most pain when the data is wrong. The departments that suffer operational consequences from poor data quality typically have the strongest incentive to improve it.

2 Determine which team is the first to identify quality issues with the data. Those closest to the data often have the most insight into its problems and potential solutions.

3 Look for the department that dictates the standards by which the data is captured. Those who establish the rules for data creation typically have the deepest understanding of its business purpose.

I use the information gathered to identify the teams who are most likely to be interested in owning the data (if a team does not care whether the data is good enough, why would they be interested in owning it?). I then approach the heads of those teams to discuss whether they are the right person to be making decisions on the data.

This method is reasonably successful, but it means that the data governance manager arbitrarily decides a list of data domains (which reinforces a commonly held, but incorrect, assumption that the data governance manager is responsible for all data). It also involves a lot of effort and constantly being passed from one team to the next, before eventually agreeing on a data owner. You then have to start the process all over again for the next data domain on the list and of course, you can get a lot of push back on whether the list of data domains is even right in the first place…

Using conceptual data models to identify and engage data owners

I had been doing data governance for about eight years when I came across conceptual data models. I had joined an insurance company as an interim data governance manager, and in the first few weeks in the role I was lucky enough to attend some conceptual data model workshops. As you may remember, I was already a fan of logical data models and I immediately liked these higher-level data models. More importantly, I noticed that in the workshops to create them, the business stakeholders were engaging easily. Getting them to talk about the data they use and create was much more effortless than the approach detailed previously. At the end of one workshop, I tentatively asked if there was any data that they would not want other departments making decisions on or changing and they immediately identified a list of datasets that they felt strongly should be owned by their department head. This was a light bulb moment for me, I realized that creating conceptual data models was not only a great way to engage stakeholders and get them thinking about data, but they enable senior stakeholders to easily identify and volunteer themselves as data owners.

Conceptual data models (CDMs) are simply a high-level diagram showing the data that a department uses and produces. They are created with a business focus to document at a high level what data exists in an organization. I like to create one for each business department or function. They are quick and simple to create and, importantly, they are incredibly powerful tools for identifying the right people to take ownership of data. You may wish to see an example of a CDM and I would have loved to have included one here for you. However, while a CDM can be easily read in A4 size, it would be far too small to read when printed in a book. So, I have included a link to an online example in the resources section of this book.

While talking about CDMs, it is useful to note that they play a far bigger role in a data governance initiative than just helping to identify data owners. When stakeholders engage in creating these models, they begin to articulate their understanding of the data and the collaborative process of building the model becomes as valuable as the model itself. During the workshops, you gain wider insights into the data being discussed: challenges experienced with the data, or maybe new systems being implemented. This information is invaluable in determining where to focus your early efforts in implementing data governance.

The resulting CDMs are a great level at which to assign the criticality classifications (covered in Chapter 4) and a good place to start data catalogue development (which will be covered in the next chapter).

You have probably gathered from this section that I love conceptual data models and highly recommend them as a tool to support your data governance initiative. Sadly, I have not been able to convince every organization that I have worked with to embrace them. I still use my original approach to identifying data owners occasionally, but my experience is that those initiatives take longer and stakeholder engagement is harder to achieve and maintain. However, despite these challenges, some companies/clients do not want to do conceptual data models, because they perceive them to be complex IT items and do not comprehend the business value of them.

The one data owner rule

A cardinal rule I've established through years of implementation experience is never to assign more than one data owner per dataset. Multiple owners inevitably lead to delays, disagreements and data governance paralysis as competing interests make consensus difficult to achieve.

Having only one data owner per dataset is crucial for several reasons:

- Clarity in accountability: When there is one designated data owner, it creates clear accountability. This means if there are issues related to data quality or usage, everyone in the organization knows exactly who to approach. Without this clarity there can be confusion, leading to blame-shifting and prolonged resolution of problems.

- Avoiding deadlock: When multiple individuals are designated as data owners for the same data, it often leads to discussions and debates that stall the decision-making process. Disagreements can prevent progress. A single data owner can make clear decisions, ensuring that the data governance initiative moves forward and data quality issues get solved.

- Avoiding inconsistent decisions: With multiple data owners, one can make a decision which is later countered or overturned by another data owner of the same dataset. Confusion and inconsistency will ensue.

Establishing a single data owner for each dataset is not only best practice for data governance but also a strategic necessity to ensure effective management and utilization of data across the organization. By doing so, you create an environment where data governance can thrive, ultimately benefiting the overall business objectives of implementing data governance in the first place.

When organizations struggle to identify a single owner for a dataset, I recommend breaking down the data into smaller subsets with different owners. For example, in one insurance company I helped, we split the 'customer details' dataset. Both the head of underwriting and the marketing director felt that they owned the dataset. As both were strong supporters of the data governance initiative, I did not want to alienate either of them. Through discussions about which data within that dataset they were keen to own, we were able to agree that 'customer risk details' (e.g. age/date of birth) would be owned by underwriting and 'customer contact data' (e.g. Email address) would be owned by marketing.

Final advice on data owners

It is vital that data owners are named individuals, not job titles, teams or departments. I discovered that unless the role is allocated to you personally, you are unlikely to be particularly engaged in it. After all, there will always be someone else who might do it, so you don't have to!

Do not assume that, once agreed, the data owners will only change for staff turnover reasons. As you progress on your data governance journey, it may well become clear that one or more data owners are no longer correct. This usually manifests itself in them not being able to make the decisions they need to. Sometimes this arises because the wrong person took the role in the first place, or because the organization structure has changed. If this happens, do not stress; work with the existing data owner to find a more appropriate stakeholder for the role. This is usually a straightforward task as your senior stakeholders have a better understanding of what you are doing by this point and the present incumbent is always incentivized to help you identify the correct person to take over the responsibility.

When finding your data owners, please do not use the words assign, allocate, appoint or anything similar. To be successful, you have to find and engage the right people for the role. Arbitrarily allocating the role will not win you friends and supporters! You may well know who the data owners should be, but telling them that they are a data owner rarely gains their support. It will take time, but follow the steps detailed in this section to engage and speak to potential data owners, work with them and support them as they come on the journey with you. Help them to understand that, while accountability for data comes with the role, it also brings the power to be able to make decisions and fix problems with data that has probably been causing their teams issues for years.

The hard work is in finding and engaging the data owners. Do not rush or even worse skip this step. Once you have the right data owners in place, the rest of the roles are easier to allocate (yes, you can use that word for the remaining roles) and you should have engaged senior stakeholders supporting you on the next phases of your data governance journey.

Data stewards

While data owners provide accountability and authority, they often lack the time and detailed subject matter expertise to handle day-to-day governance activities. This is where data stewards play a crucial role, serving as the operational backbone of data governance implementation. Like data owners, data stewards are not typically part of the general data team. They are subject matter experts who understand the business context and practical use of the data they are the stewards for.

The relationship between data owners and stewards

Data stewards act as deputies for data owners, taking responsibility for the practical implementation of data governance decisions. While data owners are accountable for outcomes, data stewards are responsible for execution. This distinction follows the RACI model (responsible, accountable, consulted, informed), where accountability remains with the data owner while responsibility is delegated to the data steward.

To illustrate this, consider the process of creating data definitions. The data owner is accountable for ensuring appropriate definitions exist and represent business reality. However, the data steward researches current usage, drafts proposed definitions, gathers feedback from stakeholders and presents recommendations to the data owner for approval. The data owner makes the final decision, but the data steward performs the detailed work that enables informed decision-making.

This partnership extends across all data governance activities, from quality monitoring to issue resolution to policy implementation. The data steward executes, coordinates and recommends, while the data owner approves, prioritizes and decides. Although I say the data owners 'approve', they can of course 'reject' proposed definitions or remediation activities, it's just that this rarely happens in practice. If the data owner has chosen the right subject matter experts to be their data stewards, they are likely to trust and approve their recommendations.

Effective data stewards

Data stewards typically have deep operational knowledge of the data they oversee. They understand both the business context and some technical aspects of the data, allowing them to translate between business requirements and technical implementation. Effective data stewards need good communication skills, as they frequently need to facilitate discussions between diverse stakeholders with different perspectives on data.

Once I have one or more data owners in place, I ask them to identify their data stewards. Usually, they will select more than one, splitting their data domain into smaller datasets to appoint the correct subject matter experts.

In selecting data stewards, data owners should look for individuals who demonstrate:

- subject matter expertise within their data domain
- strong analytical and problem-solving capabilities
- excellent communication and facilitation skills
- attention to detail while maintaining strategic awareness
- respect among colleagues across business and technical teams

Unlike data owners, who are always senior executives, data stewards typically occupy mid-level positions with sufficient experience to understand business operations but close enough to day-to-day activities to understand the practical implications of data decisions.

Final advice on data stewards

As with data owners, data stewards must be named individuals who have been identified as being the subject matter experts for specific datasets. Since identifying, engaging and confirming data owners can be a considerable task, many people decide to leave that until later and appoint data stewards first. You may already have a good understanding of who the data subject matter experts are in most areas of your organization, and of course, being less senior, they are easier to approach and broach the topic of data governance with. However, identifying data owners before data stewards is crucial for successful data governance.

Consider the analogy of a ship that needs a captain to define the course before the crew can set sail. Similarly, in the early phases of a data governance initiative, you need to engage your data owners to agree that they want to do data governance and get them to prioritize the implementation. You need them to have accountability so that they make time for their data stewards to complete data governance tasks. If they are delegating data governance responsibilities to these people, they need to choose who they are delegating to, not you!

As with all things, you may need to be flexible in how you define and use these roles. In small organizations, the roles of data owner and data steward might be combined, or a data owner might appoint just one data steward as a deputy data owner to assist with all data governance activities for their datasets. In large global organizations, this simple two-layer approach may not be enough and another layer may need to be introduced, perhaps 'senior data stewards' or 'data governance coordinators', to ensure that data governance is undertaken successfully. Your specific choice of role structure should reflect your organization's structure and complexity, while maintaining clear distinctions between accountability and responsibility.

For the first few years I was doing data governance, I used only the data owner and data steward roles. I had some successes, but I always felt that I could be achieving more. I came to the conclusion that whilst those two roles are undoubtedly the most important when it comes to data governance, everyone at an organization has a part to play in managing data better. That is where the next two roles come in.

Data producers

Data producers are those responsible for creating or capturing data within an organization's systems. This might include frontline staff entering customer information or operational teams recording production metrics. It can also be a data analytics team that creates new data to provide valuable insights. While often overlooked in data governance frameworks, data producers directly influence data quality at its source and, if the role is implemented and communicated properly, can act as a foundation for good-quality data that prevents long-term issues.

The impact of data producers

Data quality issues frequently originate at the point of data creation. When data producers lack understanding of the data requirements of the users of the data they capture, do not understand the importance of accuracy, or face system limitations that prevent proper data capture, they inadvertently create data quality issues that can cascade throughout the organization.

Consider a financial services representative who does not understand the importance of accurate customer classification. Their incorrect category selection (a mandatory system field that probably no one has explained the purpose of) might seem inconsequential during data entry, but it could later affect regulatory reporting, marketing campaigns and product eligibility. What begins as a simple entry error becomes a systemic issue with far-reaching consequences.

It is therefore vital that data producers are effectively engaged and briefed, helping them understand both the mechanics of proper data entry and the importance of good-quality data. This engagement transforms data producers from potential sources of data problems into the first line of defence in data quality management.

Engaging data producers

Unlike the data owner and data steward roles, most employees of an organization produce some data as part of their role. It is not feasible or useful to meet with everyone to agree whether they produce data or not, so we have to engage and educate producers with organization-wide communications. Effective engagement strategies for data producers include:

- providing clear data entry procedures that explain both how and why data should be captured in specific ways
- developing intuitive interfaces that guide proper data entry and prevent common errors
- creating data quality reports (which will be covered in Chapter 7) that alert data producers to quality issues in their data entry
- recognizing and rewarding contributions to data quality improvement
- involving representative data producers in the development of data standards and procedures

It is really important that everyone involved in data entry understands that they need to capture data following the requirements of the stakeholders consuming that data. This is often a missed step, which can lead to bad quality data. In my experience, data producers rarely deliberately capture data incorrectly. It's just that no one took the time to tell them what was needed, which segues nicely onto the next role of data consumers.

Data consumers

Data consumers use data as part of their operational responsibilities to make decisions, generate reports or perform analysis. As with the data producer role, it is likely that most people in your organization consume some data and again, we need to reinforce the role with organization-wide communications and training.

This role applies to virtually everyone in the organization, though some specialist users, such as data scientists, data analysts and actuaries, depend more heavily on specific or specialist datasets than others. From executives reviewing dashboards to analysts preparing forecasts to operations staff following data-driven procedures, data consumers represent the ultimate beneficiaries of data governance efforts.

The data consumer perspective

Data consumers should approach data use with a fundamental question: 'Is this data good enough for my purpose?' Their definition of 'good enough' will vary widely depending on their particular needs. A marketing analyst performing customer segmentation may require different data quality levels than a compliance officer preparing regulatory reports or a sales representative checking product availability.

These varying requirements create a challenge for a data governance initiative, you need to balance diverse data consumer needs while maintaining coherent and obtainable standards. Successful data governance involves data consumers defining data quality requirements for their specific use cases. Data stewards then need to work with a variety of other consumers of the same data, along with the producers of the data, to integrate all requirements into achievable standards that address the organization's full use of that data.

Establishing a data consumer and data producer partnership

Data consumers play a vital role by articulating data quality expectations. By clearly defining their requirements, they provide valuable input into the standards against which data quality is measured. I have found it common for the users of data to blame those entering the data for data quality issues, but often they have not explained why they need the data captured in a certain format. It is almost as though they think that the data producers are telepathic! This scenario is common in larger organizations who frequently work in silos, disconnected from other functions.

A partnership between data consumers and data producers is essential for data governance success. When data consumers articulate their needs clearly and data producers understand those needs, data quality improves naturally. Data governance provides the framework for this communication, creating channels for defining requirements, providing feedback and facilitating continuous improvement.

To facilitate this partnership, you need to create and deliver training, briefings and communications explaining these roles and the importance of managing data better across the whole organization. Even using tools such as e-learning, this is a huge task and should not be underestimated. Despite the magnitude of the task, building a strong partnership is critical. Building a data culture across your organization is the key to sustainable success. Business users talking to each other about data is key to delivering the benefits that data governance brings.

This relationship between data consumers and data producers creates a feedback loop that drives continuous improvement. Data consumers identify issues and articulate their needs, while data producers adjust their practices to better meet those requirements within the standards established by data owners and data stewards. When functioning effectively, this cycle becomes self-reinforcing, with each improvement building greater trust in data.

In practice, most people are both producers and consumers of data. I've had some clients ask if they can just have one role name that covers both. I have not found that approach to be successful in terms of breaking down silos and getting users to talk to each other about data. Separating the two roles helps individuals to understand that, while they may undertake both roles at different times, there are other people producing or consuming the same data whom they need to speak to in order to ensure that everyone has good enough data to do their job properly.

Data custodians

As mentioned early in this chapter, before having data governance in place, it is common for many business stakeholders to believe that IT own all data because it often resides on IT systems. Having read to this point in the chapter, you understand that senior business users need to own data. Your IT department cannot be responsible for making business decisions about data. They are, however, responsible for the technical management of data. They need to ensure that data is held, transferred and transformed in accordance with business requirements while it is on IT supported systems. Of course, this is not news to your IT department. They have known this for years. I use the data custodian role not to add new responsibilities to IT, but to reinforce the new responsibilities the business stakeholders have acquired and to explain the interaction between IT and business users when it comes to data.

Effective data governance clearly separates ownership (a business function) from custodianship (a technical function). This distinction resolves much of the confusion about data responsibility that exists in organizations without formal governance. Before an organization has data governance in place, it is rare that business users have been trained in articulating their data requirements, and therefore it is often down to IT to interpret or make decisions in order to help the business. However, once you have a data governance framework in place, business users get much better at explaining their data requirements and IT's job gets easier.

This evolution represents a significant cultural shift for some organizations. IT departments accustomed to making unilateral decisions about data management must transition to implementing business requirements defined through data governance processes. Simultaneously, business units must accept greater responsibility for clearly articulating their data needs rather than delegating these decisions to technical teams.

Unlike the data owner and data steward roles that apply to specific individuals, data custodians are often defined as a collective role for the entire IT department. This approach as it recognizes that different technical specialists may be involved in managing different aspects of the data infrastructure.

Data governance manager

The data governance manager (sometimes called a data governance lead) provides the dedicated resource needed to design, implement and support the data governance framework. This role coordinates all data governance activities and ensures that the initiative delivers value to the organization. The data governance manager serves as both architect and facilitator, designing the data governance framework while building stakeholder engagement to drive adoption.

The data governance manager is typically the only new role which is created when implementing data governance, as the other data governance roles assign new responsibilities to existing positions. This role requires a unique blend of data governance understanding, business acumen and interpersonal skills to navigate the organizational complexities of data governance. Interpersonal skills are of the utmost importance, since a lot of your time will be spent engaging and influencing stakeholders.

In larger organizations, a data governance team might support the manager, with team members focusing on different aspects of the initiative. However, even in large organizations, it is common for just one person to be tasked with setting up data governance initially. That person often has to work alone for some time before delivering enough value for the organization to invest more in data governance. For example, one client had just the data governance manager for two years before the team was quadrupled to support the growing demand for data governance to be implemented in other parts of the business.

Facilitating data governance

Beyond establishing the data governance framework, the data governance manager facilitates ongoing operations by:

- coordinating communication between data owners, data stewards and other stakeholders
- providing guidance and training on data governance processes

- monitoring and reporting on data governance activities and outcomes
- identifying and addressing barriers to data governance adoption
- mediating conflicts between stakeholders with different perspectives
- ensuring data governance activities align with organizational priorities
- advocating for resources to support data governance initiatives
- supporting the data governance forums (covered in the next section)
- ensuring that the data governance framework evolves to meet the evolving needs of the organization

This facilitation role is critical because governance inherently crosses organizational boundaries, requiring coordination between departments with different priorities and perspectives. The data governance manager serves as a neutral party who can mediate and influence to get good data outcomes for the organization.

A critical success factor for this role is avoiding the trap of taking on responsibilities that should belong to data owners or data stewards. The data governance manager and team will build knowledge and expertise as part of their roles, but do not let key stakeholders assume that means you will do their role for them! I have seen this happen on numerous occasions, resulting in business stakeholders disengaging from the roles which we need them to fulfil.

Ultimately, success depends on business stakeholders embracing their data governance responsibilities. Finding this balance requires careful management of expectations and boundaries from the outset of the data governance initiative.

Notes on naming the roles

As mentioned briefly at the start of this chapter, the names assigned to data governance roles can significantly impact adoption and engagement. While this chapter uses standard terminology, these terms may not resonate equally well in all organizational cultures. As Shakespeare's Juliet famously observed, 'What's in a name? That which we call a rose by any other name would smell as sweet.' This principle applies equally to data governance roles, where responsibilities matter more than title. The critical consideration is selecting role titles which promote understanding and engagement rather than creating resistance or confusion.

Organizations develop their own cultural norms which influence how formal titles are perceived. Terms like 'owner' or 'steward' may carry unexpected connotations in certain environments. Some organizations prefer alternative terms that better align with their culture:

- 'data trustee' or 'data accountable executive' instead of 'data owner'
- 'data champion', 'data advocate' or 'subject matter expert' instead of 'data steward'
- 'data office' or 'data enablement team' instead of 'data governance team'

The key consideration is selecting role titles which align with your organization's culture and promotes engagement. It doesn't matter if they aren't called a data steward as long as they act like one!

PERSONAL ANECDOTE: WHEN ROLE TITLES NEED CHANGING

Early in my data governance career, I encountered significant resistance to the term 'data owner' when implementing governance at a financial services firm. The executive team felt uncomfortable with the ownership concept. Some believed that the company owned the data (which is not helpful for data governance, as the company is not in a position to make decisions about data).

Several executives explicitly stated they couldn't 'own' customer data since it belonged to the customers themselves. Despite my explanations about the functional meaning of the term within data governance, the semantic barrier remained insurmountable.

It took several frustrating meetings where I made no progress on engaging anyone to this critical role before I realized that it was the role title which was creating an unnecessary barrier. Rather than force a term that didn't fit their culture, we retitled the role as 'executive data steward'. This simple change eliminated resistance immediately. The executives clearly understood the accountability and readily accepted their new responsibilities. The responsibilities had not changed at all, just the role title, but the new name resonated with their corporate vocabulary. We quickly moved from debating terminology to implementing substantive data governance activities. Within weeks, I had engaged executive data stewards for all of their key data domains and begun developing data governance processes.

This experience taught me a valuable lesson about pragmatism in data governance implementation. While role definitions matter greatly, flexibility in terminology can make the difference between adoption and rejection. Focus on getting the right people doing the right things; what you call them is secondary.

Data governance forums

Data governance requires formal mechanisms for decision-making, issue resolution and strategic oversight. Data governance forums, whether called committees, councils or steering groups, provide those mechanisms. These forums represent the collective decision-making component of a data governance framework, ensuring consistent approaches across data domains while providing necessary oversight.

Types of governance forums

Depending on your organization's size and complexity, there are several types of forums you could establish to address different aspects of data governance. I prefer to keep it as simple as possible:

DATA GOVERNANCE COMMITTEE

The data governance committee serves as the primary decision-making body, mainly comprising data owners who set strategic direction and resolve cross-domain issues. This executive-level group provides the ultimate oversight for the data governance initiative, approving the policy, resolving escalated issues and ensuring alignment with your organization's corporate strategy.

DOMAIN FORUMS

An approach I would only recommend in particularly large and complex organizations, domain forums focus on data governance within particular data domains such as customer, product or finance data. These groups address domain-specific issues and standards while ensuring consistency with enterprise data governance principles. They typically include the domain data owner and relevant data stewards, along with key stakeholders who produce or consume that data. In most organizations, this would be covered in the data governance committee meetings. In very large or complex organizations, it can work better to have these additional forums in place for key data domains, each reporting into the data governance committee.

DATA STEWARD WORKING GROUP

The bank where I started doing data governance had a very formal structure for official committees. For every committee, there had to be a working group that did detailed work and reported to the committee. So I did not hesitate to set up a data steward working group to bring together data stewards from across the division to address operational data governance challenges and data quality issues.

In theory, these forums facilitate knowledge sharing, issue resolution and collaborative problem-solving among the people most directly involved in day-to-day data governance activities. In practice, I have found that they have too many attendees with a vast array of different interests. It is impossible to run it as an effective and productive forum. You only have time to discuss a few things and they are likely to interest only a handful of the attendees. Over time, a large number of data stewards stopped attending as we never discussed topics that interested or impacted them. I tried the approach a few more times before coming to the conclusion that, on the whole, these are not useful forums and it is better to use online collaboration tools or other communications methods with the data steward community. Instead, I prefer to create data quality working groups as and when needed.

DATA QUALITY WORKING GROUPS

I like to create these transient working groups, as and when needed, to bring the right stakeholders together to investigate and resolve particularly complex or widely impacting data quality issues. I invite all the data stewards who are impacted by the issue, along with representatives from the areas that capture the data and any other consumers of that data. Depending on the nature of the issue, I may also invite someone from IT to advise on technical constraints and options. The group works together for the period it takes to investigate and resolve the issue.

How you structure your data governance forums and what you call them needs to reflect your organization's needs, culture and complexity. Smaller organizations might implement a single governance committee that addresses all aspects, while larger enterprises may require multiple forums with clearly defined relationships and escalation paths.

Establishing a data governance committee

Whatever you choose to call your forum of data owners, it is important to also consider when you are going to set it up. The timing of its establishment can significantly impact its effectiveness. Some organizations create such committees at the outset of data governance initiatives, while others wait until the framework is more developed.

A data governance committee established too early may struggle to find purpose and maintain engagement. Things move slowly at the start of a data governance initiative and it can be challenging to keep all the attendees engaged if you do not have much progress to report.

However, waiting too long to establish forums can hamper decision-making and limit stakeholder engagement. The best approach involves creating a minimal initial structure focused on framework development, then expanding to a more comprehensive agenda as you progress on your data governance journey.

Once it is set up, in order to add value and support the success of your initiative, it will require careful planning and management. In my experience, several factors significantly influence how effective your committee will be:

LEADERSHIP

Leadership selection is critical. The chairperson should be a senior supporter of data governance, ideally the executive sponsor of the initiative. They must have sufficient authority to drive decisions and secure resources. The data governance manager should support, but not chair, the committee. They do not have the seniority and authority in the organization to act as a useful chairperson. Instead, they should act as facilitator and subject matter expert.

TERMS OF REFERENCE

For a committee with such senior attendees, it is important to document clear terms of reference. This will define purpose, scope, membership, decision authority and operating procedures. These documents establish boundaries and expectations, preventing confusion about responsibilities or authority. They should include provisions for evolving the committee's role as data governance matures from design and implementation to operational phases. Having a formal terms of reference document sends a clear message to the attendees that this is a committee with a clear purpose.

MEETING CONTENT

What is discussed at the meetings can significantly impact the effectiveness of the committee. Agendas should focus on decisions and actions rather than information sharing and updates. I have been asked for help numerous times to revive a disengaged data governance committee. The cause is nearly always the same thing: the meetings are just an update from the data governance manager on what has been done since the last meeting and what will be done next. It's no wonder the data owners stop turning up to the meetings in this scenario. There is nothing for them to provide updates or make decisions on. There are no meaningful discussions about direction or actions for them to take. They may as well skip the meeting and read the minutes of the meeting instead!

Make sure that you keep your stakeholders engaged. Get them making decisions and providing true oversight of your data governance initiative. Ask the data owners to provide updates on critical data issues. Make sure that these meetings are valuable and not a waste of everyone's time.

Done well, a data governance committee can be a powerful mechanism for driving organizational change through collaborative decision-making, strategic oversight and senior stakeholder engagement.

Conclusion

Establishing clear roles and responsibilities forms the foundation of any successful data governance initiative. The roles outlined in this chapter provide a starting point, but remember that flexibility and pragmatism are essential when adapting these roles to your organization's unique culture and constraints.

The most critical insight from my years of implementation experience is that people make data governance work, not processes or technology. Your success depends on finding the right individuals who understand the value of data and are willing to take on responsibilities within the data governance framework. Take time to engage stakeholders properly rather than simply assigning roles; this investment in relationship building will pay dividends throughout your data governance journey.

Key takeaways for implementing data governance roles:

- Start with data owners: Identify and engage senior business stakeholders before appointing other roles, as they provide the authority and accountability needed to drive change.

- Never assign multiple owners: Maintain the 'one data owner per dataset' rule to ensure clear accountability and avoid decision-making paralysis.

- Adapt role titles to your culture: Focus on responsibilities rather than specific names and use terminology that resonates within your organization.

- Engage, do not assign: Take time to find and convince the right people rather than arbitrarily allocating roles to unwilling participants.
- Build executive support early: Secure visible sponsorship from senior leadership to provide credibility and remove organizational barriers.
- Create meaningful forums: Establish a data governance committee that focuses on decisions and actions rather than information sharing and updates.

The hard work lies in finding and engaging your data owners. Once you have the right senior stakeholders committed to data governance, the remaining roles become much easier to establish. Don't rush this critical step, as engaged data owners will become your strongest advocates for driving cultural change across the organization.

And remember: it doesn't matter what you call these roles as long as the right people are doing the right things to improve data quality and data governance across your organization.

PART THREE

Implement

07

Data governance deliverables

Introduction

In the previous chapters we explored the foundational elements of data governance: strategy, framework design, policies, processes and roles. Now it's time to turn theory into practice. This chapter focuses on the tangible outcomes that transform your data governance framework from an abstract concept into concrete business value.

Data governance deliverables are the 'things' you'll have in place that you didn't before starting your initiative. They're the practical outputs that make data governance real and valuable to your organization. While the specific deliverables you prioritize will depend on your drivers and organizational context, certain core elements are essential for most data governance initiatives.

In this chapter, we'll explore:

- what data governance deliverables are and why they're crucial for success
- data definitions: the foundation for common understanding across your organization
- data glossaries and catalogues: where your data definitions live and stakeholders go for clarity
- data lineage: mapping the journey of data through your organization
- data quality rules and reporting: ensuring your data is fit for purpose

- data risks and controls: protecting your most valuable data assets
- creating a visual framework: why you need a diagram that shows how all these deliverables connect

Each deliverable serves a specific purpose, but their real power comes from how they work together as an integrated system. By the end of this chapter, you'll understand not just what to build, but how to structure these deliverables in a way that makes sense for your organization and resonates with your stakeholders.

Remember, without these tangible deliverables, data governance risks remaining a well-intentioned but ultimately ineffective exercise that fails to deliver business value.

What are data governance deliverables?

Data governance deliverables are key components of your data governance framework that ensure your organization effectively manages its data. I like to think of them as the things you now have in place which you didn't before you started your data governance initiative. Initially, I wasn't sure what to call this collection of data governance things. 'Things' seemed too trivial a term that would not be taken seriously, but 'artefacts' sounded too high-brow. I settled on 'deliverables' (probably influenced by the years I spent being a project manager before embarking on my data governance career) and it works well with all stakeholders.

Data governance deliverables represent the tangible outcomes and documentation produced as part of a data governance initiative. These deliverables ensure that data governance processes are effectively structured and that responsibilities are clearly defined.

It will be clear to you at this stage in the book, that why your organization is implementing data governance will influence how you have designed your data governance framework. It also impacts which deliverables you will have and at which stage in your initiative. This chapter covers the key data governance deliverables which most organizations will need: a data governance policy, an operating model, processes, data definitions, a data catalogue, data quality rules and reports, data lineage and risks and controls.

Why are deliverables important?

Data governance deliverables provide essential structure to a concept that can all too easily become an abstract or overwhelming initiative. These tangible outputs bring clarity to data governance processes by clearly defining roles, responsibilities and expectations across the organization, eliminating the confusion that often derails data governance initiatives before they gain momentum. Beyond simply providing direction, deliverables create a framework for accountability that ensures data is managed both effectively and responsibly, with clear ownership and defined processes for maintaining data quality standards.

Perhaps most critically, the deliverables transform data governance from a theoretical concept into a practical mechanism. By implementing structured approaches to documenting data and monitoring data quality, organizations can build trust in their data. For organizations operating in regulated industries, these deliverables become even more vital, as they provide documented evidence of compliance with increasingly stringent data governance requirements. Without these deliverables, data governance risks remaining a well-intentioned but ultimately ineffective exercise that fails to deliver business value.

Policy, operating model and processes revisited

Before diving into the specific deliverables, let's briefly revisit the three data governance deliverables, which we already covered in the Design section of this book, as these form the backbone of everything that follows.

Your *data governance policy* (covered in Chapter 4) establishes the overarching principles and standards that guide how your organization approaches data governance. It is not documentation for the sake of it. It is, in effect, the high-level instruction manual which states what must be done and by whom. It mandates data governance and provides a clear message that your organization understands the value of its data and describes what will be done to manage it as an asset.

Your *operating model* (also covered in Chapter 4) defines how data governance works in practice within your organization's unique structure and culture. Closely linked to your policy, the operating model gets into the practical mechanics of governance, i.e. how the things described at a high level in the policy actually get done: how decisions get made, how issues get escalated and how data governance activities integrate with existing business processes.

Data governance processes (detailed in Chapter 5) translate your policy and operating model into specific, repeatable workflows that stakeholders can follow. These are the practical step-by-step procedures that cover everything from data quality issue resolution to new data definition approval.

These three elements work together as your data governance foundation. In the rest of this chapter, we will explore the specific deliverables that bring this foundation to life and make data governance tangible and valuable to your organization.

Data definitions

Here's something that might surprise you: despite talking about data governance for many years, I was not asked to explain what a 'data definition' is until very recently. This highlights how we often assume everyone knows the basics. That assumption can lead to misunderstandings and mistakes, so I've included this section in the chapter to make sure that you understand both the importance of data definitions and, more importantly, what they are.

If you are tempted to google 'data definition', please don't. I tried it and the results are just not helpful! You'll find technical jargon like 'the origin of a field that references a data domain and determines the data type and format of data entry'. That is because most online definitions are written in the context of data dictionaries (which will be explained in the next chapter). That is not what we mean when talking about data definitions in data governance terms.

What are data definitions?

In the data governance world, we focus on making data accessible to business users who need to understand and use it for decision-making.

That means capturing simple, clear explanations of what your data means in business terms.

The problem we're solving is surprisingly common: people across your organization use the same terms but mean completely different things. Take 'customer', what does that mean in your business? Is it someone who's made a purchase? Someone who's registered interest? Someone with an active contract? Ask Bob from accounting and Sarah from marketing and you are likely to get different answers. When stakeholders aren't aligned on basic definitions, your reports and decisions become unreliable.

Some terms are straightforward, like 'date of birth', 'first name' and 'postcode', and don't typically cause debate. But venture into business-specific territory like 'active customer', 'qualified lead' or 'product category' and you'll discover just how much interpretation varies across your organization.

How to write good data definitions

Creating effective data definitions isn't rocket science, but it does require discipline. I'm talking about short, clear phrases or sentences that explain what something is and what it represents. My litmus test with clients is simple: 'Could someone who knows nothing about this organization read this definition and understand it?' If the answer is yes, you've succeeded.

Here's my practical advice for writing definitions that are useful:

- Make it unique and distinguishable. Your definition should clearly separate this term from all others. Write descriptively using proper phrases or sentence. Simply restating the term's words in a different order won't cut it. Avoid acronyms and abbreviations that could confuse readers unfamiliar with your organization's jargon. State what it is, not what it is not. Focus on positive, descriptive language that builds understanding.

- Be clear, concise and unambiguous. Every word should earn its place in your definition. Consider this poor example: 'Spoon: something to eat with.' This definition could easily describe a knife, fork or even chopsticks. A better definition would be: 'Spoon: a utensil used for eating, consisting of a small, shallow, oval or round bowl at the end of a handle.' See the difference? The improved version is specific, descriptive and leaves no room for confusion.

- Test your definitions with non-experts. If they are confused, the definitions need to be revised. Consider adding context like data usage examples where helpful but remember that clarity trumps comprehensiveness every time.

The goal isn't to create the perfect academic definition. It is about ensuring that anyone in your organization can read a definition and immediately understand it, without needing additional explanation or context.

Who should write the data definitions?

This is where many organizations get it wrong. The data governance team should not be writing definitions for the entire organization. You cannot be expert in every data item your business has, only the business users truly understand what their data represents.

This is where your data governance roles become crucial. Data owners, as senior stakeholders accountable for specific datasets, are responsible for reviewing and approving definitions. However, they are typically too senior to draft them personally. That's where data stewards step in, writing data definitions is a key part of their role.

Data stewards may need to collaborate with other business users in their area to get the full picture, but the responsibility clearly sits with them. The data governance manager or team's role is to provide guidance, training and support, not to become universal experts in every piece of data the organization holds.

DATA DEFINITIONS MATTER

Data definitions are the unsung heroes of data governance, bridging the gap between technical systems and business understanding. They are all about ensuring everyone speaks the same language when discussing data, creating the foundation for reliable reporting and decision-making. Get

> them right and you will eliminate countless hours of confusion and misalignment. Get them wrong and you'll wonder why your data governance efforts aren't delivering the value you expected. Whatever your drivers for data governance are and whatever your initial focus is, they are a key deliverable that should not be skipped or left until later.

You may be wondering where these valuable data definitions are held? That is where your data glossary or data catalogue comes in.

Data glossary/data catalogue

Of all the data governance deliverables we will cover in this chapter, none is more fundamental to your success than your data glossary, or data catalogue. These terms are often used interchangeably and cause significant confusion in the data governance world, but regardless of what you call it this deliverable serves as the cornerstone of effective data governance.

Your data glossary or catalogue is where your carefully crafted data definitions live, where stakeholders go to understand what your organization's data means and where the theoretical concepts of data governance become practical, usable resources. It's the foundation that makes all your other data governance activities possible.

Because this deliverable is so critical to your data governance success (and because there's substantial confusion about the different approaches and tools available), I've devoted the entire next chapter to exploring the data glossary or catalogue and the tools that support them. Chapter 8 will guide you through the distinctions between these and other concepts, help you choose the right approach for your organization and provide practical advice on implementation strategies that actually work.

For now, it's enough to understand that this central repository of data understanding is not optional. It's the deliverable that transforms abstract data governance concepts into concrete business value and getting it right is essential for everything else that follows.

Data lineage

In this section I want to talk about something that sounds a bit daunting but is actually very helpful when it comes to data governance and that is data lineage. I think the term makes it sound perhaps scarier than it really is, but data lineage can be a very valuable tool for your data governance initiative.

What is data lineage?

Data lineage refers to the visual representation of the flow of data within an organization. Picture it as a map that tracks the journey of data: where it begins its life, how it moves through various processes and where it ultimately resides, or even leaves your organization. At its absolute simplest, data lineage is just a diagram that shows you how data flows through an organization from the first point that it comes in. Sometimes they are also called data flow diagrams, which is often a less scary term for some stakeholders.

For instance, imagine a customer placing an order on a website. This initiation marks the beginning of the data's journey through systems like order processing and inventory management, eventually landing in a data warehouse for reporting. That might be as far as the data goes for that particular journey.

Obviously, there are much more complex scenarios than that, but I recommend starting with a very simple data lineage or data flow diagram, which just shows little boxes representing the systems your data passes through and the processes that happen to it along the way, like the one shown in Figure 7.1.

FIGURE 7.1 Simple data lineage example

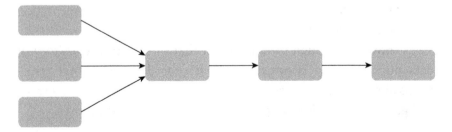

Why data lineage is important

Understanding data lineage is vital for several reasons that directly impact your data governance success. Troubleshooting and problem-solving becomes significantly more effective when you have documented data lineage. When data issues arise, data lineage allows stakeholders to trace problems back to their origins, facilitating more effective and lasting solutions. Without understanding where data originates or how it's transformed, resolving issues becomes more of a guessing game that wastes time and resources.

Data quality assurance improves significantly when you maintain a clear record of data movement and transformation. Data quality is most at risk when it moves between systems or is transformed, so understanding these transition points through data lineage is crucial for maintaining data quality and integrity. By mapping where data flows and changes, organizations can better evaluate the quality and reliability of their data, identifying potential weak spots where issues are most likely to occur.

Regulatory compliance becomes manageable rather than over-whelming. In an era of increasing data related regulations, having documented data lineage helps organizations comply with legal requirements. This is particularly crucial in sectors like finance and healthcare, where organizations must prove the reliability of their data processes to regulators. But remember, having data lineage documented not only aids in compliance with regulations but enhances overall data quality across the business.

Documenting data lineage

Despite being very valuable, creating data lineage diagrams can be challenging at times. There are automated tools made specifically to help with these challenges that can scan your databases and create data lineage for you. The problem with this approach is that they often churn out significant volumes of detailed diagrams that have been documented at data field level. While this granular level of detail is useful in some scenarios, it can be overwhelming if this level of detail isn't needed or if you're doing data lineage to support your data governance efforts.

These automated tools are certainly useful for data architecture and data engineering teams who need that technical detail for system design and troubleshooting, but they're often less useful for the business-level data lineage that provides real value in a data governance initiative.

In practice, data lineage diagrams can become very complex, especially if they are created at a very low level of detail. My preference and recommendation is for them to be created at a high level, for example tracking 'customer data' rather than individual fields like 'customer name', and only to create them for the most critical data in your organization.

START SIMPLE AND WORK BACKWARDS

If you don't need very detailed data lineage, my advice would be to choose some critical datasets that are important to your organization and work backwards. I say this because it's really hard to work forwards when you're trying to create data lineage if it's never been documented before.

Start by consulting with business users to understand where their data comes from and follow its path. Speak to a data consumer who's using the data, perhaps in a report at one of the final stages when that data is used. Ask them where they get that data and then you literally do that same process time and time again, tracing it all the way back to find out where it originates.

However, working backwards can be time-consuming and often it is possible to speed things up by using the knowledge of experienced business analysts. Business analysts who have been in your organization a long time and worked on many projects will have a lot of knowledge about how data moves between systems in your organization. You will be able to get a substantial amount of information about the data lineage of a particular data domain in a short workshop with them, which you can then share with your data stewards to review and fill in any gaps.

BUILD INCREMENTALLY

As it is time consuming and can be complicated to document data lineage, I recommend adopting an iterative approach. As recommended above, start by documenting data lineage for your critical data only. If it is classified as 'critical' your business stakeholders understand the value of this data and are more likely to support you as you trace back and document the data lineage. Once data lineage for all critical data has been completed you can iteratively add to your data lineage documentation as you investigate and resolve data quality issues. During data quality issue investigations, you will be tracing the data lineage to identify the source of the issue, so you can document this and gradually expand your data lineage repository.

THE REALITY CHECK

Data lineage is not merely a technical exercise; done well at the right level of detail it can add great value to your organization. Effective data lineage is crucial for troubleshooting, improving data quality and ensuring regulatory compliance.

Data lineage isn't scary. It's fairly simple to create high-level data lineage diagrams when you break it all down first and focus on what actually matters to your organization.

Data quality rules and reporting

In Chapter 1 we looked at the strong relationship between data quality and data governance. The two disciplines are so interrelated that I consider data quality reports and the rules needed to create them as data governance deliverables. Data quality rules and reports are pivotal in ensuring that data is of good enough quality for its intended use. Let's delve into what these elements entail, how they function and why they are crucial.

What are data quality rules?

Data quality rules are predefined criteria that specify what constitutes 'good enough' data. Rather than seeking perfection, these rules focus on essential attributes that make data usable. In Chapter 4 I mentioned the typical data quality dimensions:

- accuracy: ensures that data is correct and free from errors
- completeness: verifies that all necessary data fields are populated
- validity: assesses whether data conforms to defined formats or standards
- consistency: checks that data is consistent across different datasets
- uniqueness: confirms that there are no duplicates in critical data entries
- timeliness: evaluates whether data is up-to-date and available when needed

When you come to work on data quality rules for your organization, I recommend revisiting that section of Chapter 4 and the resources recommended there.

What are data quality reports?

Once data quality rules are established, data quality reports are generated to assess compliance with these standards. These reports provide a view of how well the data meets the agreed criteria and highlight any exceptions or areas needing improvement.

Data quality reports offer regular insights into the state of your most critical data assets. They transform abstract quality rules into concrete, measurable outcomes that stakeholders can understand and act upon. Rather than relying on assumptions about data reliability or trustworthiness, these reports provide objective evidence of the data quality.

The frequency and scope of these reports should align with your business needs. Some organizations require daily monitoring of critical operational data, while others may find weekly or monthly reporting sufficient for strategic datasets. The key is establishing a frequency that allows for timely intervention when data quality issues arise, without overwhelming teams with unnecessary reporting overhead.

Effective data quality reports don't just identify problems; they provide context that helps teams understand the significance of issues and prioritize their response efforts. They should clearly distinguish between minor inconsistencies that can be managed over time and critical failures that require immediate attention.

Why data quality rules and reports matter

Understanding the need for data quality rules and reports is crucial for any organization aiming to leverage its data as a valuable asset. Let's explore some key reasons why these rules and reports are essential.

Enhancing decision-making becomes dramatically more reliable when you have good-quality data foundations. Data quality rules act as your aids, ensuring that the data guiding your decisions is accurate and trustworthy. High-quality data supports better strategic decisions and can significantly influence better business outcomes.

Operational efficiency improves when data quality issues are caught early. When data quality is poor, errors can cascade through business processes, leading to inefficiencies. By implementing data quality reports, organizations can identify and rectify inaccuracies before they disrupt operations. A robust approach to data quality allows for smoother workflows, reducing time spent on corrections.

In an era where regulatory requirements are increasing, maintaining data quality is not just beneficial but often necessary. Organizations in regulated sectors risk facing hefty penalties if they fail to comply with data governance and quality standards. Data quality reports provide oversight, helping ensure regulatory compliance and protecting the organization from potential legal ramifications.

Data quality reports help communicate the state of data across the organization, much like a regular health check-up. These reports highlight issues and trends, fostering an environment where stakeholders are informed and can collaboratively address data discrepancies. This transparency builds trust and enhances team collaboration.

A focus on continuous improvement becomes a natural outcome of regular data quality monitoring. Setting data quality rules encourages business stakeholders to reflect on their data practices. By regularly assessing data through reports, teams can identify recurring issues, leading to ongoing refinements in data governance processes.

REAL-WORLD EXAMPLE

How data quality rules transformed financial reporting

A financial services client was struggling with month-end reporting delays caused by data inconsistencies. After implementing data quality rules that flagged incomplete customer records and duplicate transactions, their reporting cycle improved from 15 days to 5 days. The data quality reports also helped them identify a systematic issue with their CRM data entry, leading to improved training and processes.

When to start creating data quality reports

I'm often asked when you should start looking at data quality rules and data quality reporting, and in my experience many organizations try to tackle this too early in their data governance initiative (or even worse before they have commenced data governance). This premature approach almost always leads to frustration and wasted effort.

The reason I say this comes down to two fundamental issues. First, if you haven't got your data catalogue or data glossary in place with your data definitions, how do you know what that data is properly? You haven't agreed on basic definitions or had those crucial conversations about what the terms mean. How can you possibly agree on what makes that data 'good enough' if you don't even know what it represents?

Second, as we have already established, not all data is equal. Do you need data quality rules and reporting on all of your data? In my opinion, probably not. You only need them for the data that's most important or most critical to your organization. But until you've actually agreed on a criticality approach, the criteria and got all your data assessed against those criteria, how do you know which is the most important data that should have data quality rules and reporting?

You can see where I'm going with this. Data quality work is a very valuable activity that we need to do, but we need to undertake it after we have put the foundations in place, to avoid wasted effort and rework.

Writing effective data quality rules

Once you've laid the proper groundwork, you can proceed to creating data quality rules, but it comes with a warning. It sounds like a simple thing to do. 'Let's just get the business users to write some data quality rules', you might think. The trouble is, our business users have never had to write data quality rules before, so they often don't know where to start.

THE WRONG APPROACH: TECHNICAL LISTS

Giving your business stakeholders a technical list of options like 'You can have completeness rules, validity rules or consistency rules' is really not going to help them. I do not recommend that you ask your stakeholders to state the rules in terms of the data quality dimensions detailed above. You are unlikely to get a favourable or useful response. What we need to do is ask them what makes their data 'good enough' and we want this information to be in business language or business rules.

THE RIGHT APPROACH: BUSINESS-FOCUSED QUESTIONS

I have found it far easier and more effective to ask the consumers of the data to describe what makes the data fit for the purpose they use it. We might give them some clues by asking questions like: Does that data always have to be complete? Does it have to be accurate? Do you have a particular format that it has to be in to be considered valid? We can ask questions to help tease out the business rules, but it is never a good idea to ask our business users to give us fully formed technical data quality rules.

For instance, for customer data, a data consumer might specify that all customers must have a valid email address format (which translates to validity), customer names cannot be left blank (completeness) and postcodes must be checked against an authoritative postcode list (accuracy). Notice how these business rules describe actual business needs without getting bogged down in technical terminology.

THE COLLABORATIVE PROCESS

Whilst responsibility for setting data quality rules rests with data stewards, the data governance manager or team will work collaboratively with data stewards and consumers of the data to document the data quality rules. Please note that while the data steward should draft and propose the data quality rules, it's crucial to involve data consumers in this process as well, since they may have requirements that the data steward is not aware of, so hasn't considered.

Additionally, it's essential to canvas the views of data producers to ensure that the desired standards are achievable before any rules are approved and set. Data producers have intimate knowledge of the source systems, data creation processes and technical constraints that may impact the feasibility of proposed quality rules. Their input helps prevent the establishment of unrealistic standards that could lead to frustration and non-compliance.

For example, at an insurance company I worked with, a 100 per cent complete data quality standard was approved for a field that had not previously been considered mandatory. The call centre agents, in order to keep calls as short as possible, had never asked customers for this information and left the field empty. When the head of the call centre discovered this new requirement, he was horrified. He explained that this seemingly small change, requiring just one additional field to be completed, would necessitate an expansion of the call centre and significant recruitment to handle the increased call duration. These are changes that require substantial investment and time to implement. This example illustrates why consulting with data producers, particularly in environments like call centres where efficiency metrics are critical, is essential before finalizing data quality rules.

The business rules, once approved, are given to a data quality analyst to convert into technical specifications and reports. The business stakeholders define what good looks like; the technical team figures out how to measure and monitor it.

APPROVAL AND ACCOUNTABILITY

Of course, before being turned into data quality reports, the rules should be formally approved by data owners, ensuring that senior stakeholders take ownership of the standards being established. This approval process creates accountability and gives the rules the authority needed for effective implementation across the organization.

ACTING ON THE REPORTS

With data quality rules established and approved by data owners, you might think the hard work is done. However, even after the reports are produced, your business stakeholders still need to be involved. Those reports provide the exceptions against the rules you've established and those exceptions shouldn't just be reviewed by a central team. They need to go back to the data stewards and the consumers of that data, so they're aware when the data may not be good enough for them to complete their tasks. They also need to be sent to the producers of the data (if it is not the data steward) so that they can correct the exceptions.

However, it is important to have a process whereby people not only fix the immediate exceptions but also try to identify and fix the underlying causes. We do not want to be perpetuating activities that result in tactical, regular manual fixes. We want to be using data quality reports to identify where there might be broken processes, bugs in systems or gaps in user training.

When you're delivering data quality reporting, make sure that you put in place a process that clearly defines who's going to get the reports, and who's responsible for looking into the exceptions and doing something about them. Without that process, it's pointless to produce the reports in the first place.

The role of generative AI

With all the current hype around generative AI, I'm increasingly asked whether AI can be used to create data quality rules. While AI tools can be extremely helpful, we must be very careful to use them appropriately as part of a human-driven process rather than as a replacement for human judgement.

The ironic thing about using AI for data quality is that the artificial intelligence is only as good as the data it learns from. To get AI to give you really good-quality data quality rules, your data quality has to be really good to begin with. If it's not, the AI will learn from what you give it and make its best guess about what may be right or wrong, potentially correcting data in incorrect ways.

That said, I do think AI can be useful, in a similar way to how I've always encouraged clients to use data profiling tools when setting up data quality rules. These tools look at the data and identify what they think might be outliers or anomalies. But time and time again, when you present profiling results to business users, they might say, 'Oh, those outliers are okay. They don't happen very often, but we don't need to change the data quality rule. It's just less common for that to happen.'

Business users can spot that those items aren't really exceptions and that those outliers are perfectly acceptable. But what is AI going to do? It's going to assume that because 90 per cent of the data fits within a certain range and 10 per cent falls outside it, clearly the 10 per cent must be wrong.

One area where AI is proving particularly valuable is in no-code data quality rule creation. No-code solutions allow organizations to define and implement data quality checks without requiring coding skill. This makes creating the technical data quality rules essentially as easy as filling out a form. The AI backbone of these solutions can interpret business requirements and automatically generate the necessary technical code for data quality checks.

The benefits of no-code approaches include speed (dramatically reducing implementation time), accessibility (enabling non-technical stakeholders to participate directly), efficiency (freeing up analysts for more strategic work) and scalability (easily adapting to new requirements). However, even with no-code solutions, the same principle applies – AI should accelerate and simplify the process, but human judgement remains crucial for validating that the generated rules make business sense.

Use AI and profiling tools to help speed up the process and give your business users ideas about what may be right or wrong with your data, but do not let AI run your data quality processes entirely on its own. The human element remains essential for making informed judgements about what constitutes acceptable data quality for your specific business context.

THE BOTTOM LINE

Implementing robust data quality rules and generating regular reports not only enhances the quality of data used but also drives overall organizational success. By adopting a proactive stance towards data quality, you can unlock the true potential of your organizations' data, driving better insights and performance.

Further data quality reading

This has been a high-level overview of data quality rules and reports, focusing on how they fit within your broader data governance initiative. For a detailed approach to implementing comprehensive data quality practices, I recommend Robert Hawker's excellent book: *Practical Data Quality*.[1] Robert provides the in-depth technical guidance and practical strategies that will help you implement effective data quality management beyond the data governance foundations covered here.

Data risks and controls

Data risks and controls are essential elements in managing data effectively within an organization, but unless required for regulatory purposes they are best left until later stages of your data governance initiative. Let's delve into each aspect and understand how they fit into your overall data governance framework.

DATA RISKS

Data risks encompass a variety of challenges that could arise from improper handling or management of data. Risks to data quality represent one of the most common risks organizations face, where poor-quality data can lead to unreliable analyses and poor decisions. Missing or inaccurate data can significantly impair operational effectiveness, leading to customer dissatisfaction, regulatory issues or financial losses.

Understanding the risks to your data and its quality enables you to take action to prevent those risks turning into real issues.

DATA CONTROLS

To mitigate the risks with the worst potential impact, organizations need to implement a set of controls that safeguard data quality and ensure data remains appropriate, complete and accurate throughout its lifecycle. Your data governance framework serves as the foundation by establishing a structured approach that defines roles and responsibilities around data, ensuring accountability and clarity across the organization.

As already covered earlier in this chapter, effective data quality management processes involve continuous assessment through monitoring. These practices are the key controls that are used to mitigate data risks but not the only ones. Training and awareness programmes play a crucial role in ensuring your staff are equipped with the knowledge to manage data effectively, preventing many risks associated with human error. When people understand their role in maintaining data quality, they become an active part of your control environment rather than a potential source of risk.

A risk-based approach

This approach to data risks and controls represents an operational risk way of thinking: identifying the risks to your data at any point in time, determining where the risks are highest for data you consider critical and then putting controls in place to mitigate the risk of problems occurring.

Because this is fundamentally an operational risk approach, I don't suggest that you work in isolation when looking at risks and controls for your data. It's much better to work with the operational risk team in your organization and try to align what you want to do around data risks and controls, with how they manage operational risks. After all, risks relating to data are operational in nature, they're just a very specific type of operational risk. This is yet another example of making it easier for everyone to do the right thing when it comes to data. Business stakeholders do not want reviews of operational risks one week and data risks the next – it is a duplication of effort and a waste of everyone's time. By working together, both you and the operational risk team can work more efficiently and your key stakeholders are only asked once about their risks (some of which will undoubtedly be data risks).

By thinking about data risks and controls as part of your broader operational risk management, you create a more integrated and sustainable approach to data governance that aligns with existing business processes and risk management frameworks.

Just remember the goal is not to eliminate all data risks. That's impossible and often impractical. Instead, focus on identifying your most critical data assets, understanding the specific risks they face and implementing proportionate controls that provide effective protection without creating unnecessary bureaucracy or operational burden.

Why you need a diagram of your deliverables

The adage 'a picture is worth a thousand words' is popularly attributed to Confucius but is thought to have been born much more recently. It is believed that the modern use of the phrase stems from an article by Fred R Barnard in an advertising trade journal in 1921, promoting the use of images in advertisements. Whatever the source, one thing that is certain is that when the saying was first used, no one was thinking about data governance! But they easily could have been.

Over the years, one important thing I've learned is that most people respond well to pictures. I'm a list person; my brain likes long lists of activities and ordering them in the most logical and efficient order. I once confounded a boss because I produced a project plan off pat without first having drawn a conceptual diagram of what the project was trying to achieve (something he assumed that I would have to do to work out what tasks were needed and in which order). Because of my fondness for lists, it took me a while to realize that a lot of people not only do not like lists, they find them off-putting.

Whilst working with a team of business architects many years ago, it became very apparent that whilst they did not like my lists and wordy documents, I could easily understand their diagrams, and so started my experimentation with using diagrams to sell new concepts to people.

Gaining stakeholder understanding

You need to be comfortable that you can articulate your data governance deliverables, how they fit together and how they form part of your data governance framework. If you can't do that, you're going to struggle to communicate your data governance deliverables to your stakeholders. If you can't get that across to them in a way that they understand and can see how it fits into the bigger picture, then you're going to struggle to get their buy-in and support. That is going to impact your ability to successfully implement data governance.

If you speak about or share your deliverables as separate items without showing their relationships, they don't actually mean anything, they're just a number of random items. Remember, most of your stakeholders will not have come across data governance before, so it's really important that you're able to communicate these in a way that people can understand.

Creating your structure

I wish I could give you the perfect diagram that you could re-use. But remember what we covered in Chapter 3 about custom-building your own data governance framework. There isn't one size or one standard approach that fits everybody. Your organization isn't standard. So, a standard data governance framework won't work for you. In the same manner, how you choose to structure these deliverables will depend on several factors. It depends on which deliverables you're focusing on delivering. It depends on your organizational culture. It depends on how you traditionally manage these things. It depends on what existing frameworks and structures you have in place in your organization. You might want to align to these existing structures. You might even want to hang some of your data governance deliverables off them (for example, the data risks and controls becoming part of your organization's approach to operational risk management).

In the many such diagrams I've created, one approach I've used successfully is to have the data governance policy at the top (see Figure 7.2). This is the mandate, the overarching authority that says your organization is going to govern and manage your data properly. Below that sits the operating model, which provides the detail of how you are going to implement that policy. You might then structure the remaining deliverables by having data lineage, risk and controls and data quality rules all forming part of your overall data catalogue, while keeping data quality reports as a separate output that flags data quality issues.

Alternatively, I've worked with clients where data quality rules and the data quality issue resolution process formed part of their operating model, with the data catalogue sitting separately alongside standalone risk and controls documentation that integrated with their existing operational risk systems (see Figure 7.3).

FIGURE 7.2 Data governance deliverables diagram option 1

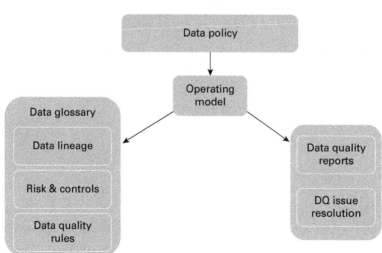

FIGURE 7.3 Data governance deliverables diagram option 2

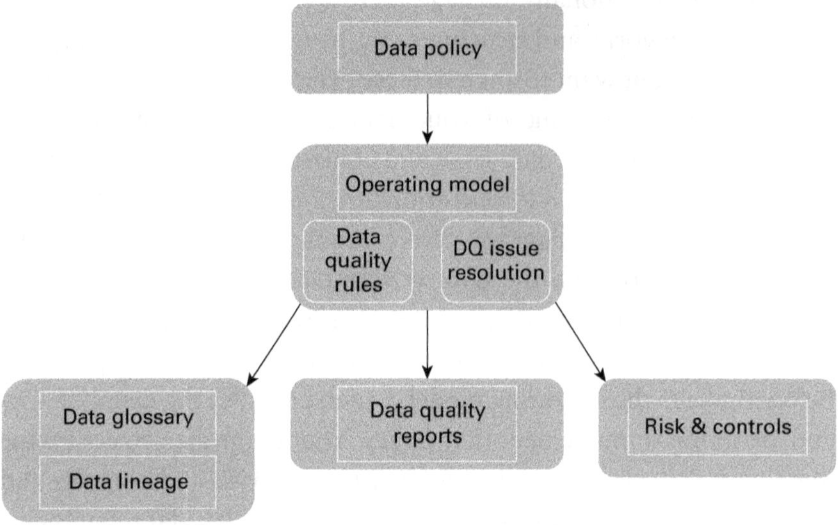

The key thing to remember is that when you're designing a structure, it doesn't matter if it does not look like either of the diagrams shared here. Over the years I have seen numerous different and very creative diagrams. It's just important that you have one. It's a way of articulating your deliverables and being able to explain them in a structured way that engages your stakeholders and helps them understand what your initiative is delivering. If you're not able to communicate these successfully, your stakeholders are not going to understand what you're doing and are likely to resist it. If that happens, it's going to be very hard to get buy-in and get the support you need.

A simple diagram showing how your deliverables relate to each other can transform confusion into clarity, resistance into understanding and scepticism into support. It's worth the effort to create one that works for your organization.

Conclusion

Data governance deliverables are what transform your initiative from theory into practice. They're the tangible proof that data governance is working in your organization, providing structure to what can otherwise feel like an overwhelming or abstract concept. More importantly, they create the foundation for everything else that follows in your data governance journey.

Throughout this chapter, we've seen how each deliverable serves a specific purpose while contributing to the broader goal of making data a trusted and valuable asset. From the foundational data definitions that ensure everyone speaks the same language, to the data quality reports that provide ongoing assurance, each element plays a crucial role in your overall framework.

Key takeaways from this chapter:

- Start with the foundations: Data definitions and your data catalogue must come before data quality rules and reporting.

- Focus on your critical data: Not all data needs the same level of governance; prioritize what matters most to your organization.

- Involve the right people: Data stewards draft, data owners approve and data consumers inform the requirements.

- Think incrementally: Build your deliverables gradually, starting simple and expanding over time.

- Connect to existing processes: Integrate with operational risk management and other established frameworks where possible.

- Create a visual representation: A diagram showing how your deliverables connect is essential for stakeholder understanding and buy-in.

Remember that these deliverables don't exist in isolation. Their value comes from how they work together as an integrated system that supports decision-making, ensures compliance and builds trust in your organization's data. Get the relationships right, communicate them clearly and you'll have created something truly valuable.

The specific deliverables you choose and how you structure them will be unique to your organization. What matters most is that you have them, that they serve your business needs and that your stakeholders understand their purpose and value. With these foundations in place, you're ready to move on to the practical challenges of implementation and evolution covered in the remaining chapters.

Note

1 R J Hawker (2023) *Practical Data Quality: Learn practical, real-world strategies to transform the quality of data in your organization*, Packt, Birmingham

08

Your data catalogue

Introduction

The data catalogue sits at the heart of your data governance initiative, yet it's also one of the most misunderstood and poorly implemented components. While vendors promise revolutionary change and IT teams get excited about sophisticated features, the reality is that most data catalogues become expensive digital dust collectors because organizations rush into tools before understanding the fundamentals.

This chapter cuts through the confusion and gives you a practical roadmap for creating a data catalogue that people actually want to use. We'll start by clarifying the terminology that causes so much confusion in our profession, then guide you through a proven approach that begins with simple spreadsheets and evolves strategically towards more sophisticated tools.

In this chapter, you'll learn:

- how to distinguish between data catalogues, data glossaries and data dictionaries: getting the terminology right matters more than you think

- why starting with spreadsheets isn't just about saving money, it's about building organizational capability and proving value before investing in expensive software

- the critical questions to ask when evaluating data catalogue tools, including how to avoid the common pitfalls that derail implementations

- how to get business users to actually want and use your data catalogue by connecting it to their real problems rather than theoretical benefits
- a proven phased approach to implementation that dramatically increases your chances of sustainable adoption and long-term success
- real-world lessons from failed implementations – including a detailed example of what happens when you introduce tools too early

The goal isn't to have the most sophisticated data catalogue; it's to have one that solves real problems and gets used daily by the people it's designed to help. By the end of this chapter, you'll know exactly how to build that foundation and avoid the expensive mistakes that have derailed countless data governance initiatives.

A critical data governance deliverable

While we touched on the data catalogue briefly in Chapter 7 as one of the key data governance deliverables, its importance and complexity warrant a much deeper exploration. The data catalogue serves as the cornerstone of understanding and data discovery within your organization, yet it's often one of the most misunderstood and poorly implemented components of a data governance framework.

Data glossary/data catalogue/data dictionary

These interlinked but distinct data governance deliverables cause a lot of confusion in the data governance world. The three terms are thrown around constantly, often interchangeably and usually incorrectly. I've lost count of how many times I've walked into organizations where people confidently talk about their 'data dictionary' when they mean something completely different or assume a 'data catalogue' and 'data dictionary' are the same thing. They are not, and getting it wrong causes mixed messages and bewilderment in the very stakeholders we are creating them for!

The confusion exists because terminology in data governance is surprisingly subjective, varying dramatically between organizations. What one company calls a data catalogue, another might call a data or business glossary.

There's a certain irony in the data governance profession that I find both amusing and frustrating: we're the people telling our data stewards to define their terms clearly and consistently, yet we're terrible at doing this ourselves. The confusion around data glossary, data catalogue and data dictionaries isn't just an unfortunate side effect of rapid technological change; it's a direct result of data governance practitioners failing to practise what we preach.

I've lost count of how many conferences I've attended where one speaker talks about 'data glossaries' as being one thing, while the next speaker uses the exact same term to describe something completely different. We've created a profession full of jargon that means different things to different people, then act surprised when our stakeholders get confused.

The problem is that many of us in the data governance space came from different backgrounds – some from IT, others from project management and business analysis, some from compliance, others from data warehousing. We have all brought our own terminology and definitions with us and never bothered to standardize them across the profession. The result is confusion for our stakeholders and this isn't just academic confusion; it has real consequences. When a data governance manager talks about implementing a 'data catalogue', but the IT team thinks that means something completely different, you end up with misaligned expectations, wasted effort and frustrated stakeholders. We've inadvertently created the very problem we're supposed to solve, unclear definitions leading to poor communication and failed initiatives.

The good news is that awareness of this problem is the first step to solving it. By acknowledging that our profession has been sloppy with terminology, we can start being more deliberate about defining our terms clearly. But it means we need to check our assumptions, ask clarifying questions and resist the urge to assume everyone means the same thing we do when they use familiar terms.

REAL-WORLD EXAMPLE
When terminology goes wrong

I once worked with a financial services company where the business team proudly announced they were building a 'data dictionary' (more on what this is later) to support their new data governance initiative. The IT team heard this and immediately assumed the business was stepping into their territory. After all, IT had always owned data dictionaries and they already had several for their various systems.

The IT manager became defensive, arguing that the business didn't understand the technical complexities involved and shouldn't be creating data dictionaries without IT oversight. Meanwhile, the business team couldn't understand why IT was being so resistant to what they saw as a simple business project.

The confusion escalated when IT started insisting that any 'data dictionary' needed to include technical metadata like table schemas, field lengths and database constraints, exactly the kind of technical detail that would have made the tool unusable for business users. The business team pushed back, saying they just wanted clear definitions of business terms, which IT dismissed as 'not a proper data dictionary'.

What should have been a straightforward data governance deliverable turned into a territorial dispute that nearly killed the entire initiative. The breakthrough came when we sat everyone down and clarified that the business was actually building what most people would call a data catalogue or data glossary, not a technical data dictionary at all.

Once we agreed on terminology and clarified that this was a business-owned tool for business users (with IT providing technical support rather than ownership), the initiative moved forward smoothly. But the weeks of confusion and conflict could have been avoided entirely if the data governance team had been clearer about terminology from the start.

This is exactly why I always recommend establishing clear definitions of these terms within your organization before you start working on them or even talking about them.

Understanding metadata

In keeping with the spirit of the previous section, before we dive deeper, we need to address a term that gets thrown around constantly when discussing data dictionaries, glossaries and catalogues, but is rarely explained properly: metadata. At its essence, metadata is simply 'data about data', but that definition is about as helpful as describing a car as 'a thing with wheels'.

Think of metadata as a library catalogue system. When you walk into a library looking for a specific book, you don't wander the aisles hoping to stumble across it. You use the catalogue system that tells you not just where the book is located, but who wrote it, when it was published, what it's about and how it relates to other books. That's exactly what metadata does for your organization's data, it provides the context and navigation information that makes your data usable rather than just accessible.

WHAT METADATA INCLUDES

Metadata comes in different flavours, each serving a distinct purpose in helping you understand and use your data effectively.

Technical metadata is the domain of IT professionals and provides the structural blueprint of your data. This includes details about where data resides, its format, data types, relationships with other datasets and technical constraints. Think of this as the architectural plans for your data, essential for building and maintaining systems, but not particularly useful for business users trying to understand what the data means.

Business metadata focuses on the practical, human side of data. It answers the fundamental questions that business users actually care about: What is this data? How is it used? Who owns it? Who's responsible for maintaining its quality? Who should I speak to if I have a question about it? Think of this as the user manual for your data. It is the information that helps people understand not just what they're looking at, but whether they can trust it and how to use it appropriately.

METADATA MATTERS

The importance of good metadata becomes crystal clear when you see what happens without it. I've worked with a bank that suffered significant reputational damage because of a misunderstanding about a single data field. The technical metadata was perfect, everyone knew where the data lived and how to access it. But the business metadata was missing, so nobody understood what the field actually represented or how it should be interpreted. The result was a regulatory report that painted a completely inaccurate picture of the bank's risk exposure.

In another case, a retail company shut down what they believed was an unprofitable product line, only to discover six months later that the line was actually highly profitable. The problem wasn't with the data itself; it was with the metadata. The report they used to make the decision contained a field labelled 'profit margin', but nobody had documented that this particular calculation excluded certain overhead costs. Without that crucial context, they misinterpreted the numbers and made a catastrophic business decision.

This is why metadata sits at the heart of every successful data governance initiative. You can have the most sophisticated data catalogue in the world, but if the metadata held in it is poor, incomplete or misleading, your users will either ignore the tool entirely or make decisions based on misunderstood or potentially the wrong data.

Good metadata transforms data into a valuable business resource. Data definitions are a key part of metadata, which can be held in a variety of different places, as we are about to cover.

Data dictionary: The technical foundation

Let's start with the data dictionary because it's been around the longest and has the clearest definition. According to the *DAMA Dictionary of Data Management*, a data dictionary is 'a place where business and/or technical terms and definitions are stored, typically designed to store a limited set of metadata concentrating on the names and definitions relating to the physical data and related objects.'[1]

This is fundamentally an IT-owned document that focuses on the technical aspects of data: where it lives in databases, what format it takes and what constraints apply to it. If you've ever worked on a data platform or data warehouse project, you've probably encountered one. They should be created for every system and database built or implemented in your organization, though sadly, they are often forgotten once the implementation project ends or, worse, lost entirely over time.

While data dictionaries should include business definitions and involve business stakeholders in their creation, the reality is they're primarily referenced by IT and analytics teams, so they often lack meaningful business input.

Data catalogue: Finding the data you need

A data catalogue is essentially a searchable inventory of all your organization's data assets, to help data professionals find what they need quickly. Think of it as solving the 'needle in a haystack' problem when you're dealing with vast amounts of organizational data.

The catalogue's core functions include dataset searching (with keyword functionality) and facilitating data discoverability. It's designed primarily for data analysts, data scientists, data consumers and data stewards who need to discover and understand datasets to extract business value.

Data catalogues evolve with your organization, with metadata becoming richer over time to support better data discovery, data governance and data quality management.

Data glossary: Your business vocabulary

A data glossary is a guide to the terminology used in your organization. In an ideal world, it would be an exhaustive list of terms used across the company with clear definitions. The glossary solves a fundamental communication problem: people across your organization use the same terms but mean completely different things. It defines the terminology used when discussing concepts, processes and data, ensuring everyone speaks the same language and eliminating the confusion that leads to unreliable reports and poor decisions.

Unlike data dictionaries, a data glossary should be created and maintained by the business, not IT. They focus on improving business understanding rather than technical specifications. As your data governance matures, your glossary should capture data owners and data stewards for each term and potentially include data quality rules and known issues with that data.

The practical reality: I prefer one data catalogue/data glossary solution

I'm going to be honest with you: while data glossaries and data catalogues are semantically different, in practice most organizations use the terms to mean exactly the same thing. Technically, a data catalogue helps you find datasets while a data glossary defines business terms, but the reality is that both end up serving as the central place where people go to understand their organization's data.

I'm not a fan of having both a data glossary and a data catalogue; it just adds confusion about where users should look things up. Do they check the glossary or the catalogue for the definition of 'customer'? Where do they find information about the data owner? The result is usually two half-populated tools that nobody uses effectively.

My preference is to pick one approach and stick with it. Call it either a data glossary or a data catalogue (I don't really mind which) and make it the single source of everything you know about the data in your organization. You can build in the discovery capabilities of a catalogue alongside the definitions of a glossary, but having one place to go eliminates the confusion that kills user adoption.

This isn't just about user convenience. There's a fundamental data governance reason why you should have only one data glossary or catalogue for your organization. The moment you have multiple glossaries or catalogues, you lose the ability to identify when there are conflicting definitions for the same term across different parts of your business.

One of the most valuable exercises in developing a data glossary is discovering where the same term means different things to different teams, or where different terms actually mean the same thing. This visibility is crucial because it forces conversations about whether you need to agree on a common definition or whether there are legitimate reasons for the differences (in which case you should rename the terms to make the distinctions clear).

If your HR team has their own glossary defining 'employee' one way and your finance team has a separate glossary defining it differently, you'll never spot this conflict. The result? Continued confusion and misaligned reporting; the very problems you're trying to solve with data governance in the first place.

While you might have multiple data dictionaries (one per system), you absolutely must have only one central tool for business data understanding to make data governance work effectively.

A WORD OF CAUTION ABOUT 'COMMON' DEFINITIONS

Many people advocate for using a data glossary to create common definitions across the organization. While that sounds sensible in theory, most organizations are just not mature enough to jump straight into this approach. Instead, use your glossary development to identify where different teams use different definitions for the same term, or where different terms mean the same thing.

Only after you've mapped this landscape can you begin the negotiation process toward standardization. Sometimes, forcing common definitions is not the right answer. If there are valid business reasons for different definitions, consider renaming terms to make the distinctions clear rather than trying to force artificial alignment. Good reasons that I have come across include:

- the term 'customer' meaning different things to a sales team when compared to the operational team's definition
- 'month' meaning a calendar month in most parts of an organization, but to finance teams the month starts on the 15th of the month for reporting reasons
- a 'large claim' being defined differently by the claims team (in an insurance company) compared to the actuarial team who use the data for a different purpose so have valid reasons for a different definition

In all these instances, we renamed the terms to make it clear that more than one definition (and therefore set of data) existed. For the last example you could have 'operational large claim' and 'actuarial large claim'.

Remember, the biggest cause of data quality issues I've encountered is simply people not understanding what their data means. Whether data producers don't understand what should go in a field or data consumers misinterpret what they're seeing, clarity of definition and ease of finding those definitions are fundamental to data quality.

Data glossary/data catalogue tools

The market for data governance tools has exploded in recent years, with numerous software products promising to revolutionize how you manage your data catalogue (in the interests of simplicity I will use only the term data catalogue from this point onwards and use it to mean a combined data catalogue and data glossary). These tools have become incredibly popular, and if you have the budget to purchase one, they can genuinely accelerate your data governance initiative. But if you select the wrong tool or implement it poorly, it won't just fail to help, it could actively derail your entire data governance effort.

Starting simple: The case for spreadsheets

Before you even think about purchasing expensive data governance software, let me share some advice that might save you from a costly mistake: start with a spreadsheet. I know that sounds almost embarrassingly simple, but there's solid strategic reasoning behind this approach that goes beyond just saving money.

The fundamental issue with introducing data governance tools is that you are asking stakeholders to use a new tool to perform a new task they've never done before. Usually, when organizations introduce new software, it's replacing an old, clunky system or streamlining a laborious manual process that people are already familiar with. Users understand the value proposition immediately because they've been struggling with the old way of doing things.

Data governance is different. Most business users have never maintained a data catalogue, drafted data definitions or formally documented data ownership before. When you hand them a sophisticated software platform and ask them to start doing these activities, they see it as additional work with unclear benefits. The result is resistance, poor adoption and another expensive tool gathering digital dust.

SPREADSHEETS ARE YOUR SECRET WEAPON

Building your initial data catalogue in a spreadsheet is both practical and strategic, serving several critical purposes.

Simplicity and familiarity are your allies here. Nearly every business user knows how to use Excel or Google Sheets. There's no learning curve, no training requirements and no technical barriers to entry. You can create a structured format quickly, organizing terms, definitions, data owners and usage notes in a way that's immediately accessible to anyone in your organization.

An iterative process becomes natural with spreadsheets. You can start with a handful of columns for your data stewards to complete. If there is a column that no one ever completes, perhaps they do not understand what it means, or do not see the value of capturing that particular piece of metadata. Conversely, you may find that many people add an extra column for 'comments' or 'notes', basically other information they know about that data which they wish to document. In each case, it is very simple to delete or add a column to the spreadsheet based on user feedback. Using a tool in the early stages of building a data catalogue, while the stakeholders are still working out which metadata it will be useful to document, can result in the overhead of complex tool amendments and administration.

Collaboration and engagement tend to improve when you are not intimidating people with unfamiliar software. Different data stewards and other stakeholders can contribute their insights and definitions easily, creating a sense of ownership over the data catalogue. This engagement is crucial because it develops a proactive mindset toward data governance that will be essential if you eventually move to more sophisticated tools.

Handling complex definitions becomes more manageable when you can easily flag terms that require additional discussion. Spreadsheets allow for deeper exploration and consensus-building around definitions, improving overall clarity without the constraints of rigid software workflows.

Immediate utility is perhaps the most important benefit. A well-structured spreadsheet can serve immediate needs by providing a centralized location for commonly used terms, reducing the misunderstandings that arise from ambiguous definitions. This saves time and reduces frustration when different departments refer to the same data points, demonstrating tangible value to stakeholders.

A PRACTICAL STARTING POINT

Here's how to build your initial data catalogue in a spreadsheet effectively:

- Identify key terms: Brainstorm the terms that your organization frequently uses and that cause the most confusion or debate. Start small, maybe 20-30 terms maximum. Starting from a conceptual data model (as covered in Chapter 6) is also a good starting point.

- Define a simple structure: Work out the column headings needed. Consider using: term, definition, data owner, data steward and examples. Keep it straightforward and resist the urge to overcomplicate.

- Engage stakeholders: Invite your data stewards to complete the spreadsheet. Make this collaborative from the start, not something you do for or, even worse, to them.

- Review and revise: Regularly revisit the format of your catalogue, refine and improve it based on data steward and other user feedback.

- Plan to scale up: As your glossary grows and stakeholders become comfortable with the concept, then consider transitioning to a more robust tool that can handle advanced workflow and monitoring capabilities.

THE EVOLUTION STRATEGY

The beauty of starting with spreadsheets is that you're building both content and organizational capability simultaneously. By the time you're ready to invest in proper data governance software, your stakeholders will understand what they're trying to accomplish, why it matters and how the activities fit into their daily work. They'll see the tool as an upgrade to something they're already doing, not as an additional burden.

This approach also gives you real requirements for tool selection. Instead of guessing what features you might need, you'll have concrete experience of what works, what doesn't and what limitations you've hit with your spreadsheet approach. Your tool selection will be informed by actual usage patterns rather than theoretical needs.

Starting simple isn't about being cheap, it's about being smart. By establishing the foundation properly, you'll dramatically increase your chances of success when you do eventually invest in more sophisticated data governance technology.

The advantages of data catalogue tools over spreadsheets

While spreadsheets are excellent for getting started, if your organization is large and complex there comes a point where their limitations become clear and the advantages of proper data catalogue tools become compelling. Remember, it is important to recognize when you've outgrown your spreadsheet approach and move to a tool at the appropriate time, rather than jumping to expensive software prematurely.

SCALE AND PERFORMANCE

Spreadsheets work brilliantly when you have dozens or even a few hundred terms, but they become unwieldy as your data catalogue grows. Data catalogue tools are designed to handle thousands of data assets with sophisticated search capabilities, filtering options and performance that doesn't degrade as your content expands. When your stakeholders start complaining that finding information takes too long, it's time to consider an upgrade.

WORKFLOWS

Perhaps the most significant advantage of dedicated tools is their ability to support formal data governance workflows. While spreadsheets rely on informal processes and email chains for reviews and approvals, data catalogue tools can enforce approval workflows, track changes, maintain version history and ensure accountability through automated notifications and deadlines. This becomes essential as your data governance initiative matures, and you need audit trails and formal change management.

INTEGRATION AND AUTOMATION

Data catalogue tools can integrate with your existing systems to automatically capture technical metadata, reducing the manual effort required to keep information current. They can connect to databases, data warehouses and other systems to pull in structural information, data lineage (which was covered Chapter 7) and usage statistics. Such capabilities, while not impossible with spreadsheets (if you use automation apps), are not straightforward and require skills and support that you and your team may not have.

This automation capability becomes invaluable as you collect higher volumes and more diverse metadata. It also enables the integration of your data catalogue with your data dictionaries, increasing the wealth of metadata available to users of the data catalogue.

USER EXPERIENCE AND ACCESSIBILITY

While everyone knows how to use spreadsheets, data catalogue tools are designed specifically for data discovery and understanding. They offer intuitive search interfaces, relationship mapping and presentation features that make information more accessible to business users. The ability to link related terms, visualize data lineage and provide rich context goes far beyond what's practical in a spreadsheet format.

The right time to transition

The transition point typically comes when you find yourself spending more time managing the spreadsheet than using it, when multiple people need simultaneous access, or when you need to enforce consistent processes across different teams. By starting with spreadsheets, you will have developed the content and organizational maturity needed to make informed tool selection decisions and ensure successful adoption.

Remember, the goal isn't to have the most sophisticated tool, it's to have the right tool for your current needs and organizational maturity. Spreadsheets teach you what you need; proper tools help you scale what works.

The pitfalls of tool selection

When you are ready (and have the budget) to purchase a data catalogue tool, please proceed in a careful and considered manner. I've seen too many organizations get seduced by impressive demos and feature lists, only to end up with expensive software that nobody uses. The problem isn't usually with the tools themselves; it's with how organizations approach the selection and implementation process.

Little or no business user involvement

The biggest mistake is organizations making tool decisions in isolation, involving business users only after the purchase is complete or even during implementation. This is absolutely catastrophic and I cannot stress enough how important it is to avoid this pitfall at all costs.

I've witnessed several implementations go horribly wrong because the eventual business users were completely excluded from the selection process. Think about it from their perspective for a moment. They haven't asked for this tool, they don't understand why they need it and it doesn't help them do any existing task more quickly or easily. Unlike other software implementations where you're replacing something clunky or automating a manual process they already understand, data governance tools often introduce entirely new activities and responsibilities.

When you finally roll out your shiny new software after months of IT-led procurement, business users immediately see it as yet another technology initiative being forced upon them by people who don't understand their daily reality. Their first reaction is typically, 'Great, another system I have to learn that's going to make my job harder.' This resistance isn't unreasonable. From their viewpoint, you're asking them to spend time learning new software to perform tasks they've never done before, with benefits that aren't immediately obvious to them.

I have seen more than one data catalogue implementation that had to go completely back to the drawing board because business users were excluded from initial tool selection. Once they understood what they were expected to use the tool for, their requirements were vastly different from what had been delivered.

Early and meaningful business user involvement isn't just about avoiding resistance, though that's certainly important. Business users bring essential insights about how work actually gets done, what information they need and what barriers exist to adoption. They can identify potential workflow issues before implementation begins rather than after significant time and money have been invested.

The organizations that succeed with data governance tools are those that treat business users as partners in the selection process from the very beginning, ensuring the tool serves their needs rather than imposing IT-driven solutions that nobody wants to use.

Remember this tool will be introduced to help your business stakeholders, not the data governance manager and team. So, make sure that you capture their requirements of the new tool before making any selection.

UNCLEAR REQUIREMENTS

The second pitfall is being unclear on what you require of the tool and this is where I see organizations waste the most money and time. Often someone has latched onto the fact that a tool could help them and dived straight into procurement without being really clear about what they want the tool to accomplish. They've seen an impressive demo, heard success stories from other companies, or been pressured by vendors, but they haven't done the hard work of defining their specific objectives.

'We need a data catalogue' is not a requirement. It's barely even a starting point. What does success look like? Are you trying to reduce the time spent clarifying data definitions in meetings? Improve report accuracy? Support regulatory compliance? Enable self-service analytics? Each of these objectives would lead to different tool requirements and implementation approaches.

I've worked with organizations that spent months evaluating vendors and ultimately purchased expensive software, only to discover that what they really needed was a simple shared vocabulary for customer data, not a comprehensive enterprise data catalogue. In another case, a company bought a sophisticated tool thinking they needed advanced data lineage capabilities, when their actual problem was basic data quality issues that could have been solved much more simply.

The problem compounds when requirements gathering becomes a wish-list exercise. Data governance teams start adding every feature they can imagine needing rather than focusing on what they actually need to solve today's problems. I've seen requirement documents that read like vendor feature lists, including automated data profiling, machine learning-powered recommendations and advanced visualization capabilities, without any connection to real business problems or current organizational maturity.

This approach inevitably leads to tool selection based on feature comparison rather than fit-for-purpose analysis. Organizations end up choosing the tool with the most checkmarks against their inflated requirements list, often the most complex and expensive option, when a simpler solution would have delivered better results.

Another common mistake is failing to consider organizational readiness. Your requirements might technically be achievable, but if they require sophisticated data governance processes that don't exist yet, or demand high levels of user engagement that your culture doesn't support, even the best tool will fail.

Before you begin any vendor evaluation, invest time in understanding what specific problems you're solving, what success would look like and what your organization is realistically capable of adopting. Clear, focused requirements don't just help you choose the right tool, they dramatically increase your chances of successful implementation.

OVERLY COMPLEX INITIAL IMPLEMENTATION

Finally, another common pitfall is trying to make the initial implementation too complex. Some of the more established tools on the market have been around for a while and have evolved over time to provide a multitude of functionalities, all of which can facilitate and enable your data governance and data quality activities. The vendor demos showcase impressive capabilities. It's easy to get seduced by the possibilities and want to implement everything immediately.

But, please, when you're looking at selecting a vendor initially be very clear what you want a tool to do now. Also, consider what you definitely want it to do in the future. Finally, you can make a 'nice to have' list. Just make sure you take a thorough approach to determine clear requirements, because the temptation to implement every available feature is overwhelming and almost always disastrous.

I've seen implementations fail spectacularly because organizations tried to boil the ocean from day one. One organization I spoke to attempted to implement data cataloguing, automated data quality monitoring, full data lineage tracking and workflow management simultaneously across six different business units. The project became so complex that eighteen months later, they still hadn't delivered anything useful to business users. Meanwhile, the simple data definition problems they originally wanted to solve remained unsolved.

The fundamental issue is that complexity kills adoption. When you present business users with a sophisticated platform that has multiple interfaces, complicated workflows and numerous features they don't understand, they're immediately overwhelmed. Remember, most of your users have never done data governance activities before. Asking them to navigate complex software while learning new concepts is a recipe for failure.

Just because a tool can do something doesn't mean your business really needs it, especially not immediately. Users need to understand the basic concepts and see immediate value before they'll engage with sophisticated capabilities.

Another complexity trap is trying to integrate with every possible system during initial implementation. It's often better to start with manual data entry to prove the concept and add automation incrementally.

The most successful implementations I've seen focus ruthlessly on solving one specific problem well rather than trying to address everything simultaneously. Start with your most pressing need, perhaps basic data definitions for your organizations most critical data, implement that successfully, demonstrate value and then gradually expand functionality as users become comfortable with both the tool and data governance concepts.

This phased approach takes longer to reach full functionality, but it dramatically increases your chances of sustainable adoption and long-term success.

Essential questions for vendor evaluation

When evaluating vendors, ask 'How does your tool meet our specific requirements?' not 'Does it meet our requirements?' Every vendor will say yes to the latter question. What you need to understand is whether the functionality is available out-of-the-box or requires extensive customization that could complicate future upgrades.

Ask about implementation support. These tools are inherently flexible, which means you'll need guidance on configuring them for your specific business context. Understand exactly what support is included and what costs extra – surprises here can destroy your project budget.

Finally, clarify training provisions for both your technical team and business users. The best tool in the world is useless if people don't know how to use it effectively.

To help you, here are some questions that I like to ask when I'm supporting a client to select a data catalogue tool (remember these are from a business user/data governance manager point of view and your IT department will have their own questions about technical requirements):

REQUIREMENTS AND FUNCTIONALITY

- How specifically does your tool meet our documented requirements? (Ask for detailed demonstrations, not just 'yes, we can do that'.)
- What functionality is available out-of-the-box versus requiring customization or configuration?
- Can you show us exactly how a business user would complete [specific task relevant to your needs]?
- What are the limitations or constraints we should be aware of?
- How does your tool handle [specific scenario relevant to your organization]?

IMPLEMENTATION AND SUPPORT

- What implementation support will you provide, and what's included versus additional cost?
- Who will be our main point of contact during implementation, and what is their experience?
- How long do typical implementations take for organizations similar to ours?
- What are the key milestones and deliverables during implementation?

TRAINING AND USER ADOPTION

- What training is available for business users, and in what formats?
- Do you provide train-the-trainer options so we can handle ongoing education internally?
- What user adoption strategies have worked best for your other clients?
- Can you provide examples of user guides or documentation we'd receive?

CUSTOMIZATION AND FLEXIBILITY

- How much customization is possible without affecting future upgrades?
- Can you show us examples of how other clients have configured the tool differently?
- What happens to customizations when you release new versions?
- How flexible is the user interface and workflow configuration?
- Can we modify terminology and labels to match our organization's language?

PROOF OF CONCEPT

- Can we trial the tool with our actual data and use cases?
- What's included in a proof of concept and how long would it run?
- Will you configure the tool to match our specific requirements during the trial?
- Can our business users participate in hands-on evaluation during the trial period?

Remember, the vendors you are evaluating won't be the people you work with during implementation and ongoing support. Don't let impressive sales presentations override practical considerations about functionality and long-term support quality.

Implementation realities

Even after selecting the right tool, success isn't guaranteed. Focus on implementing one area or functionality first rather than trying to deploy everything simultaneously. Your business users need time to become comfortable with both data governance concepts and the tool itself.

Think of implementation as a phased process, not a one-off project. Start with a pilot or trial, gather feedback, make necessary adjustments, then roll out gradually across the organization. This approach takes longer but significantly increases your chances of sustainable adoption.

Plan for ongoing content maintenance from the beginning. I recommend annual reviews where data owners examine the data definitions they are responsible for, confirming definitions are still accurate or providing updates as needed. Without this discipline, your expensive tool becomes an expensive repository of outdated information remarkably quickly!

The bottom line on tools

Data governance tools can be powerful enablers, but they must be implemented after your data governance initiative is already underway, not as a substitute for it. The tool should support processes you've already tested and refined, not drive them. Get your data governance fundamentals right first, then use technology to scale and sustain your efforts.

Remember, you're not just buying software, you're investing in a long-term capability that needs to integrate with your organization's culture and processes. Take the time to do it right, because the cost of getting it wrong extends far beyond the purchase price.

Getting business users to want and use a data catalogue

Putting a data catalogue in place can take a lot of hard work and effort, so it can be particularly frustrating when your business users don't truly appreciate the value it brings and either don't want to help you build it or don't use it when it has been built. I've seen too many organizations invest significant time and resources creating comprehensive data catalogues that become expensive digital dust collectors.

A big reason why this scenario happens is because we often ignore why we are creating a data catalogue in the first place. By this, I don't mean you should have one because you are implementing data governance. I mean answering the question: why should your business users want and use one?

This doesn't mean rattling off a predefined list of benefits from a vendor website, but rather taking that deep breath, stepping back and working out why exactly you are building a data catalogue in the first place and for whom. Why does your organization need a data catalogue? What value will it deliver? What problems will it solve?

I'm often asked how to engage business stakeholders with your data catalogue and the answer is always about understanding the value it would bring to them specifically. This message needs to be tailored to each group of individuals you're speaking to, as one reason won't work universally across different stakeholders. These messages need to be specific for each of your groups of stakeholders.

Let me give you a couple of examples when seeking to communicate the value of your data catalogue. The faster development of reports is a common theme, as a lot of time and effort can be wasted creating reports without agreed definitions. This can result in ongoing disputes, wasteful meetings and, ultimately, poor decision-making with damaging consequences for an organization.

Think about how many hours your teams spend in meetings debating what 'customer retention rate' actually means, or whether 'active users' includes trial accounts. These aren't productive strategic discussions; they're basic arguments about data definitions that happen repeatedly because nobody has established and documented clear, agreed-upon meanings.

Another potential benefit can be identified in the quicker implementation and deployment of new systems. Whether building a system from scratch or implementing a bought package, decisions need to be made about the data which will reside in the system and this will result in lengthy debates on the exact definitions of certain terms like 'customer'. Wouldn't it be much quicker if those debates happened just once and the agreed definitions were logged in the data catalogue to be referred to in the future instead of repeating this for each new system?

A data catalogue is invaluable for documenting and, where appropriate, streamlining definitions across an organization and ensuring a common understanding of data and how it can or should be used.

What if you already have a data catalogue?

If you have already created a data catalogue but are struggling to get business stakeholders using it, you should still follow the approach detailed here. You have to work out what value it will bring and communicate that effectively.

This means identifying what data challenges your business users are facing today and using these examples to demonstrate how a properly implemented and maintained data catalogue can solve those specific challenges. Perhaps your existing catalogue is too technical, outdated or simply not accessible to the people who need it most. These problems become your opportunities to demonstrate why a better approach would make their working lives easier.

Making it personal

The key is connecting conceptual benefits to the concrete problems your users experience daily. Instead of talking about 'improved data governance', talk about eliminating the three-hour monthly meeting where teams debate performance metrics. Instead of 'better data quality', focus on reducing the time spent reconciling conflicting reports from different systems.

When business users see solutions to their actual problems rather than theoretical benefits, engagement follows naturally. Remember, they don't care about your data governance initiative; they care about doing their jobs more effectively and with less frustration.

REAL-WORLD EXAMPLE

Using a tool too early

A number of years ago, while I was acting as an interim data governance lead for an insurance company, I experienced first-hand what happens when organizations rush into implementing sophisticated tools before establishing the fundamentals. I had taken over from a previous interim who had struggled to get the business to engage with the new data catalogue tool. He was a great person and incredibly enthusiastic about data governance. However, he had come from a technical background and felt more comfortable talking about the technical side of a data catalogue tool rather than engaging business users and understanding their actual requirements.

This was my first experience working directly with one of the then-new data catalogue tools and I was genuinely excited to see it in action. I was sorely disappointed when the feedback I received from business users was not just poor, but openly dismissive.

I sat down with the enterprise data architect, who gave me a demo of the tool. He was genuinely excited about it and explained that he and my predecessor had spent many hours designing what they believed was the perfect implementation. Not only was it going to meet the regulatory requirements that were driving the data governance initiative, but it was going to add enormous value to the organization as people would be able to look up what data they had and, more importantly, what it meant.

However, when he showed me the tool, it fell far short of my expectations given all the market hype at the time. It was clunky, seemed very technical and was clearly not designed with business users in mind. But I kept my views to myself and decided to conduct a more formal review to seek detailed feedback from business users.

Upon interviewing multiple stakeholders, the feedback was consistently damning. They didn't understand what the tool was for. They didn't understand why they had to use it. It just felt far too technical for them.

During this review, I discovered something crucial: no data catalogue had been built using a spreadsheet first. The first time these business users had encountered the concept of a data catalogue was when the project to implement the tool started up. They had been presented with the tool amid great fanfare and excitement from the project team, but they were completely bewildered about what this tool was supposed to accomplish and were very resistant to using it.

After collecting stakeholder feedback and understanding their perspectives, I had to go right back to the drawing board. I started an approach that included a comprehensive communications plan where I spent time educating various stakeholders about why the company was implementing data governance and what specific benefits it would bring to them personally, not just theoretically to the organization.

We then started capturing data definitions in a simple spreadsheet. Once we had been doing this long enough for people to understand the value and become comfortable with the activities, I approached the stakeholders again to ask for their feedback on requirements for a tool to eventually replace the spreadsheet. Only then did we start a project to reconfigure and relaunch the data governance tool.

In total, I estimate nearly two years were wasted while the tool sat unused because it was unsuitable for the users' needs and had not been communicated effectively. There was also additional time lost while we worked to engage business stakeholders and get them to undertake data governance activities, before they were able to understand what they would want from a tool to support those activities.

When the tool was eventually relaunched, it was much better received and stakeholders were genuinely grateful for it, although somewhat frustrated that it had taken so long to get it right for their needs.

The lesson

This experience reinforced my belief that tools should support established processes, not create them. The technical team had fallen into the trap of thinking that a sophisticated tool would somehow make data governance happen automatically. Instead, they needed to help people understand why data governance mattered, get them comfortable with the basic activities and then introduce technology to make those activities more efficient and scalable.

The tool wasn't the problem; the approach was. By starting with fundamentals and building data governance capability before introducing technology, the eventual implementation was not only successful but genuinely valued by the people who had to use it daily.

Conclusion

Your data catalogue should be a valuable business asset, not an expensive burden. The organizations that succeed are those that resist the temptation to jump straight into sophisticated tools and instead build their foundation properly. They start simple, prove value and evolve strategically based on real user needs rather than vendor promises.

The path forward isn't about having the most features or the biggest budget. It's about understanding your users, solving their actual problems and building something they genuinely want to use. When you get this right, your data catalogue becomes the central nervous system of your data governance initiative. The place people naturally turn to when they need to understand their organization's data.

Key takeaways from this chapter:

- Terminology matters: Establish clear definitions within your organization before you start building anything and stick to one unified approach rather than confusing users with multiple tools.
- Start with spreadsheets: They are not just a budget-conscious choice, they are a strategic way to build capability, prove value and understand real requirements before investing in software.
- Focus on user problems, not tool features: Connect your data catalogue to specific pain points your business users experience daily and communicate value in terms they actually care about.
- Take a phased approach to tool selection and implementation: Involve business users from the beginning, be crystal clear about requirements and resist the urge to implement everything at once.
- Plan for the long term: Your data catalogue needs ongoing maintenance, regular reviews and continuous engagement to remain valuable rather than becoming outdated quickly.
- Remember the real goal: It's not about having a data catalogue, it's about enabling better decision-making through clearer understanding of your organization's data.

The most successful data catalogues aren't the most technically impressive ones; they're the ones that solve real problems and get used every day. Focus on that outcome and the rest will follow.

Note

1 DAMA (2011) *DAMA Dictionary of Data Management*, 2nd edn, Technics Publications, New Jersey

09

Measuring your progress and evolving your data governance framework

Introduction

Successfully implementing data governance is just the beginning of your journey. Once you've established your framework and started seeing initial results, two critical questions emerge. How do you know if you're making meaningful progress? And how do you ensure your framework remains effective as your organization evolves?

This chapter addresses both challenges by providing practical guidance on measuring your data governance success and adapting your framework to meet changing needs. You'll discover why measurement is essential for maintaining stakeholder support, learn how to distinguish between progress and value metrics, and understand when and how to evolve your approach.

In this chapter, you will learn:

- why measurement matters: understanding the critical role of tracking progress in maintaining momentum, securing ongoing support and demonstrating return on investment
- what to measure: distinguishing between value delivered, progress made and stakeholder engagement to create a comprehensive measurement strategy
- how to measure effectively: practical approaches including maturity assessments, key performance indicators (KPIs) and stakeholder feedback mechanisms

- recognizing when change is needed: identifying the signals that indicate your framework requires evolution, from business strategy shifts to regulatory changes
- your data governance weathervane: finding and using key stakeholders as early warning systems for framework adjustments
- evolution strategies: systematic approaches to updating your framework while maintaining stability and stakeholder confidence
- implementation timelines: realistic expectations for framework development and the factors that influence implementation speed

Remember, data governance is not a destination but an ongoing practice. This chapter will equip you with the tools to ensure your framework continues delivering value as your organization grows and changes.

How long does it take to implement a data governance framework?

One of the questions I'm most frequently asked is how long it takes to implement data governance, particularly by those doing it for the first time.

First things first: data governance is not just an agenda item that can be crossed off once implemented. Data governance is a long-term, ongoing practice that constructs a healthier data environment in an organization to support its goals. Data governance extends beyond a single activity or initiative.

The initial implementation of data governance is a journey that can vary widely in duration, depending on several factors. Let's look at some key insights around the timeframe for establishing a data governance framework.

Factors influencing implementation time

- Organizational size and complexity: The size of your organization, the number of systems in place and the overall system complexity will significantly impact the timeline. Larger and multifaceted organizations may face a lengthier process due to the diverse systems and stakeholders involved.

- Phased approach: Adopting a phased approach is always recommended. This method, on the face of it, may take longer but allows for prioritization and the gradual implementation of data governance principles. This makes implementation both easier to manage and more successful in the long term.

- Typical duration: On average, designing your framework and starting to realize benefits from a data governance initiative typically takes between one year and 18 months. This timeline is a rough estimate and may extend further for more complex organizations.

- Continuous nature of data governance: It's important to emphasize that data governance should not be seen as a one-off project. Instead, it's an ongoing practice that requires continual refinement and adaptation as organizational needs evolve. For this reason, it is never complete or 'done'.

- Team size versus stakeholder pace: While having a larger team to implement data governance can be helpful, it doesn't necessarily accelerate the process. Progress is ultimately governed by the pace at which your business stakeholders are able and willing to engage. Their availability, decision-making timelines and capacity to participate alongside their regular responsibilities are the true limiting factors in how quickly implementation can move forward.

Choosing your implementation strategy

Many people think that the implementation of data governance can be approached in one of two ways. That it can be introduced all at once, like a seismic shift. Alternatively, you might decide to tackle it by business function, data domain or a combination of both, depending on where the greatest need for data governance lies within your organization at the time.

I'm a fan of the latter approach, having never seen it be successful when the first approach is attempted!

Why the big bang approach rarely works

The 'all at once' or 'big bang' approach might seem appealing on paper. The logic is simple: implement everything simultaneously across the entire organization and achieve comprehensive data governance quickly. However, this approach typically fails because it overwhelms stakeholders by introducing all the data governance processes and roles and responsibilities at once, creating confusion and resistance. Your organization's ability to absorb change is limited and a big bang approach often exceeds this capacity while straining available resources. Additionally, you miss the chance to refine your approach based on early feedback and lessons learned. Perhaps most critically, if something goes wrong, it affects the entire initiative rather than just a pilot area, creating a higher risk of complete failure.

The phased approach

A phased roll-out offers a much more sustainable path forward. It allows you to start where the pain is greatest, focusing initial efforts on areas with the most pressing data issues or highest business impact. This approach helps you build momentum through early wins, as success in one area creates advocates who can champion the initiative elsewhere in your organization. Each phase provides valuable insights that can be used to improve subsequent phases and stakeholders can see the benefits before being asked to participate fully, making change management far more effective.

Selecting your roll-out strategy

When deciding how to phase your implementation, consider several key factors. Business criticality should guide you toward data domains that directly impact key business decisions, operational processes or regulatory requirements. Stakeholder readiness is equally important, beginning with departments or teams that are most receptive to change rather than fighting an uphill battle from the start. Data complexity also matters; consider starting with simpler data domains before tackling those which are complex. Finally, align your roll-out with periods when key stakeholders have capacity to engage, as resource availability will significantly impact your success.

It's crucial to understand the natural rhythms and busy periods of different business functions when planning your roll-out timeline. Finance teams, for example, are typically overwhelmed during month-end and year-end closing periods, making these poor times to introduce new processes or expect active participation in data governance activities. Similarly, retail organizations may find their teams stretched thin during peak shopping seasons, while HR departments often have limited availability during annual performance review cycles.

Marketing teams may be less available during major campaign launches and operations teams might be focused entirely on delivery during peak production periods. Understanding these cyclical demands allows you to schedule data governance roll-out activities when stakeholders have the mental bandwidth and time to engage meaningfully with the process.

Taking the time to map out these business cycles and align your roll-out accordingly demonstrates respect for your stakeholders' workloads and significantly increases your chances of securing their engagement and buy-in.

Common phasing approaches

You might choose to implement by business function, rolling out data governance in finance first, then marketing, followed by operations. Alternatively, you could phase by data domain, starting with customer data, then product data, then financial data. For multi-location organizations, piloting in one region before expanding often works well. Some organizations prefer to begin with their most critical data systems and expand outward from there.

The key is to be strategic about your sequencing while remaining flexible enough to adapt as you learn what works best in your organization's context. Remember, there's no single right way to phase your implementation. The best approach is the one that fits your organization's unique circumstances and constraints.

Expected milestones in the first six months

In the initial six months, while you may not have a fully embedded framework, you can expect to achieve several foundational milestones that will set the stage for long-term success.

ESTABLISH STAKEHOLDER BUY-IN

This involves more than just getting approval from senior leadership. You'll need to identify and engage key stakeholders across different business functions, helping them understand the value proposition of data governance for their specific areas. This period should include conducting awareness sessions, addressing concerns and misconceptions and beginning to build a coalition of data governance champions throughout the organization. You may also establish your data governance steering committee or forum during this time.

BEGIN DRAFTING ROLES AND RESPONSIBILITIES

Rather than trying to define every role perfectly from the outset, focus on clarifying the key roles needed for your initial phase. Start by identifying potential data owners and data stewards for your pilot areas and begin having conversations about what these roles will entail. You are likely to find that role definitions need to be adjusted based on your organization's culture and existing responsibilities, so treat this as an iterative process. Document draft role descriptions and begin socializing them with potential role holders for their review and feedback.

COMMENCE WORK ON A DATA CATALOGUE

Begin capturing definitions for critical data in your pilot area. This doesn't mean creating a comprehensive enterprise-wide data catalogue immediately, but rather starting with the most important business terms that cause confusion or disagreement. Focus on data elements that are frequently used in decision-making or key reports. This early work often reveals the extent of data definition challenges across the organization and helps build the case for more comprehensive data governance.

ADDITIONAL EARLY MILESTONES

You should also expect to complete your initial data governance maturity assessment, finalize your governance framework design and begin developing your first governance processes. Many organizations also start identifying quick wins, small data quality issues that can be resolved relatively easily to demonstrate early value.

Remember, the goal in these first six months isn't perfection. It's progress and momentum. Focus on building solid foundations that you can expand upon as your data governance initiative matures.

FROM FRAMEWORK TO CULTURE

By understanding these elements, you can better gauge the time and effort required for your data governance journey and set realistic expectations for the stakeholders involved. Remember, it's not just about putting a framework in place; it's about cultivating a culture that values and adheres to data governance principles as an ongoing practice.

Embarking on the data governance journey requires thorough planning and a measured, phased execution. Don't let the timeframe discourage you! Data governance is an ongoing practice and keeping the wheels in motion is critical in ensuring your organization's approach to data remains adaptable and robust.

Measuring your progress

Why you need to measure your progress

Before exploring how to measure your data governance progress, it's crucial to understand why measurement is so important in the first place. Data governance initiatives often face scepticism from stakeholders who question their value, particularly when the benefits aren't immediately visible. Without clear evidence of progress and impact, your data governance initiative risks losing momentum, support and even, potentially, funding.

Measurement serves several critical purposes in your data governance journey. Firstly, it provides accountability and demonstrates that your data governance efforts are producing tangible results rather than simply consuming resources. This is particularly important when reporting to senior leadership who need to see a return on investment. Secondly, measurement helps you identify what's working well and what needs adjustment, enabling you to refine your approach and avoid wasting time on ineffective activities.

Perhaps most importantly, measurement creates motivation and engagement among your stakeholders. When people can see clear evidence of improvement, whether that's fewer data quality issues, faster issue resolution or better decision-making capabilities, they become more invested in data governance. Conversely, without visible progress, even the most enthusiastic supporters can lose faith in the initiative.

Finally, measurement provides the foundation for continuous improvement. Data governance is not a destination but an ongoing journey and regular measurement helps you understand how to evolve and adapt your approach as your organization's needs change.

Measuring the progress of your data governance implementation can feel like navigating through a maze. However, with the right approaches, it is possible to chart a clear path forward. Below are some key strategies and actionable steps you can use to effectively measure your data governance implementation progress.

Understanding what to measure

Before diving into specific metrics, it's important to distinguish between measuring value delivered and measuring progress. Both are essential, but they tell different stories about your data governance journey.

Value delivered focuses on the tangible business benefits and improvements your data governance initiative has achieved. Examples include the number of data quality issues identified and resolved, reduced time spent on data reconciliation, improved decision-making or a decrease in regulatory compliance risks. These metrics demonstrate the real-world impact of your data governance efforts.

Progress measures how well you're building the foundations and capabilities needed for long-term success. This includes the number of data owners and data stewards identified and trained, the number of data catalogue terms drafted and approved, processes documented and implemented or data quality reports created and ratified. Progress metrics show you're systematically building the infrastructure for sustainable data governance.

Engagement sits between these two categories and is equally important to measure. Monitor and track data owner attendance at data governance committee meetings, measure how many times the data catalogue is referenced or searched, track participation in training sessions and assess stakeholder feedback on data governance initiatives. Engagement metrics indicate whether your data governance initiative is gaining traction and becoming embedded in day-to-day operations.

How to measure progress

Having established why measurement matters and what to measure, it's time to put theory into practice. Here are some strategies that will enable you to systematically track and demonstrate the success of your data governance initiative.

REVISIT YOUR DATA GOVERNANCE MATURITY ASSESSMENT

As discussed in Chapter 2, a data governance maturity assessment serves as a vital tool for understanding your current strengths and identifying gaps in your data governance practices. This evaluation provides insight into what's working well and where improvements are needed. This is important at the start of your initiative, but also provides valuable insight into the progress made when repeated periodically throughout your initiative.

I recommend rerunning your data governance maturity assessment once a year. Real change takes time and frequent reassessments may overwhelm your stakeholders without offering substantial insights. Use your baseline assessment as a reference point to track meaningful progress over time, celebrating improvements while identifying areas that still need attention.

DEFINE KEY PERFORMANCE INDICATORS (KPIS)

A question I've been asked many times over the years is whether I can provide examples of good key performance indicators for data governance initiatives. While I understand the appeal of having ready-made examples to work from, I'm afraid there's no fast track when it comes to developing meaningful metrics for your data governance initiative.

The problem with providing generic examples isn't that I don't want to help; rather, it's the same challenge we face with anything considered 'standard' in data governance. What works for one organization simply won't be relevant to yours. You need to develop and track KPIs that align with your organization's specific goals. While there are no one-size-fits-all metrics, consider these categories:

- Compliance metrics: Measure adherence to your data governance policy. Examples include the percentage of data assets that have identified data owners, the completion rate of data governance training across and the number of data definitions drafted and approved.

- Stakeholder engagement: Evaluate how well stakeholders are engaging in your data governance initiative. This could include tracking attendance rates at data governance committee meetings or monitoring the frequency of data catalogue usage. You might also track the number of data quality issues reported by data consumers or measure response times to investigate and resolve data quality issues.

- Data quality metrics: As you start to develop data quality reports, you will begin to assess aspects such as accuracy, completeness and consistency. Track improvements in the metrics over time and share as evidence of improvement.

As with designing the data governance framework itself, you must involve your stakeholders in setting the KPIs. If you don't get the people who actually consume or use that data involved in setting the KPIs, they are not going to be interested in the outcomes or take action based on the results.

Involving relevant stakeholders in creating these KPIs ensures they remain relevant and actionable.

ESTABLISHING KEY RISK INDICATORS (KRIS)

When it comes to key risk indicators, you are likely to need to work closely with your operational risk team alongside your data owners. In my experience, data owners are often the same people who appear on the organization's risk register as risk owners, making this collaboration natural and productive.

Facilitate meetings with these stakeholders to discuss the risks associated with your most critical data assets. Together, you can identify what controls should be put in place to mitigate those risks and determine which of them require KRIs for ongoing monitoring. The potential risks associated with your data are diverse, affecting everything from operational efficiency to strategic outcomes. The following examples illustrate some of the most common risks organizations face:

- incomplete customer records leading to poor service delivery and complaints
- inconsistent product codes across systems causing inventory management errors
- incorrect pricing data resulting in incorrect billing or lost revenue
- poor data quality undermining analytics, resulting in misguided strategic decisions

Making your metrics matter

While there's no easy way to fast-track the development of meaningful metrics, the investment in this collaborative process is worthwhile. When you put in the work to develop KPIs and KRIs with genuine stakeholder input, you'll end up with metrics that people actually want to monitor and will take action on when standards aren't being met.

This approach creates ownership and accountability that simply don't exist when metrics are imposed by the data governance manager or copied from other organizations. Remember, the goal isn't to have the most sophisticated metrics, it's to have metrics that drive the right behaviours and improvements in your organization while demonstrating both the progress you're making and the value you're delivering.

Evolving your data governance framework

Why your framework needs to change

I can almost hear the collective groan from here! You've spent months painstakingly crafting your data governance framework. You've engaged stakeholders, documented processes, defined roles and finally got everyone aligned on your approach. You're feeling quite proud of your accomplishment and rightfully so. And now here I am, telling you that you will need to change it!

Before you close this book and throw it across the room, hear me out. I promise this isn't some cruel joke or an attempt to send you back to square one. The reality is that evolving your data governance framework is not merely an option; it's an essential strategic necessity in today's business environment. You may be wondering why, so let's dive in and make it all make sense!

THE DYNAMIC NATURE OF DATA

In our data-driven world, data is not static; it evolves continuously with new uses for it constantly being thought up. As the uses of and importance of data evolve, so must your approach to data governance. The following reasons highlight the necessity for this evolution:

- Alignment with business goals: Your data governance framework should be in step with your organization's strategy and objectives. If it isn't, your efforts may be misaligned, leading to wasted resources and missed opportunities. Traditionally, an organization would update its corporate strategy and objectives every three to five years. However, as the pace of change accelerates, I'm increasingly hearing that they are being reviewed and refreshed on a shorter cadence. You must make sure that you are aware of any updates to your organization's corporate strategy and consider whether any changes are needed to your data governance framework as a result.

- Regulatory compliance: With increasing regulations across multiple sectors, maintaining a robust data governance framework becomes imperative. While for many years it was only financial and pharmaceutical regulators that asked for data governance, it is increasingly being asked for in a range of regulated sectors, from higher education to housing. Proactively embracing these changes facilitates compliance and mitigates the risks associated with non-compliance.

- Cultural shift: Data governance is fundamentally about people. Evolving your framework means fostering a culture that values data, ensuring that everyone understands their role in managing data effectively. As the culture becomes more data-focused, you may be able to raise the bar and introduce higher standards or new activities that weren't feasible when you first implemented your framework. What seemed too ambitious or complex initially may become achievable as people become more comfortable with data governance principles and see the value it brings. This cultural maturation opens opportunities to enhance data quality standards, implement more sophisticated monitoring processes or introduce more advanced data governance practices that would have overwhelmed stakeholders in the early phases.

- Organizational change: Your organization itself is constantly evolving through mergers and acquisitions, restructures, new product or service offerings and strategic pivots. Each of these changes brings new data sources, different stakeholder groups, altered reporting lines and shifted priorities that your data governance framework must accommodate to remain relevant and effective.

COMPLEXITY AND SCALE

As your organization grows, so too does the complexity of your data landscape, making an adaptive framework crucial for continued success. With the sheer amount of data multiplying exponentially, simplistic data governance approaches that may have worked in smaller, less complex environments will inevitably fall short. A mature, evolving data governance framework allows for better management of diverse data types, ensuring both quality and usability across an increasingly varied data ecosystem.

This challenge is further compounded as organizations embrace automation and AI technologies. The data that these advanced systems rely on must be trustworthy and well-governed, requiring a framework that can evolve alongside technological advancements. What worked for traditional reporting and analytics may prove inadequate for machine learning algorithms or automated decision-making systems, necessitating more sophisticated data governance approaches that can adapt to these emerging technological requirements.

Recognizing the need for change

With all these forces at play, evolving business goals, expanding regulatory requirements, organizational transformations, growing data volumes and advancing technologies, how do you know when your framework needs to adapt? The challenge isn't just understanding that change is necessary; it's recognizing the right moment to act and knowing what adjustments to make.

Many data governance practitioners get so focused on implementing their carefully crafted framework that they miss the early warning signs that evolution is needed. Others become overwhelmed and paralysed by the constant stream of potential changes, unsure which ones deserve immediate attention and which can wait.

The key is developing a reliable system for sensing when change is required, something that can help you distinguish between temporary growing pains and genuine signals that your data governance framework needs updating. Fortunately, there's a simple but effective tool that can help you navigate these decisions.

Your data governance weathervane

Just as knowing the direction of the wind is important if you are a pilot, gauging the sentiment of your organization towards your data governance initiative while you are implementing it is vital.

The times of predicting the weather using seaweed are long gone and these days meteorologists have a wide range of increasingly sophisticated tools available to them to forecast the weather. As a data governance practitioner, you do not have a vast array of tools available to help you do your job, but there are some simple devices which can help you greatly when implementing data governance.

One such tool is a weathervane. In meteorological terms, a weathervane is a mechanical device attached to an elevated structure which rotates freely to show the direction of the wind. The data governance version is less mechanical, but nonetheless rotates freely to show the direction of sentiment towards your data governance initiative. Do not underestimate the usefulness of this simple tool. If the prevailing sentiment is positive, this could indicate that it is a good time to tackle some of the more challenging activities on your plan. If things are not looking so good, you need to know so that you can take remedial action quickly.

Having grasped the value in having a data governance weathervane, I'm sure you are wondering where you can buy one. If only it were that easy! Sadly, it is not something you can simply purchase, install and immediately start reaping the benefits of. However, the good news is that you already have one; you just have to find it. You see, my data governance weathervane is a person and not just any person. The value in having such a device is only realized if you have identified the correct person.

FINDING THE RIGHT PERSON

Generally, my weathervane is a fairly senior person, usually a data owner or other senior stakeholder, but never someone who was an immediate supporter of my data governance activities (such a strong supporter would be no good as they will tend to pass on only good feedback to you). Equally, someone who is resisting your efforts is not useful, as they will only tell you what is going wrong (whether perceived or actual). The person you want is someone who you've had challenging conversations with initially, but has eventually been persuaded to see the value in data governance. Such a person makes a perfect weathervane. If you are doing the right things at the right pace and communicating well, they are likely to feel comfortable with what you are doing. If things are not going so well (or as I usually find is the case, I haven't communicated how things are going for a while), then they will start getting twitchy and it's time for you to take some action.

Importantly, their sentiment can also flag that something fundamental has changed in the organization that requires you to take action to adapt your data governance framework. When your weathervane starts expressing concerns about new business priorities, changing regulatory requirements or shifts in organizational structure, this is often an early indicator that your current framework may need evolution to remain relevant and effective in the new environment.

BUILDING YOUR EARLY WARNING SYSTEM

One important thing to note is that, although it is obviously important to maintain a good relationship with your weathervane, it is equally (if not more so) important to build good relationships with the people around your weathervane. These people are often your early warning alarm. When you bump into someone and they tell you that 'Joe' is getting worried about data governance or is wondering what he has to do next, you get a very good indication of which way the wind is blowing and you can take appropriate action. If 'Joe' tells you he is worried himself, then it is imperative that you find out what is worrying him and take action promptly. If your weathervane is worried, the chances are that other data owners also have concerns, but just haven't told you yet.

In my experience, my weathervane usually highlights that with progress being slow (as is often the case with any business change initiative), there has been nothing concrete for me to communicate and so, being wrapped up in numerous other activities, I haven't thought to communicate anything at all. Someone who is not 100 per cent comfortable with what you are doing will take the silence or lack of communication as worrying, whereas your most positive of supporters will realize that you are engrossed in your work and will assume that, unless they've heard to the contrary that everything is going well.

REAL-WORLD EXAMPLE

The weathervane in action

A number of years ago, when I was working at an insurance company, my data governance weathervane proved an invaluable tool and flagged that I needed to not only adapt my data governance framework but also align it with another initiative entirely.

This was early on in my experience of selecting one of my senior stakeholders as a weathervane, and at that stage I'd only had vague grumblings about how much I was expecting them to do on top of their day jobs, nothing really concrete. My weathervane was the finance director ('Jim'), who had been quite resistant to taking on the role of data owner. I had to have a number of conversations using every influencing tactic in my book to convince him to take the role.

One day, his business manager turned up at my desk and explained that Jim was very unhappy about data governance and that I needed to come with him right away to speak to him, because he was threatening to stop the whole data governance initiative. I was very worried and rushed off to see him.

When I met him, Jim was very frustrated about someone he thought I had sent to meet him, who had told him that he wasn't a data owner, he was an information owner. It sounded as though this person had used lots of jargon that he didn't understand. He felt that this person must be working for me and had been sent to explain added complexities to the data governance framework and the role that he was not overly happy to have in the first place.

Once he'd vented and let off steam about his frustration, I was able to have a really useful conversation with him. I assured him that I had not sent anybody to meet him and change his data owner role, but that I would go and find out what was going on and report back.

After some investigations, I discovered that the company had recently hired a records manager whose role was to implement a record management policy for the company. It was the new records manager who had met with not only my finance data owner, but also other of my data owners (none of whom had thought to let me know that this had happened) and told them that their role was not data owner, but information owner.

I was able to track this new records manager down and discovered that he had assumed that data owner role related to a previous failed attempt at records management. Of course, I was frustrated at this, but through a series of conversations with him, his boss and my line manager, we were able to agree that records management and data governance would work way better if they were aligned. Instead of asking the same senior stakeholders to take on yet another role, it would be better to evolve the data governance framework to include provisions that made it possible for the records manager to get these senior stakeholders to take on the additional responsibilities without creating another role. Included in that change was the decision to drop the data owner title and call them information owners so that they owned both the data and the information which was created from it.

This example illustrates how a weathervane can alert you to changes in your organization that require framework adaptation, changes you might have missed entirely if you'd only been focused on your own data governance activities.

Staying informed about change

As well as having a weathervane to gauge internal sentiment, you need to keep up to date with everything that is happening in your industry and organization. Regular monitoring of industry trends, regulatory developments, technological advances and organizational announcements will help you anticipate when your data governance framework might need to adapt to cope with changes. This proactive approach allows you to plan your framework evolution rather than react to it, ensuring your data governance programme remains ahead of the curve rather than constantly playing catch-up.

REAL-WORLD EXAMPLE
Adapting to organizational restructure

Many years ago, I was working at a financial services company as an interim data governance manager. After 18 months, data governance was progressing well, with engaged data owners attending the data governance council regularly. The company then announced a major restructuring, moving from a hierarchical reporting structure to a matrix management approach. Since there were no personnel changes involved, I assumed it wouldn't significantly impact the data governance framework.

A few weeks later, when I approached the finance data owner with a question about finance data, he seemed unsure whether he was still the right person to make decisions. He explained how finance had been reorganized regionally, with each region reporting into a consolidated group level. I spoke with my other data owners and discovered similar restructuring across most business functions.

All the data owners I spoke to had similar concerns. While they were happy to make decisions about data for their domain and region, they felt that they could not make decisions for their data domain in different regions. It seemed that I needed a data owner in every region for each data domain! The implications were clear: if I applied the new structure to the existing data governance framework, it would quadruple my data owners from 20 to 80 people. Our data governance council meetings were already challenging with just over 20 attendees; expanding to over 80 would be unmanageable for a global organization where finding suitable meeting times was already difficult.

The impact of the restructuring was a clear signal that our current data ownership approach needed fundamental revision. Rather than working in isolation, I conducted one-to-one sessions with each existing data owner to understand how the restructure affected their role and gathered their input on potential solutions. While most couldn't suggest specific solutions, involving them in the process ensured they felt heard and were then supportive when I proposed a new approach based on their feedback.

The result was a revised data ownership structure that maintained our council at just over 20 attendees, preserving our ability to have meaningful discussions and make decisions effectively. It also allowed for stakeholders in all regions to be consulted and involved in decision-making.

This example demonstrates how organizational changes can combine with internal signals from stakeholders to clearly indicate when framework evolution is necessary. Without staying alert to both the announced restructure and the resulting confusion among data owners, the data governance initiative would quickly have become unwieldy and ineffective.

Practical steps to evolve your framework

Whenever you decide it is time to evolve your framework, you must remember to use the same approach covered in Chapter 3 to design your framework in the first place. The fundamental principles of thoughtful design, stakeholder engagement and systematic implementation remain just as important when modifying an existing data governance framework as they were when creating it initially. These steps will guide you through this evolution process:

1. ENGAGE WITH STAKEHOLDERS

Involve senior stakeholders to gather insights and secure buy-in, ensuring that any revisions to the framework align with organizational goals. This engagement should be systematic and ongoing, not just a one-off consultation. Schedule regular check-ins with key stakeholders to understand how their priorities are shifting and what new challenges they're facing. Consider including a quarterly agenda point for your data governance committee to review the performance of your data governance framework and discuss potential changes.

Remember that different stakeholders will have different perspectives on what needs to change, so create opportunities for diverse voices to be heard. Document their feedback and concerns and be transparent about which suggestions you can implement immediately versus those that require longer-term planning.

2. START SMALL AND ITERATE

Implement changes in manageable phases, allowing for adjustments based on feedback and results. Rather than attempting a complete framework overhaul, identify specific areas that need attention and tackle them one at a time. This might mean updating a single process, revising role definitions for one role or piloting a new tool in a limited scope before rolling it out enterprise-wide. Each small change should be tested, evaluated and refined before moving to the next iteration. This approach reduces risk, allows for learning and helps maintain stakeholder confidence by demonstrating that changes are thoughtful and controlled rather than disruptive.

3. FOCUS ON TRAINING

Cultivate a knowledgeable workforce through comprehensive training to empower employees with data governance principles. As your framework evolves, your training programmes must evolve too. This means updating existing training materials to reflect new processes, creating targeted sessions for people taking on new roles and developing refresher courses for those whose responsibilities have expanded. Consider different learning styles and delivery methods, from formal workshops to informal lunch-and-learn sessions, online modules to hands-on demonstrations. Don't forget to train the trainers, ensuring that data stewards and data owners have the skills and confidence to cascade learning within their teams.

4. CONTINUOUS MONITORING AND ADAPTATION

Make it clear that data governance is an ongoing journey rather than a one-off project. Regularly review the framework to adapt to new challenges and opportunities as they arise. Establish formal review cycles, perhaps annually for major framework assessment and quarterly for minor adjustments. Use the metrics you've established to track both progress and value delivery, looking for patterns that suggest areas needing attention. Create feedback loops that capture insights from day-to-day data governance activities and ensure there are clear processes for escalating issues that might require framework changes. Most importantly, communicate that evolution is expected and positive, not a sign of failure in the original design.

5. DOCUMENT AND COMMUNICATE CHANGES

Ensure that all framework modifications are properly documented and communicated across the organization. Update all relevant documentation, from high-level framework diagrams to detailed process instructions. Develop a communication plan for each significant change, tailoring messages for different audiences and ensuring that everyone understands how the changes affect their roles and responsibilities. Consider creating version control for your framework documents to help track evolution over time.

6. LEARN FROM OTHERS

Stay connected with the broader data governance community to learn from others' experiences and avoid reinventing solutions to common problems. Join professional networks, attend conferences, participate in industry forums and maintain relationships with peers in similar organizations. However, remember that while you can learn from others' approaches, any changes to your framework must still be customized for your organizational context. Use external insights as inspiration and validation, but always filter them through your own stakeholder needs and business requirements.

Core principles for evolution

Having covered why change is necessary and how to manage it effectively, here are the core principles to remember as you navigate the evolution of your data governance framework:

- By evolving your data governance framework, you ensure your organization stays agile and maximizes the strategic value of its data.
- Remember the 'why' behind your governance efforts to drive engagement and success.
- Embrace a culture of continuous improvement to ensure your framework adapts to the changing data landscape.

In essence, improving your data governance framework is not just about managing data; it's about empowering your organization to harness the full potential of its data-driven capabilities. So what are you waiting for? Identify your weathervane and find out in which direction your data governance wind is blowing! Understanding the sentiment around your data governance programme is the first step in recognizing when your framework needs to evolve to meet changing organizational needs and expectations.

Conclusion

Measuring progress and evolving your data governance framework are not optional activities. They are essential practices that determine the long-term success of your data governance initiative. Without proper measurement, you risk losing stakeholder support and missing opportunities for improvement. Without evolution, your framework will become outdated and ineffective as your organization changes.

Throughout this chapter, we've explored practical approaches to both challenges, from establishing meaningful metrics to recognizing when change is needed. The concept of a data governance weathervane provides you with an early warning system, while the systematic evolution steps ensure changes are managed thoughtfully and effectively.

Key takeaways from this chapter:

- Measurement drives success: Regular tracking of progress, value delivery and stakeholder engagement maintains momentum and demonstrates the worth of your data governance efforts.

- Start with stakeholder involvement: Meaningful metrics can only be developed with input from those who will use and act upon them.

- Expect and embrace change: Your framework must evolve to remain relevant as business strategies, regulations and organizational structures shift.

- Use your weathervane: Identify a key stakeholder who can provide early signals about sentiment and the need for framework adjustments.

- Implement changes gradually: Small, iterative improvements are more successful than major overhauls and help maintain stakeholder confidence.

- Plan for the long term: Data governance implementation typically takes 12 to 18 months, with ongoing evolution being a permanent feature.

- Document and communicate: All changes must be properly recorded and clearly communicated to ensure continued buy-in and understanding.

Remember, data governance is a journey, not a destination. By measuring your progress and adapting your approach, you ensure that your framework continues to deliver value and support your organization's evolving data needs. The investment in measurement and evolution will pay dividends in sustained stakeholder engagement and improved data outcomes.

10

Learning from what goes wrong

Introduction

Before we conclude this book, I want to share with you the most common mistakes I've seen organizations make when implementing data governance. Why start with the mistakes? Because in my experience, understanding what can go wrong is often more valuable than simply knowing what to do right.

Throughout the book, I've shared real-world examples of clients who struggled with various aspects of their data governance initiatives. The prospective client who created an overly complex framework, the client who thought they had to do everything at once, the client who implemented a tool too early. These weren't isolated incidents. They represent patterns I see repeatedly across different organizations and industries.

Over the years, I've identified 10 critical mistakes that can derail even the most well-intentioned data governance initiatives. Some of these mistakes are subtle and might not become apparent until months into your implementation. Others are more obvious but surprisingly prevalent. What they all have in common is that they can be avoided if you know what to look for.

The beauty of learning from these mistakes is that they naturally point us toward the solutions. Each mistake I'm about to describe has taught me something valuable about what successful data governance actually requires. These lessons have shaped the principles that act as safeguards against these common pitfalls.

The 10 critical mistakes

- Mistake 1: Failure to address culture. The biggest mistake organizations make, failing to address culture change as part of their data governance initiatives.

- Mistake 2: The initiative is IT-led. When IT leads data governance, it becomes technology-focused rather than value-focused.

- Mistake 3: Not understanding organizational maturity. Implementing data governance without assessing whether your organization is ready for it.

- Mistake 4: Treating data governance as a project. Managing data governance as a traditional project rather than an ongoing change programme.

- Mistake 5: Misalignment with strategy. Failing to clearly connect data governance to organizational strategic objectives.

- Mistake 6: Not understanding the data landscape. Implementing changes without mapping how data flows through your organization.

- Mistake 7: Failure to embed the framework. Creating impressive frameworks that never become integrated into daily business operations.

- Mistake 8: The big bang approach. Trying to implement everything at once, overwhelming stakeholders and creating resistance.

- Mistake 9: The tick-box approach for compliance. Doing the absolute minimum required to satisfy regulators rather than building sustainable capabilities.

- Mistake 10: Thinking a tool is the answer. Believing that purchasing the right software will solve data governance challenges.

So let's start with what can go wrong. Think of this section as your early warning system, a way to recognize potential problems before they become costly failures. Then, armed with this knowledge, we will look at the principles that will help you navigate around these obstacles and build a data governance framework that truly works for your organization.

Mistake 1: Failure to address culture

If you take away just one thing from this entire section on mistakes, let it be this: the biggest mistake I see organizations make is failing to address culture change as part of their data governance initiatives. This mistake is so fundamental and so common that it can single-handedly cause the failure of an otherwise well-designed data governance framework.

I've worked with clients who have invested significant time and resources in creating frameworks that are genuinely ideal for their organization. The policy is well-written, the processes are clearly defined and the roles and responsibilities are perfectly mapped out. Yet, despite all this excellent preparation, their initiatives fail because they neglected the human element. They focused on the 'what' and the 'how' of data governance but forgot about the 'who'.

What this looks like in practice

When organizations fail to address culture change, their business users and stakeholders feel that data governance is being done to them rather than for them or with them. This creates an adversarial relationship from the start. People see data governance as yet another burden imposed by management or IT, rather than as something that will genuinely help them do their jobs better.

The result is predictable. Stakeholders do the absolute minimum they can get away with. They might attend the mandatory training sessions, but they won't truly engage. They might complete the required documentation, but they won't embrace the underlying principles. In the worst cases, they'll simply ignore the new processes entirely if they think they can avoid consequences.

This isn't because people are difficult or resistant to change by nature. It's because no one has taken the time to help them understand why data governance matters to them personally, or how it will make their working lives easier rather than harder.

The real cost of this mistake

Simply put, you cannot start to manage your data as an asset and realize its value if you don't address culture change. Data governance is fundamentally about changing how people think about and interact with data. Without bringing people along on this journey, you're essentially trying to implement a framework that exists only on paper.

I've seen organizations spend thousands of pounds on data governance initiatives that ultimately deliver no lasting value because they treated it as a technical or process challenge rather than a people challenge. The framework documentation sits on a shelf, the training materials go unused and within months everyone reverts to their old ways of working.

How to avoid this mistake

The solution starts with applying good change management techniques. If you're not well-versed in change management, find someone in your organization who is to provide advice or even support. Most established organizations have people with these skills, whether in HR, organizational development or project management offices.

At its core, avoiding this mistake comes down to high-quality communication with all your business stakeholders. But this isn't a one-size-fits-all communication strategy. Different groups of stakeholders need different messages about their role in the data governance implementation.

Your data owners need to understand how data governance will help them better manage their areas of responsibility. Your data stewards need to see how the framework will make their day-to-day tasks more efficient. Your senior executives need to understand the strategic benefits. Each group requires tailored communication that speaks to their specific concerns and motivations.

Training is equally important, but it needs to be practical and relevant. Don't just teach people about your framework in abstract terms. Show them how it applies to their actual work. Use real examples from their department. Let them practise with scenarios they'll genuinely encounter.

Most importantly, involve people in the design process wherever possible. When stakeholders help create the framework, they're much more likely to support its implementation. This doesn't mean letting everyone design everything by committee, but it does mean seeking input, testing ideas and making people feel like partners in the process rather than passive recipients of change.

Remember, if you don't address culture change, your data governance initiative will never deliver the benefits you're hoping for. The framework might look perfect on paper, but without people who believe in it and actively use it, it's worthless.

Mistake 2: The initiative is IT-led

When I perform a data governance review for companies that are struggling with their initiatives, one pattern emerges time and again: IT is leading the data governance effort. This always happens with the best of intentions. IT teams are often the first to recognize that proper data governance is desperately needed because they see first-hand the chaos that poor data management creates.

The logic seems sound. IT understands the technical implications of bad data. They see the downstream effects when systems can't talk to each other because of inconsistent data formats. They're the ones who get called when reports don't match or when data integration projects fail. So when senior management decides something needs to be done about data governance, it's natural to hand the problem to IT.

But here's the fundamental issue: IT doesn't own the data, the business does; and true data governance will only happen when the business takes ownership of their data and leads the initiative themselves.

Why IT-led initiatives struggle

I've seen this pattern numerous times. An IT-led data governance initiative typically focuses heavily on tools and technology solutions. This makes sense from IT's perspective because that's their area of expertise, and they're often getting advice from vendors who want to sell them data cleansing tools, data quality software or master data management platforms.

The problem is that these tools, no matter how sophisticated, can only address the symptoms of poor data governance, not the root causes. Unless the business changes the way data is captured at the point of entry, the quality of the data will never fundamentally improve. You can cleanse data all you want, but if it is still being entered incorrectly or inconsistently, you're fighting a losing battle.

I remember working with a large financial services company where IT had spent a significant amount to purchase and implement a comprehensive data quality platform. The tool could identify and fix thousands of data errors every day. But the business users who were creating the data had never been trained on proper data entry procedures and they had no understanding of why data quality mattered to their daily work. The tool was essentially applying never-ending, expensive Band-Aids to a wound that never stopped bleeding.

The deeper cultural problem

An IT-led initiative also reinforces the dangerous misconception that data governance is a technical problem rather than a business problem. When IT runs the show, business stakeholders often assume they can delegate all responsibility for data quality and data management to the technology team. This completely undermines the culture change we discussed in the first mistake.

Business users start to think, 'Well, if IT is responsible for data governance, then data problems are IT's fault.' This creates an adversarial relationship where the business points fingers at IT when things go wrong, rather than taking accountability for their role in creating and maintaining good data.

Making the transition to business ownership

The solution is to get the business to recognize that they need to take ownership of their data and lead the data governance initiative. This is often easier said than done, particularly in organizations where IT has traditionally been seen as responsible for 'anything to do with data'.

It doesn't mean IT should be excluded from data governance. Far from it. IT plays a crucial role in providing the technical infrastructure and tools that support data governance. But they should be enablers and supporters, not the owners and drivers of the initiative.

At a minimum, the business must take ownership of the policy and processes relating to how data is created and managed. They need to define what good data looks like in their context, establish the business rules that govern data quality and take responsibility for training their people on good data practices.

The key insight here connects back to our discussion of business strategy in Chapter 2. Data governance must be driven by business needs and business objectives, not by IT capabilities or constraints. When IT leads the initiative, it becomes technology-focused rather than value-focused and that's a recipe for failure.

Mistake 3: Not understanding organizational maturity

This mistake comes down to a fundamental question that many organizations skip over: are you ready for data governance? It's a question that makes some people uncomfortable because they assume that if they've identified a need for data governance, they must be ready to implement it. But readiness and need are two very different things.

I learned this lesson the hard way early in my career when I was working with a client who was absolutely convinced they needed a comprehensive data governance framework immediately. They had all the right motivations: regulatory requirements, data quality issues and senior management support. But when we started implementing even basic data governance concepts, it became clear that the organization simply wasn't mature enough to handle what we were trying to introduce.

The problem wasn't a lack of intelligence or capability. It was that the organization hadn't yet developed the foundational understanding of how to think about data strategically. They were still treating data as a by-product of their business processes rather than as an asset that needed to be actively managed.

What organizational maturity looks like

Data governance maturity isn't just about having the right systems or processes in place. It's about having an organizational culture that recognizes the value of data and understands that managing data properly requires intentional effort and ongoing commitment.

In mature organizations, people naturally think about the downstream impact of their data-related decisions. They understand that the way they capture data today will affect the reports their colleagues need tomorrow. They recognize that data quality is everyone's responsibility, not just IT's problem to solve.

In less mature organizations, data is often seen as something that just 'happens' as part of doing business. People enter data into systems because they're required to, but they don't think about data as something that needs to be carefully created, consistently maintained and strategically leveraged.

This reminds me of the client I mentioned in Chapter 3 who had tried to implement a standard data governance framework. Part of their challenge was that they were trying to implement advanced data governance concepts before they had established the basic cultural foundations. It was like trying to build the top floor of a house before laying the foundation.

The communication challenge

When there's a lack of clarity about organizational maturity, communication becomes much more difficult. Your messages about data governance need to land differently depending on where your organization sits on the maturity spectrum.

If you're dealing with a less mature organization, you need to start with education about why data matters and how it connects to business outcomes. If you jump straight into discussions about data steward roles or data quality metrics, it's likely that you will get blank stares or, worse, people will assume you're talking about something that is IT's responsibility.

On the other hand, if your organization is more mature, starting with basic concepts about why data is important will feel patronizing and waste valuable time. They're ready for more sophisticated discussions about data governance frameworks and implementation strategies.

Plotting your journey

You need to know your starting point so you can plot your journey effectively. If you don't understand how mature your organization is in terms of data generally, you risk trying to introduce something that your organization isn't ready for.

I've spoken with numerous organizations that spent months developing a detailed data governance framework only to discover that their people didn't even have a common understanding of basic data concepts. The framework sat unused because it was written for an organization that was more mature than the one that actually existed.

How to assess and address maturity

The first step is to assess your current level of maturity honestly. This doesn't need to be an expensive or time-consuming exercise. There are plenty of maturity assessment frameworks available, including some free resources that can give you a good starting point.

But assessment alone isn't enough. You also need to be clear about what you hope to achieve with data governance. If you're clear about your objectives, it becomes much easier to work out what stakeholders need to hear and understand in order to welcome data governance rather than resist it.

This connects directly to the strategy work we discussed in Chapter 2. Once you've defined why your organization is doing data governance and how stakeholders will benefit from it, you can create a document that ensures everyone involved clearly understands what the initiative is trying to achieve and how it will positively impact their part of the organization.

The key is to meet your organization where it is, not where you wish it were. Start with their current level of understanding and build from there. Sometimes this means taking smaller steps than you'd ideally like, but it also means building a solid foundation that will support more sophisticated data governance practices as your organization matures.

Mistake 4: Treating data governance as a project

This mistake seems logical on the surface. After all, most organizations are used to implementing new initiatives as projects. You define the scope, create a project plan, assign resources, execute the tasks and deliver the outcomes. It's a tried and tested approach that works well for many business initiatives. So why wouldn't it work for data governance?

The answer lies in understanding what data governance actually is. Unlike implementing a new software system or launching a new product, data governance is fundamentally about changing how people think and behave. It's about shifting attitudes toward data, establishing new habits and embedding new ways of working into the fabric of your organization. These kinds of changes can't be achieved simply by ticking tasks off a checklist.

I've seen organizations create elaborate project plans for data governance with detailed timelines, deliverables and milestones. On paper, everything looks perfect. The project appears to be making excellent progress as tasks get completed and deliverables get signed off. But when the project officially 'ends', nothing has really changed. People revert to their old ways of working because no one addressed the underlying behaviours and attitudes.

The illusion of progress

When data governance is managed as a project, there's often an illusion of progress that can be dangerously misleading. You might successfully deliver a data governance policy document, complete a series of training sessions and even agree individuals for the data owner and steward roles. All of these are important components of data governance, but they're not data governance itself.

Real data governance happens when these components are actively used and embedded in daily business operations. It happens when people naturally consider data quality implications before making decisions. It happens when data stewards proactively identify and resolve issues rather than waiting for problems to escalate. It happens when data governance becomes so integral to how the organization operates that people can't imagine working any other way.

This transformation requires winning hearts and minds, not just completing deliverables. You need to help people understand not just what they're supposed to do differently, but why these changes will make their working lives better. This is sophisticated change management work that extends far beyond traditional project management approaches.

The reversion problem

Without proper change management and stakeholder engagement, organizations almost inevitably revert to their old ways of not managing data well once the 'project' is complete. I've worked with companies that have attempted to implement data governance multiple times because they treated it as a project each time, achieved some short-term improvements, but failed to create lasting change.

This pattern is particularly damaging because each failed attempt makes subsequent efforts more difficult. Stakeholders become cynical about data governance initiatives because they remember that previous attempts made no lasting improvement, or they assume they're just another temporary initiative that will soon be forgotten.

Moving from project to change programme

The solution is to approach data governance as a change programme rather than a traditional project. This means organizing your effort into different work streams that address both the practical and behavioural aspects of the transformation.

Some work streams will focus on the deliverables, like the policy, processes and role descriptions. These are important and can be managed using traditional project techniques. But other work streams must focus specifically on the behavioural changes, stakeholder engagement and culture transformation that make data governance sustainable and effective.

This approach requires a team with diverse skill sets. You'll need people who can facilitate workshops and manage stakeholder relationships. You'll need a communication specialist who can craft messages that resonate with different audiences. You'll need someone with training experience who can help people develop new skills and habits.

Sadly, many organizations start their data governance journey with just one person working on the initiative. It's unlikely that all these capabilities will reside in one person, so you'll need to build a team, identify allies in your organization or bring in external support where necessary. One of my recent clients has worked extensively with a specialist communication company, who has helped them develop and deliver impressive communication campaigns. Not everyone has the budget for this, but your organization may have a communications manager who can give support and advice.

The change programme should clearly outline the transition from your current state to a future where data governance is business as usual. This isn't something that happens overnight or can be achieved by a specific end date. It requires ongoing commitment and a realistic timeline that acknowledges the time it takes for new behaviours to become embedded.

Don't underestimate the importance of soft skills in this process. Communication, facilitation and influencing skills are critical to successful data governance implementation. These skills are more important than technical expertise, yet they're frequently overlooked when organizations assemble and train their data governance teams.

Mistake 5: Misalignment with strategy

This mistake is particularly common when the business isn't fully engaged with the data governance initiative, which often happens when IT is leading the effort, as we discussed earlier. But it can also

occur even when the business is involved if there hasn't been sufficient thought given to how data governance connects to the
organization's broader strategic objectives.

I learned this lesson the hard way in my early days of implementing data governance. I was working with a European manufacturing
company that had data quality issues affecting their supply chain
operations. The problems were obvious, the solutions seemed clear
and I assumed that everyone would naturally see the value of fixing
these issues. But when we presented our data governance proposal to
the executive team, we were met with polite interest rather than
enthusiastic support.

The problem wasn't that our analysis was wrong or that our
proposed solution was inadequate. The problem was that we had
failed to clearly articulate how the data governance initiative would
help the company achieve its strategic priorities, which at that time
were focused on international expansion and cost reduction. We were
talking about data quality improvements, but they were thinking
about market penetration and operational efficiency.

Of course, data governance would support both of these, but, not
being aware that these were their areas of focus, we did not explain
data governance in that context.

Why strategic alignment matters

Corporate strategic objectives drive the day-to-day management of
any business. Resources get allocated based on strategic priorities.
People even get promoted based on their contribution to strategic
goals. Projects get funded or cancelled based on their alignment with
strategic direction.

Unless stakeholders can see how data governance will help them
achieve their strategic objectives, it becomes irrelevant to their daily
concerns. They'll always prioritize activities that they perceive as
directly contributing to strategic success and they'll resist anything
that seems like a distraction from those priorities.

This isn't because people are short-sighted or don't care about
data quality. It's because they're being rational. If you can't explain
how data governance supports the organization's strategic agenda,
then from their perspective it probably doesn't.

The funding risk

When data governance isn't clearly aligned with strategic objectives, there's a real risk that the initiative will lose funding or support, especially when budget pressures arise. I've seen this happen more times than I care to count. An organization starts a data governance initiative with good intentions, but when economic conditions tighten or other strategic priorities emerge, data governance gets pushed aside because no one can articulate its strategic value.

This is particularly frustrating because data governance often delivers some of its greatest benefits during challenging times. When organizations need to make data-driven decisions quickly, when they need to reduce operational costs or when they need to identify new revenue opportunities, good data governance becomes invaluable. But if you haven't made this connection clear from the beginning, it's too late to make the case when the crisis arrives.

Making the strategic connection

The key to avoiding this mistake is being crystal clear about why you're implementing data governance and how it will help your organization achieve its strategic objectives. This requires doing your homework about what those strategic objectives actually are, not just assuming you know.

In Chapter 2 we discussed the importance of understanding your corporate strategy and building a business case for data governance. This is where that work pays dividends. You need to be able to articulate clearly and succinctly how your data governance initiative will contribute to specific strategic outcomes.

For example, if your organization's strategy focuses on customer experience improvement, you need to explain how better data governance will lead to more personalized service, faster issue resolution or more accurate customer insights. If the strategy emphasizes operational efficiency, you need to demonstrate how data governance will reduce manual effort, eliminate duplicate data entry or improve decision-making speed.

The connection must be specific and measurable wherever possible. Vague statements about 'improving data quality' or 'enabling better decision-making' aren't enough. You need to explain exactly how these improvements will translate into strategic value.

Communicating value to different stakeholders

Different stakeholders will care about different aspects of your strategic alignment. Senior executives will want to understand the big picture impact on organizational performance. Department heads will want to know how it will help them achieve their specific objectives. Team members will want to understand how it will make their daily work easier or more effective.

This connects back to the communication challenges we discussed in the culture change and organizational maturity mistakes. Your messaging needs to be tailored to your audience, but it all needs to be grounded in a clear understanding of how data governance supports the organization's strategic direction.

The bottom line is that data governance must be positioned as a strategic enabler, not as a compliance exercise or a technical improvement project. When stakeholders understand how data governance will help them achieve their most important objectives, they become advocates rather than obstacles.

Mistake 6: Not understanding the data landscape

You might think that before implementing data governance organizations would naturally start by understanding what data they have, where it lives and how it flows through their systems. But you'd be surprised how often this fundamental step gets skipped or done superficially. Organizations often dive straight into creating a policy and defining roles without taking the time to map out their data landscape.

This mistake often happens when there's pressure to show quick progress or when leadership wants to see immediate action on data governance. The thinking seems to be, 'We know we have data problems, so let's start fixing them.' But without understanding the broader context of how data moves through your organization, you often end up addressing symptoms rather than root causes.

I remember working with a retail client who was frustrated because they kept fixing the same data quality issues over and over again. Every month, they would identify problems with product information and clean up the data. Yet the same types of problems kept recurring. When we finally mapped out their data landscape, we discovered that the root cause was much earlier in their supply chain data capture process. They had been treating symptoms downstream instead of addressing the source of the problem upstream.

The domino effect of changes

When you don't understand how your data landscape fits together, even small changes can have unexpected consequences throughout your organization. You might fix a data quality issue in one system, only to discover that it breaks a report that someone in a different department relies on daily. Or you might standardize a data format to solve one problem, only to create integration issues with a third-party system that no one remembered to mention.

These unintended consequences don't just create technical problems – they can seriously damage the reputation of your data governance initiative. When people start experiencing unexpected disruptions to their work because of data governance changes, they begin to see the initiative as a source of problems rather than solutions. Word spreads quickly in organizations and soon you have stakeholders actively avoiding or resisting data governance efforts.

This connects to the data governance framework design principles we discussed in Chapter 3. When that prospective client created an overly complex approach, part of their problem was that they were trying to design solutions without fully understanding their data landscape. They created elegant theoretical frameworks that didn't work in practice because they didn't account for the real complexities of how data flowed through their organization.

The implementation challenge

Without a clear understanding of your data landscape, implementation becomes much more difficult and risky. You're essentially trying to navigate without a map. You might know your destination, but you don't understand the terrain you need to cross to get there.

This is particularly problematic when you're trying to prioritize your data governance efforts. If you don't understand how different data domains connect and depend on each other, you might start with an area that seems straightforward but turns out to have complex dependencies that make implementation much more challenging than expected.

Building your data map

The solution is to define your data landscape before you start implementing significant changes. But this doesn't mean you need to document everything in exhaustive detail before you can begin. That would be both impractical and unnecessary.

Instead, start with a high-level overview of your data landscape. Identify the major systems, the primary data flows between them and the key business processes that depend on this data. You can then add detail progressively as you work through different phases of your implementation.

This connects to the custom-build principle we'll discuss later. Every organization's data landscape is unique, shaped by their history, their business model, their technology choices and their growth patterns. A framework that works perfectly for one organization might be completely inappropriate for another because their data landscapes are fundamentally different.

The conceptual data models, which were covered in Chapter 6, can be particularly valuable for this exercise. They help you to quickly document your data landscape in a way that's accessible to business stakeholders, not just technical teams. More importantly, they become powerful communication tools for explaining and selling data governance concepts to your business colleagues.

Impact analysis before changes

Once you have a basic understanding of your data landscape, make sure you undertake some form of impact analysis before making any significant changes. This doesn't need to be a lengthy formal process, but you do need to think through the potential downstream effects of any modifications you're planning.

Remember that implementing data governance is too significant to tackle all at once. It's too big and too complex to understand everything before you start. The key is to work in phases, starting with the highest-level conceptual understanding and drilling down into detail only when you need to.

Sometimes, detailed documentation isn't needed at all, so this approach saves you from wasting valuable time documenting things that may never be relevant to your data governance implementation. Focus your energy on understanding the parts of your data landscape that are most critical to your initial priorities.

This phased approach also helps you avoid the big bang mistake we'll discuss later. By understanding your data landscape in manageable chunks, you can implement data governance in a way that minimizes risk and maximizes your chances of success.

Mistake 7: Failure to embed the framework

This mistake is closely related to treating data governance as a project rather than a change programme, but it deserves its own discussion because it's so commonly overlooked. You can design a brilliant framework, get stakeholder buy-in, train people on their roles and even see some initial improvements in data quality. But if you don't effectively embed the framework into your organization's daily operations, all of these gains will be temporary.

I've worked with organizations that achieved impressive quick wins with their data governance initiatives. Data quality improved, people seemed engaged and leadership was pleased with the progress. But when I returned six months later, it was as if the initiative had never happened. People had gradually drifted back to their old ways of working because the new processes hadn't become genuinely integrated into how the business operated.

This happens because there's a fundamental difference between implementing a framework and embedding it. Implementation is about introducing new processes and getting people to use them initially. Embedding is about making those processes so integral to daily operations that people can't imagine working without them.

The slow reversion

The failure to embed typically doesn't happen suddenly. It's a gradual process that can be easy to miss if you're not watching for it. At first, people follow the new data governance processes because they're fresh in their minds and there's still attention from leadership. But as time passes and other priorities emerge, adherence starts to slip.

Maybe data stewards start skipping their regular data quality reviews because they're busy with other tasks. Perhaps new employees don't receive proper training on data governance procedures because a formal data induction training programme hasn't been established. Or data owners stop participating in data governance forums because the meetings aren't seen as essential to their core responsibilities.

Each individual lapse seems minor and understandable. But collectively, they represent the framework slowly becoming disconnected from actual business operations. Eventually, you end up back where you started, except now you have the added challenge that stakeholders may be sceptical about future data governance efforts because they've seen the previous attempt fade away.

The accountability gap

One of the most common reasons frameworks fail to embed is a simple but critical oversight: no one has been specifically assigned responsibility for making it happen. Organizations spend considerable effort defining data owner and data steward roles, but they often forget to designate someone whose primary job is to ensure the framework becomes embedded in daily operations.

This connects directly to the roles and responsibilities work we discussed in Chapter 6. It's not enough to define what data owners and data stewards should do. You also need someone who's responsible for monitoring whether these roles are actually functioning as intended and taking corrective action when they're not.

Without this accountability, embedding becomes everyone's responsibility, which in practice means it becomes no one's responsibility. Data owners assume data stewards are handling it. Data stewards assume data owners are driving it. Meanwhile, the framework gradually loses momentum because no one is actively maintaining its integration with business operations.

Documentation and training gaps

Even when roles are properly assigned, embedding often fails because of gaps in documentation and training. People may receive initial training on their data governance responsibilities, but there's no ongoing reinforcement or support when they encounter situations that weren't covered in the training.

I've seen organizations create beautiful process maps and role definitions that look impressive in presentations but are useless in practice because they don't provide enough detail for people to actually use them. Or they create detailed procedures that are so complex that people can't follow them without constant support.

The documentation needs to strike the right balance between being comprehensive enough to be useful and simple enough to be practical. More importantly, people need to know where to go for help when they encounter situations that aren't clearly covered by the documented processes.

MAKING EMBEDDING HAPPEN

The solution requires several components working together. First, you need to designate someone specifically responsible for embedding the framework. This might be a data governance manager or even a data governance team, depending on the size and complexity of your organization.

This person or team needs to be actively monitoring how well the framework is working in practice, not just whether people are following the processes. They need to identify where the framework is becoming disconnected from daily operations and take action to address these gaps before they become serious problems.

Training and support need to be ongoing, not just a one-time event during implementation. People need refresher training, new employees need to be brought up to speed and everyone needs access to support when they encounter unusual situations.

Most importantly, the framework needs to become integrated with existing business processes rather than being seen as something separate and additional. When data governance procedures become a natural part of how people do their regular work, embedding happens almost automatically.

This is why the launch principle we'll discuss in the next chapter is so critical. It's relatively easy to design a framework and get initial buy-in, but turning that framework into business-as-usual operations requires sustained effort and attention. The organizations that succeed are those that recognize embedding as a specific challenge that needs dedicated focus and resources.

Mistake 8: The big bang approach

I need to be honest about this mistake: I've made it myself and I still have the scars to prove it was a terrible idea. There's something appealing about the big bang approach to data governance. The logic seems compelling: if you're going to implement data governance, why not do it comprehensively? Why not address all your data challenges at once and transform your entire organization in one major initiative?

The appeal is understandable, especially when you're facing pressure from senior executives to deliver results quickly. A big bang approach promises dramatic transformation and comprehensive solutions. It sounds bold and decisive, qualities that often resonate with senior leaders who want to see their organizations tackle challenges head-on.

But here's what I learned from my painful experience: if you're a business user trying to get on with your day-to-day job, having everything related to your work change massively in one go isn't exciting or efficient. It's overwhelming and stressful. And when people feel overwhelmed and stressed, they don't embrace change. They resist it.

The overwhelm effect

Think about it from your stakeholders' perspective. They're already juggling their regular responsibilities, dealing with their usual workload and managing their existing priorities. Then suddenly, data governance arrives and asks them to learn new processes, take on new roles, attend new meetings, use new tools and fundamentally change how they think about and interact with data.

Even if each individual change makes sense and will ultimately benefit them, the cumulative effect can be paralyzing. People simply can't absorb that much change at once while still doing their regular jobs effectively. The result is that they either ignore the new requirements entirely or comply in the most superficial way possible just to get through it.

This connects back to the client I mentioned in Chapter 1 who thought they had to do everything at once and was feeling overwhelmed. Their instinct to be comprehensive was understandable, but it was also counterproductive. They were trying to solve every data challenge simultaneously instead of taking a strategic, phased approach.

The resource trap

The big bang approach also creates practical problems that can doom the initiative before it really gets started. When you try to implement everything at once, the initiative becomes a massive undertaking that requires enormous amounts of time and resources. This makes it much harder to get the funding and support you need in the first place.

More problematically, it puts you in direct competition with other business priorities for people's time and attention. When stakeholders have to choose between their regular job responsibilities and data governance activities, guess which one usually wins? The work that directly affects their performance reviews and day-to-day success.

I've seen organizations create data governance initiatives that were so ambitious and resource-intensive that they collapsed under their own weight before delivering any meaningful results. These organizations often had to start over with a much more modest approach after their big bang attempt failed.

The fear factor

Perhaps most damaging of all, the big bang approach can make data governance seem much scarier and more disruptive than it actually needs to be. When you present data governance as a massive transformation that will change everything about how people work, you create resistance and anxiety.

This can have lasting effects on your organization's receptivity to data governance. Even if you eventually adopt a more sensible phased approach, people may remain sceptical because their first impression was that data governance meant massive, disruptive change.

Taking a structured approach

The alternative is to take a methodical, phased approach to implementation. This starts with the strategy work we discussed in Chapter 2: being clear about why you're doing data governance and what you want it to achieve for your organization.

Once you have that strategic clarity, you can break your implementation into manageable phases that are directly related to your organization's priorities. Instead of trying to address every data challenge at once, you focus on the areas that will deliver the most value with the least disruption.

This doesn't mean being unambitious. It's about being smart about how you sequence your ambitions. Each phase should build on the previous one, creating momentum and confidence rather than overwhelming people with too much change at once.

The phased approach also allows you to learn and adapt as you go. When you implement everything at once, you don't have opportunities to refine your approach based on what's working and what isn't. But when you work in phases, you can incorporate lessons from early phases into later ones, improving your chances of success.

Managing expectations and timelines

One of the most important aspects of avoiding the big bang approach is never underestimating the amount of time that data governance implementation will take. Cultural change doesn't happen overnight. New habits don't form instantly. People need time to absorb new concepts, practise new skills and integrate new processes into their daily routines.

When you're honest about these timelines from the beginning, you set realistic expectations with stakeholders and leadership. This prevents the disappointment and impatience that can arise when people expect immediate transformation but encounter the inevitable challenges of real organizational change.

Remember, you shouldn't be doing data governance because someone told you it's a good idea. You should be doing it to help your organization achieve its strategic objectives. A phased approach aligned with those objectives is much more likely to deliver sustainable value than a big bang approach that tries to change everything at once.

Mistake 9: The tick-box approach for compliance

When regulatory pressure is the driving force behind a data governance initiative, there's a temptation to do the absolute minimum required to keep the regulator happy. This seems like the practical, efficient approach. After all, why do more than you have to? Why not just focus on satisfying the specific regulatory requirements and move on to other business priorities?

I understand this thinking completely. Compliance requirements can feel like unwelcome burdens imposed from outside the organization. When you're already dealing with multiple regulatory frameworks, each with their own specific requirements and deadlines, the idea of doing more than the minimum can seem like unnecessary effort and cost.

But this tick-box approach is actually a false economy. Organizations that take this route typically end up doing significantly more work in the long run than those who use compliance requirements as a springboard for a broader data governance initiative. They also miss out entirely on the substantial business benefits that come from managing data properly.

The task-focused trap

The fundamental problem with the tick-box approach is that it focuses entirely on completing specific tasks rather than achieving meaningful change. Organizations create checklists of requirements that need to be satisfied and then issue directives to ensure these tasks get completed, often with threats of consequences if people don't comply.

This creates exactly the wrong dynamic for sustainable data governance. People go through the motions because they have to, not because they see any real benefit to their day-to-day work. They complete the required documentation, attend the mandatory training and submit the necessary reports, but none of this translates into genuine improvements in how they think about or manage data.

The result is a hollow shell of data governance that exists only on paper. The policy gets written, the processes get documented and the roles get assigned, but the underlying data practices remain unchanged. You end up with perfect compliance documentation alongside continued data quality problems, inefficient processes and missed opportunities for data-driven insights.

The moving goalposts problem

Regulators are notorious for changing requirements over time. What satisfies them today may not be adequate tomorrow as their understanding evolves, as new risks emerge, or as industry best practices advance. When you've built your data governance around the specific requirements of a particular regulation, every change means going back to square one.

I've spoken to organizations that have had to completely rebuild their data governance frameworks multiple times because they designed them too narrowly around specific regulatory requirements. Each time the requirements changed, they discovered that their approach wasn't flexible enough to accommodate the new demands without starting over.

However, the organizations that take a broader approach to data governance find that regulatory changes typically require only minor adjustments to their existing frameworks. When you build good foundational data governance practices, compliance becomes a natural by-product rather than a separate effort.

Missing the business value

Perhaps most importantly, the tick-box approach completely ignores the substantial business benefits that proper data governance can deliver. When you focus solely on regulatory compliance, you miss opportunities to improve operational efficiency, enhance decision-making, reduce costs and identify new revenue streams.

These missed opportunities represent real economic value that could more than justify the investment in data governance. But when stakeholders only see data governance as a compliance burden, they never get to experience these benefits, which makes them even more resistant to future data governance efforts.

Leveraging compliance as a driver

The smarter approach is to use regulatory requirements as your starting point and business case, but not as your limiting factor. Look for ways to satisfy the regulatory requirements while also delivering meaningful business value.

This doesn't necessarily mean dramatically expanding the scope of your initial implementation. It means thinking strategically about how you design your framework so that it can grow and evolve beyond the immediate compliance needs.

For example, instead of creating data documentation solely to satisfy regulatory requirements, design a data catalogue that serves both compliance and data analysis needs. Instead of implementing data quality monitoring just for regulatory reporting, create processes that also support critical operational processes.

Building for the future

When you adopt sound data governance principles from the beginning, regulatory compliance becomes much more manageable over time. A well-designed framework can typically accommodate new regulatory requirements with relatively minor modifications rather than requiring a fundamental redesign.

This connects back to the custom-build principle we'll discuss in the next chapter. Your data governance framework needs to be designed specifically for your organization's context, including both your regulatory environment and your business objectives. A framework that addresses only compliance requirements isn't truly custom-built because it ignores the majority of your organization's data governance needs.

The key is to get stakeholders to see data governance as something that benefits them directly, not just something that satisfies external regulators. When people understand how data governance will make their jobs easier, improve their department's performance or help them achieve their objectives, they stop seeing it as a burden and start seeing it as a valuable business capability.

Start with a basic data governance framework that addresses your immediate compliance needs, but design it with the flexibility to expand into other areas of your organization. Get the whole organization engaged from the beginning, not just the people who are directly affected by regulatory requirements. This creates a foundation for sustainable data governance that delivers both compliance and business value.

Mistake 10: Thinking a tool is the answer

A number of years ago, I was quite vocal about my belief that there were no tools that could really help with data governance. I've since changed my position as the market has evolved and genuinely useful data governance tools have emerged. Today's tools can be fantastic enablers and facilitators that help you implement, manage and support data governance so it becomes integral to your business operations.

However, I want to be absolutely clear about something: these tools are not the answer to implementing good data governance. They're enablers, not solutions. The distinction is crucial because I still regularly encounter organizations that believe they can solve their data governance challenges simply by purchasing the right software.

This connects directly to the real-world example I mentioned in Chapter 8 about the client who used a tool too early in their data governance journey. They invested significant money in a sophisticated data governance platform before they had established the basic organizational foundations that would make the tool useful. The result was an expensive piece of software that nobody used effectively because the underlying processes and culture weren't ready to support it.

The business engagement problem

When an organization centres its data governance initiative around a tool, the business often disengages because they assume the tool will do all the work for them. This creates a dangerous misconception that data governance is primarily a technology problem rather than a people and process problem.

I've seen this happen repeatedly. An organization announces they're implementing data governance, demonstrates an impressive software platform with beautiful dashboards and automated capabilities and then wonders why nothing really changes. The business stakeholders attended the software demonstrations, but they never truly understood their role in making data governance successful.

The tool becomes a crutch that prevents the organization from developing the fundamental data governance capabilities they actually need. Instead of learning how to identify and resolve data quality issues systematically, they wait for the tool to flag problems. Instead of developing data stewardship skills, they assume the tool will manage data definitions and standards automatically.

Tools don't change culture

This mistake connects back to our very first mistake about failing to address culture change. No tool, no matter how sophisticated, can change how people think about data or convince them to take responsibility for data quality. Tools can make it easier for people to execute their data governance responsibilities, but they can't create those responsibilities or motivate people to fulfil them.

If you don't achieve stakeholder buy-in for the underlying data governance principles, tools sit unused or underutilized because people don't understand why they should care about the capabilities they provide.

Even when people do use the tools, they often use them in ways that defeat the purpose of data governance. They might use a data cataloguing tool to document definitions that satisfy a compliance requirement, but never reference that data catalogue when making actual data-related decisions. Data quality reports might be run regularly but no one reviews them and takes action to address the issues those reports identify.

The timing question

One of the most critical considerations is when to introduce tools into your data governance initiative. The organization I mentioned earlier made the mistake of leading with a tool before they had established the basic data governance framework, processes, role descriptions and stakeholder engagement that would make those tools valuable.

This connects to the organizational maturity covered in Mistake 3. Your organization needs to be mature enough to understand what data governance tools are supposed to accomplish before those tools can be effective. If people don't understand the fundamental concepts of data stewardship, data quality management or data lineage, giving them sophisticated tools to support these activities is pointless.

The right time to consider tools is after you've established your basic data governance framework and demonstrated that people can and will follow data governance processes manually. When people are already committed to data governance principles and understand their responsibilities, tools can significantly enhance their effectiveness and efficiency.

Choosing the right approach

Before you start evaluating potential tools, make sure you fully understand what you're trying to achieve with data governance and why you're trying to achieve it. This strategic clarity is essential for making good tool selection decisions.

You also need a clear understanding of what specific capabilities you want the tool to provide. Are you looking for help with data cataloguing? Data quality monitoring? Workflow automation? Different tools excel in different areas and trying to find one tool that does everything well is often a recipe for disappointment.

Most importantly, remember that tools don't relieve anyone of responsibility for making data governance successful. They should be positioned as enablers that make it easier for people to execute their data governance responsibilities, not as replacements for human judgement, accountability and engagement.

Remember that implementing tools successfully requires the same change management and stakeholder engagement skills that data governance itself requires. The most sophisticated tool in the world won't help if people don't understand how to use it effectively or why they should care about using it at all.

This final mistake brings us full circle to the themes we've explored throughout this section: the paramount importance of people, culture and change management in data governance success. Tools can amplify and enhance good data governance practices, but they can never substitute for the fundamental work of getting people to think differently about data and take responsibility for managing it properly.

Conclusion

These 10 mistakes represent the most common ways that data governance initiatives fail, but they're also entirely preventable. What's particularly valuable about understanding these pitfalls is that they point us toward the solutions. Each mistake teaches us something important about what successful data governance actually requires: the critical importance of culture change, the need for business ownership, the value of understanding organizational maturity and the power of treating data governance as an ongoing capability rather than a one-time project. Organizations that recognize and avoid these mistakes position themselves for data governance success, while those that fall into these traps often find themselves starting over repeatedly. The key insight is that data governance is fundamentally about people and change management, not just processes and technology. Armed with this knowledge of what can go wrong, you're now equipped to navigate around these obstacles and build a data governance framework that truly works for your organization.

The following key takeaways outline important lessons from the mistakes:

- Culture change is non-negotiable: Without addressing how people think about data, even perfect frameworks will fail.

- Business ownership is essential: IT can support data governance, but the business must lead and own the initiative.

- Maturity matters: Understanding your starting point allows you to plot an effective journey.

- Change programmes beat projects: Sustainable data governance requires ongoing commitment, not just task completion.

- Strategic alignment drives success: Data governance must clearly support organizational objectives to maintain momentum.

- Data landscape understanding prevents surprises: Mapping your data flows before making changes avoids unintended consequences.

- Embedding requires dedicated focus: Someone must be specifically responsible for making the framework stick.

- Phased approaches work better: Manageable chunks of change are more sustainable than overwhelming transformations.

- Compliance alone isn't enough: Use regulatory requirements as a starting point, not a limiting factor.

- Tools enable, they don't solve: Technology supports good data governance practices but can't create them.

Armed with this knowledge of what can go wrong, you're now equipped to navigate around these obstacles and build a data governance framework that truly works for your organization.

11

The principles of successful data governance

Introduction

After examining the 10 most common mistakes that derail data governance initiatives in Chapter 10, this final chapter focuses on what organizations need to do to get data governance right.

Rather than simply avoiding pitfalls, successful data governance requires following proven principles that consistently lead to lasting results. These aren't theoretical concepts but practical guidelines distilled from real-world experience across dozens of implementations, refined through years of learning what works and what doesn't.

Throughout this book, we've explored the essential building blocks of effective data governance from understanding what it is and developing strategy, through designing frameworks and processes, to implementing and evolving your approach. Now we bring it all together with six fundamental principles that successful organizations consistently apply.

What makes these principles particularly valuable is that they work as an integrated system, providing both a foundation for design decisions and a framework for navigating challenges as they arise. They represent the difference between data governance initiatives that struggle and those that deliver transformational results.

In this chapter, you'll discover:

- how to identify and leverage genuine opportunities that create lasting motivation for data governance

- why building the right capabilities is essential before you begin implementation
- how to design frameworks that work with your organization rather than against it
- why simplicity often delivers better results than comprehensive complexity
- how to implement successfully through phased, iterative approaches
- why treating data governance as an evolving system is crucial for long-term success

Each principle directly addresses the mistakes we explored in Chapter 10, transforming those cautionary tales into actionable guidance for building data governance frameworks that deliver genuine business value and stand the test of time.

The six principles: What successful data governance looks like

We explored the 10 most common mistakes that can derail data governance initiatives in Chapter 10, so now it's time to turn our attention to what successful data governance actually looks like. Those mistakes aren't just cautionary tales but valuable insights that have shaped my understanding of what organizations need to do to achieve effective data governance.

Over many years of implementing data governance across dozens of organizations (with varying degrees of success in the early days), these hard-won lessons have crystallized into six fundamental principles. These principles underpin every successful data governance initiative I've witnessed and I'm confident that if you follow them, your organization will achieve the business value and benefits that effective data governance delivers.

Each principle directly addresses one or more of the mistakes we explored in the previous chapter. More importantly, these principles work together as a cohesive system. You can't cherry-pick one or two while ignoring the others. Organizations that achieve lasting data governance success consistently apply all six principles throughout their journey.

The six principles, as shown in Figure 11.1, are:

1 Opportunities: Identify the benefits of data governance for your organization.

2 Capability: Set yourself up for success by ensuring that you have the right resources and knowledge.

3 Custom-build: Design a data governance framework which is tailor-made to your organization.

4 Simplicity: Avoid complexity and make it easy to embed data governance.

5 Launch: Implement on an iterative basis and start to see the benefits of your work.

6 Evolve: Develop your framework as your organization evolves, to continue making gains.

What makes these principles particularly powerful is that they're interconnected. When you focus on genuine opportunities, you naturally create the motivation needed for successful culture change. When you honestly assess your capability, you avoid the trap of implementing solutions your organization isn't ready for. When you custom-build your approach, you create frameworks that work with your data landscape rather than against it.

FIGURE 11.1 The principles of successful data governance

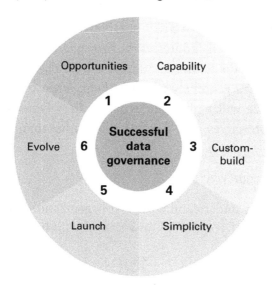

The principles also provide a framework for making decisions throughout your data governance journey. When you're faced with choices about scope, timing, tools or processes, you can evaluate your options against these principles to guide your decision-making.

In the sections that follow, we'll explore each principle in detail, examining what it means in practice and how you can apply it in your organization. We'll also look at how each principle helps you avoid the specific mistakes we've just discussed.

By the end of this section, you'll have a clear roadmap for implementing data governance that learns from the failures of others and builds upon the practices that consistently lead to success.

Opportunities

Why is your organization doing data governance? What's the value proposition? These are fundamental questions that many organizations skip over in their eagerness to get started with implementation. But if you can't answer them clearly and compellingly, your data governance initiative is already in trouble.

You need to be absolutely clear about what benefits you hope to deliver and why those benefits are important for your organization. In my experience, starting data governance for best practice purposes alone is doomed to failure. 'We should do this because it's a recommended approach' simply doesn't create the motivation and commitment needed to drive real organizational change.

This principle directly addresses the first mistake we explored in the previous chapter: the failure to address culture change. When people understand what's genuinely in it for them, when they can see how data governance will make their working lives better or help them achieve their objectives, they become allies rather than obstacles.

Understanding your 'why'

You need to truly understand why your organization is implementing data governance. If you don't know the 'why', it becomes easy to get side-tracked and distracted when challenges arise. The 'why' is what will guide you on your journey and ensure your organization gets what it needs from your data governance initiative.

Those leading data governance initiatives often mention generic benefits like 'There will be efficiencies' or 'There will be better opportunities if we do data governance', but they can't explain specifics when challenged. This vagueness is a serious problem because when you're meeting with stakeholders at the start of a data governance initiative, particularly your senior ones, they want to know, 'What's in it for me?' If you can't answer that question in a way that genuinely interests them and shows clear benefits, they're simply not going to engage.

This connects directly to our discussion in Chapter 2 about building the business case for data governance and aligning with corporate strategy. The opportunities you identify must be real, specific and tied to what your organization actually cares about achieving.

Making it personal and relevant

The most effective way to identify genuine opportunities is to understand the specific challenges and objectives of different stakeholder groups. Your finance team might be struggling with month-end reporting that takes too long because of data quality issues. Your sales team might be missing opportunities because they can't get reliable customer data quickly enough. Your compliance team might be spending enormous effort manually gathering data for regulatory reports.

These are real problems that cause real frustration and cost real money. When you can show how data governance will address these specific pain points, you create genuine motivation for change. People stop seeing data governance as an additional burden and start seeing it as a solution to problems they already care about solving.

Beyond compliance and risk management

While regulatory compliance is often a driver for data governance initiatives, it shouldn't be your only opportunity focus. As we discussed in Mistake 9 in the previous chapter, the tick-box approach and compliance-focused initiatives miss enormous potential value and struggle to maintain momentum once the immediate regulatory requirements are met.

Look for opportunities that deliver operational value, strategic advantage or competitive differentiation. Perhaps better data governance will enable faster product development cycles, more personalized customer experiences, or more agile decision-making. These opportunities create sustainable motivation because they connect to ongoing business priorities rather than one-time compliance requirements.

Testing and validating your opportunities

Once you've identified potential opportunities, test them with your stakeholders. Do they agree that these are genuine problems worth solving? Do they believe that data governance can realistically address these issues? Are they willing to invest time and effort to achieve these benefits?

If you can't get stakeholders excited about the opportunities you've identified, you probably haven't found the right ones yet. Keep digging until you discover opportunities that create genuine enthusiasm and commitment.

Remember, the opportunities principle isn't just about identifying benefits at the start of your initiative. It's about continuously reinforcing why data governance matters throughout your implementation journey. When you encounter challenges or resistance, coming back to these core opportunities helps maintain focus and motivation.

The organizations that succeed with data governance are those that never lose sight of the genuine business value they're trying to create. They use these opportunities not just to justify their initiative, but to guide every decision about scope, priorities and implementation approach.

Capability

So many people, myself included, find themselves doing data governance by accident, usually without any previous experience or knowledge of what exactly they should be doing. One day you're working in your regular role and the next day someone has decided you're responsible for 'sorting out data governance'. Sound familiar?

This principle directly addresses Mistake 3 (not understanding organizational maturity), but it goes beyond just assessing where your organization sits on the maturity spectrum. It's about honestly evaluating and building the capabilities you need to be successful, both at an individual and organizational level.

Individual capability building

If you're the person tasked with leading data governance in your organization, the first question is: do you have the knowledge and skills needed to be successful? This isn't about having all the answers from day one. It's about understanding what you need to learn and being honest about the gaps in your knowledge.

Data governance requires a unique combination of technical understanding (note I say understanding not expertise), business acumen and people skills. You need to understand how data flows through systems, but you also need to understand how organizations work and how to motivate people to change their behaviours. Most people don't naturally have all these skills, and that's fine as long as you recognize what you need to develop.

The key is finding reliable sources of practical guidance rather than getting lost in theoretical frameworks that don't translate to real-world implementation.

Organizational capability assessment

Beyond individual skills, you need to assess your organization's readiness for data governance. This connects directly to the organizational maturity discussion in Mistake 3. Are your stakeholders ready to think about data strategically? Do they understand the connection between data quality and business outcomes? Do they have the time and bandwidth to take on new responsibilities?

Sometimes an organization simply isn't ready for a comprehensive data governance initiative and that's important to recognize. Trying to implement data governance concepts in an organization that hasn't developed basic data awareness is like trying to teach calculus to someone who hasn't learned arithmetic.

In these situations, you may need to start with organization-wide data literacy training before launching formal data governance processes. This foundational work helps everyone understand the value and importance of data to the business, creates a common vocabulary around data concepts and builds the basic awareness that makes data governance possible.

Basic data literacy training shouldn't be extensive or technical. It's about helping people understand how data affects their daily work, why data quality matters to business outcomes and how better data management can make their jobs easier and more effective. This groundwork creates the cultural foundation that formal data governance processes need to succeed.

This doesn't mean you should wait until your organization is perfectly mature before starting any data governance activities. It means understanding your starting point so you can design an approach that meets your organization where it is and builds capability progressively, whether that starts with basic data literacy education or moves directly into data governance framework design and implementation.

Building the right team

Data governance success requires diverse skills that rarely exist in one person. You need people who can facilitate stakeholder discussions, others who understand technical data quality rules, others who excel at communication and training and others who can navigate organizational politics and change management.

Look around your organization to identify where these capabilities already exist. You might find excellent facilitators in your project management office, strong communicators in your marketing team, or change management expertise in your HR department. Data governance doesn't have to be built from scratch; it can leverage existing organizational strengths.

Where capabilities don't exist internally, you may need external support. But if you do bring in consultants or contractors, make sure they work on a skills-transfer basis so your organization builds its own competency rather than becoming dependent on external resources.

Avoiding capability traps

One common trap is assuming that knowledge of data governance theory alone is sufficient for data governance success. While knowing data governance concepts and understanding the other data management disciplines is important, the people skills are often more critical. You need to be able to influence stakeholders, facilitate difficult conversations and drive organizational change. These soft skills are frequently underestimated but are essential for long-term success.

Another trap is trying to build perfect capability before starting any implementation. Like most aspects of data governance, capability building is iterative. You learn by doing and you build skills through practical experience. The key is ensuring you have enough foundational capability to getting started and a plan for building additional capabilities as you progress.

Continuous capability development

Capability building doesn't stop once your data governance initiative is launched. As your framework evolves and your organization's needs change, you'll need to develop new skills and knowledge. This might mean learning about new technologies, developing expertise in different industry regulations or building capabilities in areas like AI.

For example, many organizations are now adding AI governance to the scope of their data governance teams. This expansion requires acquiring entirely new skills around AI ethics, model risk management, algorithmic bias detection and AI regulatory compliance. Teams that were previously focused on traditional data quality and stewardship suddenly need to understand machine learning model governance, AI transparency requirements and the unique challenges of governing AI-generated content.

The most successful data governance teams are those that embrace continuous learning and aren't afraid to admit when they need to develop new capabilities. They see gaps in knowledge as opportunities for growth rather than obstacles to progress. When AI governance responsibilities are added to their remit, they proactively seek training, bring in expertise or partner with other teams to build the necessary competencies.

Remember, you don't need to be an expert in everything related to data governance before you start. But you do need to be honest about what you know, what you don't know and what you need to learn to be successful. This honesty allows you to build the right team, seek the right support and design an approach that matches your actual capabilities rather than your aspirational ones.

Custom-build

For it to be successful, your data governance framework must be designed for your organization. There is no standard framework that will work for your organization or any other organization. This is one of the most important principles to understand, yet it's also one of the most frequently ignored.

A data governance framework is a set of data rules, organizational roles and processes aimed at bringing everyone in your organization onto the same page when managing and using data. The only way to be successful with data governance is to first work out why your organization needs data governance and then to design and implement a framework that meets those specific needs.

This principle directly addresses several of the mistakes we explored in Chapter 10, particularly Mistake 6 about not understanding your data landscape. This principle also connects to the real-world example from Chapter 3 about the client who implemented a standard framework and struggled to make data governance work.

Why standard frameworks fail

I can almost guarantee that any standard framework is not going to meet your needs. It is likely to be too complex, too convoluted and too focused on things that really aren't appropriate for your organization. Standard frameworks are designed to cover every possible scenario and address every potential need, which makes them inherently complex and difficult to implement.

Think about it logically: how could a framework designed for a global manufacturing company possibly work for a small financial services firm? How could an approach developed for a healthcare organization be appropriate for a retail business? The business models are different, the regulatory environments are different, the data landscapes are different and the organizational cultures are also very different.

Yet I regularly encounter organizations that have tried to implement standard frameworks, with disappointing results. They spend months trying to adapt their organization to fit the framework rather than designing a framework that fits their organization. This backwards approach leads to frustration and failure.

Understanding your unique context

Every organization has a unique combination of factors that shape what their data governance framework should look like. Your industry regulations, business model, technology infrastructure, organizational structure, culture and strategic objectives all influence what will work for your organization.

Even organizations in the same industry can have dramatically different data governance needs. A traditional bank and a fintech start-up both operate in the financial services sector, but their data governance frameworks will look completely different because their business models, risk profiles, technology approaches and organizational structures are fundamentally different.

This is why understanding your data landscape, as we discussed in Mistake 6, is so critical. You can't design an appropriate framework without understanding what data your organization has, where your biggest challenges lie and what your most important opportunities are.

Avoiding the complexity trap

Custom-building doesn't mean making it unnecessarily complex. The goal is to design something that fits your organization, which often means making it simpler and more focused than a standard framework, not more elaborate.

This connects to our simplicity principle that we'll discuss next. The most effective custom frameworks are often surprisingly simple because they focus only on what's truly necessary for that specific organization, rather than trying to accommodate every possible scenario.

Iterative design approach

Custom-building is an iterative process, not a one-time design exercise. You start with what your organization needs today, design a framework that addresses your current needs and capabilities and then evolve it as you learn more and as your organization changes.

This approach allows you to build something that works in practice rather than something that looks good in theory. You can test components of your framework with real stakeholders, get feedback on what works and what doesn't and refine your approach based on actual experience rather than assumptions.

The organizations that succeed with data governance are those that resist the temptation to adopt someone else's solution and instead invest the time and effort to design something that's truly fit for their unique circumstances. Yes, it requires more upfront thinking, but it delivers much better results and creates a framework that stakeholders actually want to use rather than feeling forced to follow.

Simplicity

I've never yet seen an overly complex framework or approach to data governance that has worked. Don't try to allow for every possible eventuality because you will tie yourself and your business stakeholders up in knots and create something that is too complicated to implement. Everyone will resist adopting it.

Simplicity is best. Remember, you can always add detail as your data governance approach matures and you find a need for an extra level of detail, but start simple and grow from there.

This principle directly addresses Mistake 8 about the big bang approach. When you try to solve every data challenge at once, you inevitably create something so complex and overwhelming that people can't or won't engage with it.

The complexity trap

There's something appealing about comprehensive frameworks that seem to address every possible scenario. When you're designing your data governance framework, it's tempting to think about all the use cases, all the potential problems and all the possible requirements you might encounter. The instinct is to design something robust enough to handle anything.

But this instinct leads to frameworks that are so complex they're practically unusable. I've seen beautiful process maps that require a PhD to understand, role definitions that read like legal documents and policies that are so comprehensive they're intimidating rather than helpful.

The problem is that complexity doesn't just make implementation difficult; it creates ongoing resistance to your data governance initiative. When people look at your framework and feel overwhelmed by its complexity, they start looking for ways to avoid engaging with it rather than embracing it.

Why simple works better

Simple frameworks have several advantages that complex ones can't match. First, they're easier to understand, which means people are more likely to actually follow them. When someone can quickly grasp what they're supposed to do and why, participation becomes natural rather than forced.

Second, simple frameworks are easier to communicate. You can explain the basics to stakeholders without requiring lengthy training sessions or detailed documentation. This makes it much easier to get buy-in and build momentum for your initiative.

Third, simple frameworks are more resilient. When your processes are straightforward, they're less likely to break when circumstances change. Complex frameworks often fail when they encounter situations that weren't anticipated in their design, but simple frameworks can be easily adapted.

Starting with minimum viable data governance

The key is to identify the minimum viable data governance you need to address your most important opportunities and start there. What's the simplest possible framework that will deliver meaningful value? What are the essential processes and roles you absolutely need, without any nice-to-have additions?

This connects directly back to the opportunities principle. When you're clear about what specific benefits you're trying to achieve, it becomes much easier to design a simple framework that delivers those benefits without unnecessary complexity.

For example, if your primary opportunity is improving the accuracy of customer data, you might start with a simple process for data stewards to review and correct customer data, basic quality metrics to track improvement and clear accountability for maintaining data accuracy. You don't need comprehensive data lineage mapping, elaborate approval workflows or data governance committees to make meaningful progress on this specific opportunity.

Building complexity progressively

The beauty of starting simple is that you can add complexity later when and where it's actually needed. As your data governance initiative matures and proves its value, stakeholders become more willing to engage with more sophisticated processes and tools.

This iterative approach also allows you to learn what works and what doesn't before you invest heavily in complex solutions. You might discover that your initial simple process works so well that additional complexity isn't needed, or you might identify specific circumstances where more detail is needed.

Organizations that try to implement comprehensive frameworks from day one often discover that much of their carefully designed complexity is never actually used. Starting simple helps you avoid this waste and focus your energy on what truly adds value.

Avoiding the perfection trap

Simplicity doesn't mean being simplistic or cutting corners. It means being thoughtful about what's truly necessary and resisting the urge to over-engineer your data governance framework. The goal is simplicity that delivers real value, not complexity for its own sake.

Remember that your stakeholders are busy people with demanding jobs. They don't have time to navigate complex frameworks or decode elaborate processes. The simpler and more intuitive you can make their data governance responsibilities, the more likely they are to fulfil them effectively.

This principle also connects to the custom-build principle we discussed earlier. When you design something specifically for your organization's needs rather than trying to accommodate every possible scenario, you naturally create something simpler and more focused.

The most successful data governance frameworks I've seen are often surprisingly simple. They focus on delivering specific value rather than trying to be comprehensive and they prioritize usability over completeness. These frameworks succeed because people actually want to use them rather than feeling forced to follow them.

Launch

Launch is linked to simplicity. Over the years I have seen many organizations fail in their data governance initiative because they try to do everything at once. However, it really is too much to do all at one time.

It's likely that attempting to do everything at once will feel overwhelming to your senior stakeholders and you may not receive approval to do this. Even if you do, it's unlikely to succeed, as such a large change all at once can be too much for business users to absorb. It is far better to take an iterative, phased approach and, slowly but surely, roll your data governance framework out across your organization.

This principle directly addresses Mistake 8 about the big bang approach and connects to Mistake 7 about failure to embed the framework. When you launch pragmatically in phases, you create opportunities to embed each component properly before moving on to the next.

The power of iterative implementation

An iterative approach allows you to learn and adapt as you go. When you implement everything at once, you don't have opportunities to refine your approach based on what's working and what isn't. But when you work in phases, each phase teaches you valuable lessons that help you improve your next phase.

This learning is particularly important because data governance often involves changing deeply ingrained habits and ways of thinking. People need time to absorb new concepts and integrate new processes into their daily routines. Trying to change everything simultaneously overwhelms people's capacity for change.

I've seen organizations achieve success by starting with a single department or a specific data domain, proving that their approach works and then gradually expanding to other areas. The early successes create momentum and credibility that make subsequent phases much easier to implement.

Building momentum through wins

A phased implementation strategy allows you to identify and deliver wins that demonstrate the value of data governance. These early victories are crucial for maintaining stakeholder support and building enthusiasm for the broader initiative.

When you try to implement everything at once, you often have to wait months or even years before seeing meaningful benefits. During this long implementation period, stakeholders may lose confidence in the initiative or shift their attention to other priorities. But when you launch in phases, you can start delivering value relatively quickly.

These wins also provide valuable evidence that your approach is working. When stakeholders can see concrete improvements in data quality, operational efficiency or decision-making speed, they become advocates for expanding data governance to other areas.

Managing change effectively

A phased approach is also fundamentally better for change management. Rather than asking people to transform everything about how they work with data all at once, you're asking them to make manageable adjustments that build on each other over time.

This connects back to our discussion about culture change in Mistake 1. People are much more willing to embrace change when it feels manageable and when they can see clear benefits from each step. A phased approach allows you to win hearts and minds gradually rather than trying to force massive change through.

Each phase also gives you opportunities to address resistance, refine your communication strategy and build the relationships that are essential for long-term success. When you try to launch everything simultaneously, you don't have time for this important relationship-building work.

Designing effective phases

The key to successful phased implementation is designing phases that are meaningful and valuable on their own, not just arbitrary chunks of a larger framework. Each phase should deliver specific benefits that stakeholders care about and should build naturally toward your broader data governance objectives.

Your phases should be guided by your opportunities and priorities. Start with the areas where you can have the biggest impact with the least disruption, then gradually expand to more complex or sensitive areas.

For example, you might start with data domains that have clear business ownership and relatively straightforward technical architecture, then move to areas with more complex data flows or shared accountability. Or you might begin with processes that stakeholders are already motivated to improve, then expand to areas where the value proposition is less immediately obvious.

Learning and adapting between phases

One of the biggest advantages of phased implementation is the opportunity to learn between phases. After each phase, take time to evaluate what worked well, what could be improved and what you learned about your organization's readiness for data governance.

This learning should inform the design of subsequent phases. You might discover that certain communication approaches are particularly effective with your stakeholders, or that specific types of training are needed to support new processes. You might find that some aspects of your framework work better than expected while others need refinement.

The organizations that are most successful with data governance are those that treat each phase as an experiment that teaches them how to make the next phase even more effective. They're not afraid to adjust their approach based on what they learn and they see adaptation as a sign of maturity rather than failure.

Maintaining long-term vision

While launching in phases, it's important to maintain clarity about your long-term vision and how each phase contributes to that vision. Stakeholders need to understand not just what they're being asked to do in the current phase, but how it fits into the broader data governance journey.

This long-term perspective helps maintain momentum during challenging periods and ensures that each phase builds effectively toward your ultimate objectives. It also helps you make smart decisions about sequencing and prioritization, ensuring that early phases create the foundation needed for later, more ambitious phases.

Remember, the goal isn't just to implement data governance processes, but to create lasting organizational change. A pragmatic phased approach gives you the best chance of achieving this deeper transformation by allowing people to grow into new ways of thinking about and working with data.

Evolve

Do not make the mistake of thinking that designing and implementing a data governance framework is a 'once and done' activity. Remember, data governance is not a project!

You need to constantly review and evolve your framework as your organization evolves, as covered in Chapter 9. Perhaps it will restructure and you must agree a new approach to data ownership. Perhaps your organization will enter new markets or merge with another organization. All these things will impact your initiative's ability to remain relevant and provide the appropriate support to your organization, which is why your framework needs to evolve too.

This principle directly addresses Mistake 4 about treating data governance as a project and connects to several other mistakes we explored. When an organization treats their data governance framework as fixed, they inevitably find that their framework becomes outdated and less effective over time.

Data governance as a living system

Your data governance framework should be viewed as a living system that grows and adapts with your organization. Just as your business strategy evolves to respond to changing market conditions, your data governance approach must evolve to support changing business needs and capabilities.

This evolution isn't a sign of failure or poor initial design. It's a natural and necessary characteristic of any data governance framework that remains relevant and valuable over time. The organizations that struggle with data governance are often those that implemented something years ago and never updated it to reflect how their business has changed.

Organizational changes that drive evolution

There are many types of organizational change that require corresponding evolution in your data governance framework. Restructuring is one of the most common triggers. When departments are reorganized, merged or split, the data ownership and stewardship arrangements that worked under the old structure may no longer be appropriate.

Mergers and acquisitions create particularly significant challenges for data governance. Suddenly you're dealing with different data standards, different processes, different systems and different cultures around data. Your framework needs to evolve to accommodate these new realities while maintaining the data governance principles that had served your organization well.

Business expansion into new markets also often brings new regulatory requirements, new data types and new stakeholder groups that weren't considered in your original framework design.

Technology evolution and new capabilities

Technology changes also drive the need for framework evolution. The emergence of new analytics capabilities, artificial intelligence applications or new technologies creates new data governance challenges that your original framework may not have anticipated.

For example, many organizations that implemented data governance frameworks before the widespread adoption of artificial intelligence now find they need to add AI governance capabilities to their existing structures. This isn't a failure of their original design; it's a natural evolution responding to new technological capabilities and associated risks.

Regulatory and compliance evolution

The regulatory environment is constantly changing, particularly around data. New data regulations, evolving interpretations of existing regulations and emerging requirements in areas like AI governance all require corresponding evolution in your data governance framework.

Capability maturity and growing ambitions

As your organization's data governance capability matures, your framework should evolve to support more sophisticated objectives and processes. What starts as basic data quality issue resolution might evolve to include advanced analytics governance.

Building evolution into your framework

The key to successful evolution is anticipating the need for it from the beginning. This means establishing regular review cycles where you explicitly evaluate whether your data governance framework is still meeting your organization's needs and supporting your strategic objectives. For most organizations, annual reviews are appropriate, though some may benefit from more frequent six-monthly assessments, particularly during periods of significant change or in rapidly evolving industries. These reviews shouldn't wait for major organizational changes; they should be a routine part of your data governance operations.

Evolution should be driven by learning and continuous improvement, not just reactive responses to external changes. Regular feedback from stakeholders, analysis of framework performance and assessment of emerging opportunities should all inform your evolution strategy.

The most successful data governance frameworks are those that evolve continuously based on learning and experience, rather than remaining static until forced to change by external circumstances. These frameworks stay relevant and valuable because they adapt proactively to serve their organization's changing needs.

Bringing it all together

These six principles work as an integrated system. You cannot successfully implement data governance by applying just one or two of them while ignoring the others. The organizations that achieve lasting success consistently apply all six principles throughout their journey.

The principles are interconnected and reinforce each other. Most importantly, these principles provide a decision-making framework for your data governance journey. Follow these principles consistently and you'll create a data governance framework that delivers genuine value to your organization and stands the test of time.

Conclusion

These six principles represent the distillation of years of experience implementing data governance across organizations of all sizes and industries. They're not just theoretical concepts but practical guidelines that consistently distinguish successful initiatives from those that struggle or fail.

What makes these principles particularly powerful is how they address the fundamental mistakes we explored in Chapter 10. Where organizations get overwhelmed by complexity, the simplicity principle provides clarity. Where they struggle with resistance and culture change, the opportunities principle creates genuine motivation. Where standard frameworks fail to fit, the custom-build principle ensures relevance.

The key insight is that these principles work as an integrated system. You cannot achieve lasting data governance success by cherry-picking one or two principles while ignoring the others. The organizations that consistently deliver results are those that embed all six principles into their approach from the very beginning and maintain them throughout their journey.

As you embark on or continue your data governance journey, use these principles as your compass:

1 Start with opportunities that create genuine enthusiasm and commitment from stakeholders who can see clear benefits to their daily work.

2 Build capability systematically, ensuring you have the skills, knowledge and organizational readiness needed for success.

3 Custom-build your approach to fit your unique context rather than forcing your organization to adapt to generic frameworks.

4 Keep it simple by focusing on what truly adds value and avoiding unnecessary complexity that creates resistance.

5 Launch iteratively in manageable phases that build momentum and allow people to absorb changes gradually.

6 Plan for evolution by treating your framework as a living system that grows and adapts with your organization.

Remember that data governance is not a destination but a journey. The principles in this chapter provide the roadmap for that journey, helping you navigate challenges, make smart decisions and deliver the transformational benefits that effective data governance can bring to your organization.

The mistakes we covered in Chapter 10 show us what to avoid. These principles show us the path forward. Together with all the concepts covered throughout this book, they give you everything you need to build data governance that works.

I wish you every success on your data governance journey. It's challenging work, but the benefits to your organization and the satisfaction of creating real, lasting change make it incredibly rewarding. I hope this book serves as a practical guide that you can return to whenever you need direction and that it helps you avoid the pitfalls while building something truly valuable for your organization.

RESOURCES

To support your data governance journey, I've created a comprehensive collection of practical resources that complement the concepts covered in this book. These free resources are designed to help you implement effective data governance in your organization.

All resources are available at sites.google.com/nicolaaskham.com/effectivedatagovernance

These materials reflect the same practical, experience-based approach you have seen throughout this book. They focus on what works rather than theoretical ideals.

Available resources

- Data governance checklist: A detailed step-by-step guide to ensure you cover all essential elements of your data governance implementation.

- Getting started in data governance blog: A collation of blogs offering practical advice for organizations beginning their data governance journey.

- Data quality issue log template: A ready-to-use template for tracking and resolving data quality problems systematically.

- Data definitions tips: Best practices for creating clear, consistent data definitions that are useful.

- Example conceptual data model: A sample model demonstrating how to structure and document your organization's key data concepts.

- Top tips to gain stakeholder engagement: Proven strategies for building support and participation across your organization.

Additional learning

For ongoing insights and discussions about data governance challenges and solutions, you can also follow:

- The Data Governance Podcast: Regular episodes covering real-world data governance topics and guest expert interviews. Available on all major podcast platforms, including Spotify, Apple Podcasts and Google Podcasts.

- YouTube channel: Video content with practical tutorials, master-classes and data governance insights: www.youtube.com/@ TheDataGovernanceCoach

INDEX

Note: Page numbers in *italics* refer to figures or tables.

8

Looking for another book?

Explore our award-winning
books from global business
experts in Business Strategy

Scan the code to browse

www.koganpage.com/business-
strategy

More on data from Kogan Page

ISBN: 9781398617773

ISBN: 9781398619593

ISBN: 9781398622012

ISBN: 9781398614208

www.koganpage.com

From 4 December 2025 the EU Responsible Person (GPSR) is:
eucomply oÜ, Pärnu mnt. 139b – 14, 11317 Tallinn, Estonia
www.eucompliancepartner.com

www.ingramcontent.com/pod-product-compliance
Lightning Source LLC
Chambersburg PA
CBHW070938050326
40689CB00014B/3248